Thomas Aquinas

A Summary of Philosophy

Thomas Aquinas

A Summary of Philosophy

TRANSLATED AND EDITED, WITH
INTRODUCTION AND GLOSSARY, BY

Richard J. Regan

Hackett Publishing Company, Inc.
Indianapolis/Cambridge

Printed in the United States of America

09 08 07 06 2 3 4 5 6 7
For further information, please address:

Hackett Publishing Company, Inc.
P.O. Box 44937
Indianapolis, IN 46244-0937

www.hackettpublishing.com

Cover design by Listenberger Design & Associates
Composition by Professional Book Compositors, Inc.
Printed at Edwards Brothers, Inc.

Library of Congress Cataloging-in-Publication Data

Thomas, Aquinas, Saint, 1225?–1274.
[Summa theologica. English. Selections]
A summary of philosophy / Thomas Aquinas; translated and edited, with introduction and glossary by Richard J. Regan.
p. cm.
Includes bibliographical references and index.
ISBN 0-87220-658-0 — ISBN 0-87220-657-2 (pbk.)
1. Theology, Doctrinal—Early works to 1800. 2. Catholic Church—Doctrines—Early works to 1800. I. Regan, Richard J. II. Title.

BX1749.T515 2003
189'.4—dc21 2002191906

ISBN-13: 978-0-87220-658-8 (cloth)
ISBN-13: 978-0-87220-657-1 (pbk.)

The paper used in this publication meets the minimum requirements on American National Standard for Information Sciences—Permanence of Paper for Printed Library Materials, ANSI Z39.48-1984
∞

Contents

Preface

This book bears the title of a work Thomas, called Aquinas (after the town near which he was born), never wrote. But his *Summa Theologica* contains texts of major philosophical importance, and this book is a compendium of such texts from ST I and I–II. More than a decade ago, I initiated a project to translate the texts in full. That project is now complete. (See Bibliography: *God and Creation; The Human Constitution; Virtue: Way to Happiness; Treatise on Law*.) In the course of the project, I became aware that nonspecialists were likely to be overwhelmed by Aquinas' references to Scripture, church fathers, Aristotle, Augustine, and sundry others. On the other hand, I think nonspecialists can readily understand the substance of his views apart from the references, and I have sought to supply that substance in this book.

This book is principally designed for undergraduate introductory courses in philosophy, especially courses in Aquinas. For such courses, this book can provide the substance of Thomas's positions and arguments on key topics to supplement explanatory texts like those by W. Norris Clarke, Brian Davies, Ralph McInerny, and John Wipple (see Bibliography). For general introductory courses, of course, this book can and should be supplemented by representative works of other important philosophers (e.g., Plato, Descartes, Hume, Kant). The book will also be useful as a reader for nonacademics and a reference book for nonspecialists.

I have followed the question-and-answer format of Thomas. The answers are in his own words, although the texts have been severely edited. For example, almost all references and many comparisons have been omitted, and instructors will need to supply the intellectual context of many questions (e.g., the challenge of a radical Aristotelianism). Only a few objections and replies have been retained, and the numbering of the objections in this anthology is mine, not that of Thomas in the *Summa*. The objections selected have been placed after the answers and are followed by the replies. Scholars will rightly want to study the complete text and references in the *Summa*, for which there is no substitute, but beginning students and general readers may benefit more from focusing on Aquinas' own thought and argument than on the writings of those authorities he cites, comments on, or refutes. The italicized introductory notes to the chapters and to the chapter sections aim to provide the reader with helpful guidance; these are my own and not to be confused with the texts of Aquinas that follow them. In addition, the Glossary explains key terms to assist the reader, and the Select Bibliography directs the reader to works on Thomas's thought.

The Latin text on which the translations are based is the 1952 Marietti recension of the Leonine text. The translations are from the works mentioned above, and the University of Scranton Press has graciously granted permission to adopt and adapt the translations it published. I have included no selections from ST II–II, but *On Law, Morality, and Politics,* Second Edition (Hackett, 2002) contains my translation of politically relevant material from that part of the *Summa*, from the *De Regno*, and from the *Commentary on the Sentences*.

I am very grateful to several anonymous readers of the manuscript. They indicated the need for many helpful and some necessary revisions. I am thankful to Dick Rousseau of the University of Scranton Press for his permission to adapt translations published by that press. I am especially thankful to Brian Rak of Hackett Publishing Company for his encouragement, patience, and careful attention to the manuscript as it progressed from a work in process to a finished product.

RICHARD J. REGAN
Bronx, N.Y.

Biblical Abbreviations

Ex.	Exodus
Gen.	Genesis
Hos.	Hosea
Is.	Isaiah
Jer.	Jeremiah
Mt.	Matthew
Rom.	Romans
Tim.	Timothy

Other Abbreviations

A.	article
c., cc.	chapter, chapters
comm.	comment
CT	Thomas Aquinas, *Compendium Theologiae*
dist.	distinction
n.	note
nn.	numbers
Obj.	objection
PG	J. P. Migne, *Patrologia Graeca*
PL	J. P. Migne, *Patrologia Latina*
Q.	question
SCG	Thomas Aquinas, *Summa contra Gentiles*
ST	Thomas Aquinas, *Summa Theologica*
tr.	treatise

Introduction

Thomas Aquinas flourished in the second and third quarters of the 13th century of our era (A.D. 1224/1225–1274). A Dominican friar, he lectured and taught at the University of Paris and taught Dominican students at Naples. Toward the end of his life, he wrote a summary of theology, the *Summa Theologica*, to introduce beginners to the study of the discipline.

The *Summa Theologica* is divided into three parts. The first part treats of God, creatures, and human nature. The first half of the second part deals with the human end and the role of human acts and virtues in achieving it. The second half of the second part deals with specific virtues and the morality of particular acts. The third part treats of Christ's redemptive sacrifice and the role of the sacraments in communicating its merits to the faithful. General topics (questions) are subdivided into particular inquiries (articles). In the first part, for example, Question 2 takes up inquiries regarding the existence of God, and Article 1 of the question asks whether the existence of God is self-evident. The articles begin with a series of objections, state Aquinas' own position and argument(s), and conclude with replies to each objection.

In the course of summarizing Christian theology, Aquinas explicitly deals with many topics of philosophical interest and advances explicitly philosophical arguments, that is, arguments based on reason rather than on Scripture or church authority. This anthology aims to present his arguments on such topics in the first part and the first half of the second part of the *Summa*.

The Intellectual Context

To understand why Aquinas chooses to treat the philosophical topics he does, the reader needs to be conscious of the intellectual climate in which he worked.

The chief institution in which Aquinas studied and taught was the University of Paris. Beginning at Bologna in the 11th century of our era, universities arose in Western Europe to provide scholarly and professional education beyond that provided by cathedral and monastic schools.[1] The

[1]On medieval universities generally, see Hilda De Ridder-Symoens, ed., *A History of the University in Europe, Volume 1: Universities in the Middle Ages* (Cambridge: Cambridge University Press, 1991).

University of Paris, which developed from the cathedral school of Notre Dame in the last quarter of the 12th century, was, like other universities, a corporation of students and masters free to govern itself.

The University of Paris was composed of four faculties: arts, medicine, law, and theology. In addition to the arts of writing and speech (grammar, rhetoric, logic), and the mathematical arts (arithmetic, geometry, astronomy, music), the arts faculty taught Aristotelian scientific and philosophical subjects (biology, physics, psychology, ethics, metaphysics). Although Aquinas taught in the theology faculty, he strenuously contested certain positions of the philosophical arts faculty that he regarded as contrary to Christian faith or reason.

The theology faculty of the University of Paris was the most distinguished in medieval Christendom and boasted such masters as Alexander of Hales (A.D. 1170/1185–1245), Albert the Great (A.D. 1200?–1280), Bonaventure (A.D. 1217?–1274), and Aquinas himself. The lecture format in theology typically consisted of a master's commentary on the *Sentences* of Peter Lombard (A.D. 1100?–1160), but the public disputation provided the discipline's cutting edge. In these disputations, students or masters would defend theses before all comers. Those defending theses would recapitulate objections, state and explain the defenders' contrary position, and reply specifically to the objections. The *Summa* adopted this basic question-and-answer format.

The chief intellectual event of the 12th and 13th centuries of our era was the reintroduction of the texts of the major works of Aristotle into Western Europe. Aside from logic and rhetoric,[2] Aristotle's works had been lost to the West since the collapse of the Roman Empire, although early medieval thinkers knew citations of the works by Latin authors. In the 12th century, James of Venice translated the *Physics*, the *De anima*, and the *Metaphysics* into Latin. In the 13th century, Robert Grosseteste produced the first complete translation of the *Nichomachean Ethics*, and William of Moerbeke revised the translations of James and newly translated other works of Aristotle. In short, by the last quarter of the 13th century, the basic corpus of Aristotle's philosophical work was readily available to Latin-literate scholars of the universities of Western Europe.

---

[2]For an older but useful survey of the reception of Aristotle until 1277 A.D., see Fernand van Steenberghen, *Aristotle in the West: The Origins of Latin Averroism*, trans. L. Johnson (Louvain: E. Nauwalaerts, 1955). For a recent survey and annotated bibliography, see Mark D. Jordan, "Aristotelianism, Medieval," *Routledge Encyclopedia of Philosophy*, gen. ed. Edward Craig (London: Routledge, 1998).

The Arabic works of Averroes (A.D. 1126–1198) had also been translated into Latin by 1240 A.D.[3]

Reconciling Aristotle with the tenets of the Christian faith posed serious problems.[4] Aristotle held that the world was uncreated, and he could be read to hold the common Greek view that the world always existed and could not have not existed, but the Christian church taught that God freely created the world, and that the world had a beginning and could have not existed. Aristotle's Prime Mover was a self-absorbed intelligence that had no providential design for the world or its human inhabitants, but the Christian God was an intelligence that providentially created the world and each human being. Aristotle never explicitly affirmed the personal immortality of the human soul, and he considered proper human behavior exclusively as a prerequisite for happiness in this life, but the Christian unequivocally affirmed the immortality of the individual human soul and unequivocally conditioned blessedness in the next life on proper behavior in this one.

The nearly simultaneous introduction of Averroes as the most authoritative interpreter of Aristotle compounded these problems.[5] Where Aristotle could be interpreted to suppose rather than to affirm that the world was eternal and necessary,[6] Averroes explicitly affirmed that the world was such. Where Aristotle could be interpreted to hold that the individual human soul was intellectual and so immortal,[7] Averroes categorically de-

---

[3]See n. 2, supra.

[4]On Aristotle generally, see J. L. Ackrill, *Aristotle the Philosopher* (Oxford: Oxford University Press, 1981) and J. Barnes, *Aristotle* (Oxford: Oxford University Press, 1982).

[5]On Averroes generally, see M. R. Heyoun and A. de Libera, *Averroes et l'averroisme* (Paris: Presses Universitaires, 1991), and O. Leaman, *Averroes and His Philosophy*, 2nd ed. (Richmond, Eng.: Curzon, 1997). On Averroes and the intellect, see H. A. Davidson, *Alfarabi, Avicenna, and Averroes on Intellect* (New York: Oxford University Press, 1992).

[6]Aquinas so interpreted Aristotle (ST I, Q. 46, A. 1).

[7]Aquinas, partially on the basis of a faulty Latin translation, so interpreted Aristotle (*Commentary on the De anima* of Aristotle, Lecture 10, nn. 742–5). Aristotle himself seems to hold that the human soul as such perishes with the dissolution of the composite. He explicitly holds that the active intellect, and only the active intellect, is immortal (*De anima* III, 5. 430a 17–25), but he is ambiguous about whether that intellect is a faculty of each human being or a separate substance operative in human beings only during their lifetime. If he means the former, which is unlikely, the individual human soul as such would presumably not be immortal,

nied that the individual human soul was intellectual by its own power and held that it perished with the dissolution of the human being. And Averroes asserted not only that philosophical reason and religious faith are different ways of knowing, but also that the way of reason, that is, the way of philosophy, is superior to the way of faith, that is, the way of theology. (Needless to say, the latter position in particular aroused opposition from contemporary Muslim theologians.)

Some masters of the arts faculty of the University of Paris enthusiastically embraced a radical Aristotelianism regarding the world and the human soul similar to that of Averroes. Prominent among these masters were Siger of Brabant (A.D. 1240?–1281/1284) and John of Jandun (A.D. 1286?–1328). Since radical Aristotelian views about the world and the human soul were clearly in conflict with central tenets of Christian belief, masters who openly taught such views risked condemnation by church officials. Whether for this practical reason or for theoretical reasons, radical Aristotelians like Siger and John seemed to resort to what orthodox adversaries called a theory of double truth. Such a theory would involve maintaining that a proposition can be true from the perspective of reason and philosophy and simultaneously false from the perspective of faith and theology.

Augustine of Hippo (A.D. 354–430) was the foremost Western patristic theologian, and the theology faculty of the University of Paris regarded his explanation and exposition of Christian doctrine as authoritative and quasi-normative. Augustine's theology reflects the dominant Neoplatonist philosophical tradition of his time.[8] Some aspects of the Neoplatonist tradition were unacceptable to Christian thinkers. The Neoplatonist theory of emanation, for example, the theory that the material world necessarily originated by a series of hierarchically descending radiations from an infinite source, is clearly contrary to the Judeo-Christian theory of creation. But there were other elements of Neoplatonism that were attractive to Christian thinkers. The infinite perfection of the One of Neoplatonism is compatible with the infinite perfection of the Christian God. The ideal forms of Neoplatonism, if interpreted as ideas in God's mind regarding the natures of the things he created, ground the intelligibility of the world and his providence. And the Neoplatonist emphasis on the superiority of spirit over matter resonated with Christian doctrine.

---

although part of it would be. If he means the latter, which is likely, there would evidently be no immortality of any part of the individual human soul.

[8]On Augustine generally, see Henry Chadwick, *Augustine* (New York: Oxford University Press, 1986). On Neoplatonism in the Latin tradition, see S. Gersh, *Middleplatonism and Neoplatonism: The Latin Tradition* (Notre Dame: University of Notre Dame Press, 1986).

On the other hand, the Aristotelian approach to philosophy was attractive from many perspectives. Aristotle's explanation of intellection, rooted in sense perception and not merely occasioned by it, seemed to correspond more closely to human experience. Where Neoplatonists regarded material things as ephemeral and unintelligible apart from the ideal forms of which they were obscure reflections, Aristotle regarded material things as unqualifiedly real and intelligible by reason of their own proper forms. Aristotle was thereby able to study material things, including the human composite of matter and spirit, in terms of their four causes (efficient, final, formal, material) and foster physical sciences, albeit not physical sciences in the modern sense. (See Glossary, s.v. *Cause*, *Science [Aristotelian.]*) Where Neoplatonists argued to the existence of the One from internal data (ideas), Aristotle argued to the existence of the Prime Mover from external data (motion and change). Some of the arts faculty of the University of Paris embraced the Aristotelian philosophical perspective without reservation, and theologians like Albert and Aquinas adopted it cautiously.

The Problem of Universals

Human beings predicate common nouns of many things. For example, we say that John is a human being, and so is Joan. What is the ontological status of such predicates and the concepts underlying them? On the one hand, every existing thing is singular. On the other hand, existing material things and human composites of matter and spirit seem to possess common traits and specific identities that validate general concepts regarding the traits or identities. From the singularity of existing things, radical empiricists, called nominalists, argued that universal concepts represent nothing existing in external reality. In other words, nominalists held that universals are nothing more than arbitrary words or purely conceptual constructs subsuming different existing things under a common heading, as, for example, we predicate "member of the armed forces" of soldiers and sailors. Conversely, radical idealists like Plato argued that material things do indeed have common specific identities, and that universal concepts of such identities reflect ideal forms that transcend their material manifestations. The highest form was the One or Good, and the lesser ideal forms shared in the perfection of the highest form.

Aristotle took a middle position. Universals as such do not exist, since every existing thing is singular, but the content of universals, that is, what they represent, exists in things in a concrete, individual way. Aquinas and most medieval theologians accepted this explanation. (Nominalists of the arts faculty of the University of Paris, of course, disagreed.) But Aquinas and other medieval theologians grounded the content of universal ideas in God himself. If universals truly represent the natures and essences of things, and if created things partake of God's essence, then the natures or essences of things need to exist in God in an unparticipated, infinite way. The natures or essences of created things are then the different ways in which various kinds of finite things can share God's essence in finite ways. The ideal forms of Plato do exist, not as such but as the ways in which creatures can partake of God's existing.

The debate over the ontological status of universals is no mere quibble. In the 14th and 15th centuries, nominalists like William of Ockham (A.D. 1285?–1349?) concentrated philosophy on linguistics and logic, with much gain to linguistics and logic and much loss to metaphysics. The implication of nominalism for ethics is particularly important. If there is nothing in external reality corresponding to ideas of human nature and its relation to other things, including God, we cannot ground moral obligation on an order of nature—although some have striven to derive such obligation from a purely internal moral law (Kant) or from a calculus weighing subjectively desirable consequences against subjectively undesirable consequences (utilitarians). And nominalism would preclude any conceptually meaningful theology.

God and the World

Contrary to some popular and scholarly misconceptions of yesteryear, 12th- and 13th-century scholars raised and discussed central problems of human concern, not least the problem of God. There was ongoing intellectual debate both between orthodox Christian thinkers (e.g., between Bonaventure and Aquinas) and between orthodox Christian thinkers and their Muslim and Jewish counterparts. In addition to Averroes, Christian thinkers knew and studied the writings of Avicenna (A.D. 980–1030), Alfarabi (A.D. 870?–950), and Moses Maimonides (A.D. 1138–1204), among others.

From the earliest days of Christianity, Paul of Tarsus (first century A.D.), in the course of preaching to the pagans, claimed that human beings, without the aid of any special divine revelation, could perceive the invisible God in the visible things he created (Rom. 1:20). Later, Augustine advanced explicitly philosophical arguments for God's existence that he deemed demonstrative. Paul and Augustine, from different perspectives, advanced these arguments to convince pagans in a predominantly pagan world of the reasonableness of Christianity. Medieval Christian theologians, on the other hand, lived in a predominantly Christian world. Why, then, did they bother to articulate arguments for God's existence? For the believer, surely, no proof should be necessary.

There is a short and a long answer to this question. The short answer is that there were agnostics and possibly atheists in medieval Christendom, however atypical they were. Few were so bold as to assert categorically that there is no God, or that they doubted his existence. But a number of philosophers were denying the Judeo-Christian idea of a transcendent, provident God. The philosophical God of the so-called Latin Averroists was finite, purely immanent, and disinterested in human affairs. Nor did the logical inconsistency of a putative theory of double truth preclude the possibility that radical Aristotelian views about God were true. One implicit atheist regarding the Christian idea of God, David of Dinant (A.D. 1150?–1206), claimed that God was prime matter, that is, the eternal substratum of material things, and so purely immanent and potential. And the faith of the weak, of course, needed to be confirmed.

Thus there were apologetic reasons for advancing proofs for the existence of God and the chief attributes that Christians predicated of him. But there was another, ultimately more important, reason for such proofs. An intellectually vibrant faith seeks understanding. Faith transcends reason, but reason enlightens faith. Theologians were naturally concerned about what reason can say about God, and his existence was a prerequisite of such inquiry.

Aquinas, in contrast with early modern and many contemporary philosophers, devotes only a few pages of the *Summa Theologica* to questions related to knowledge of God's existence. His five ways of proving God's existence (ST I, Q. 2, A. 3) rest on two principles: (1) the principle of intelligibility or sufficient reason; and (2) the inability of contingent causes to explain adequately the existence of contingent things or their activities in various lines of causality. The more serious question for Aquinas concerned how we know God and the cognitive status of our predications about him.

If God transcends finite things, and Aquinas thought he had demonstrated that by proving that God is the uniquely necessary and perfect being, then we can know what he is not by denying intrinsically finite perfections of him. For example, we can know that God is not material, changeable, and so forth. And since we know that God is not such, we can make true negative statements denying such predicates of him.

But if God transcends finite beings, then no finite intellect unblessed with the vision of God can know what God is in himself, that is, in his infinite perfection.[9] And if finite intellects in this life do not know what God is in himself, then it would seem that human beings cannot make true affirmative statements about him except that he exists and causes everything else to exist. For example, Maimonides claimed that human beings can predicate positive perfections of God only in a metaphorical sense.[10]

Aquinas agrees with Maimonides that human beings cannot know anything about what God is in himself. Our concepts are derived from sense perception, and the senses perceive material things. And so material things are the proper objects of our intellect, and we can in this life understand the nature of human spiritual things only in relation to material things, that is, as immaterial. Moreover, although we can understand that spiritual perfections like intellection and willing, as such, imply no imperfection, we cannot know what such perfections without imperfection are in God. We necessarily understand intellection and willing as they exist in us in a finite way.

But we know God as he is reflected in created things, and we can truly predicate of God pure perfections, that is, perfections that as such signify no imperfection (e.g., intelligence), despite the fact that we have no proper knowledge of what his intelligence is in him. Predicates applied to God and human beings are not univocal, that is, they are not predicated of each in exactly the same sense, as we predicate *human* of different human beings. Nor are such predicates purely equivocal, that is, identical written or spoken words predicated of different things in completely different senses, as in the case of puns. Rather, pure predicates applied both to God and to human beings are analogous, that is, understood and predicated of each in partially the same sense and in partially different senses. We predicate *intelligent* of God and human beings in partially the same sense because God creates the human intelligence we understand, and every effect is like its cause either univocally or analogically. And we predicate *intelligent* of God and human beings in partially different senses, since the way God understands (i.e., by simply and completely understanding himself) is totally different from the way we understand (i.e., by successively and incompletely understanding material things, judging, and reasoning).

There is a paradox here. We do not have proper knowledge of God, that is, knowledge of God as he is in himself, and yet we can properly predicate pure perfections of him in a transcendently eminent way because we know him through the perfections of the things he creates. Moreover, such per-

---

[9]Even those blessed with the vision of God do not and cannot know him comprehensively. Cf. ST I–II, Q. 3, A. 8, *ad* 2.

[10]Moses Maimonides, *Guide to the Perplexed*, part 1, c. 58.

fections are not synonymous, since the multiple perfections of creatures reflect his unique uncreated perfection in different ways.

The demonstrations of God's existence indicate that he is the first cause of the existence and activity of every contingent thing. And if he is the fullness of being, then contingent things share his infinite perfection in different, finite ways. And if he is intelligent, then he creates intelligently, that is, purposefully or providentially.

In Aquinas' view, the existence of the material world depends on God, its primary cause. Contrary to the view of Aristotle and Greek philosophers generally, the finite world cannot sufficiently explain its existence, nor can finite causes sufficiently explain their activities. The world needs to be created by God, and its activities need his concurrence. In this sense of radical dependency, the world does not exist necessarily. But Aquinas does not think that one can demonstrate that the material world had a beginning, that is, that there was a first moment of time (ST I, Q. 46, A. 2). He indeed there affirms as a tenet of Christian faith based on Gen. 1:1 that the world had a beginning, and he argues in the preceding article that reason can demonstrate that the world does not have to be co-eternal with God.

The presence of evil in the world, of course, poses a severe challenge to the biblical belief in a providential creator. How can an all-wise and all-good God foreordain human suffering and death? From the faith perspective, Christians can regard such physical evils as punishment of sin, whether the collectively imputed sin of Adam (cf. Gen. 3, Rom. 5:12–13) or the actual sins of his descendants (cf. Job). Christians can then regard such physical evils as the vindication of God's justice (cf. ST I, Q. 49, A. 2). From the rational perspective, the suffering of human beings may help them to develop and exercise certain moral virtues (e.g., courage, patience, compassion). Regarded in either way, human suffering is not intrinsically evil, and God can accordingly will it for the sake of a greater good (cf. ST I, Q. 2, A. 3, *ad* 1). These explanations are not likely to convince the nonbeliever or fully satisfy the believer, but they may be the most that reason can understand about human suffering without recourse to the role of Christ's suffering and of human beings' share in it in God's salvific plan.

But reconciling the presence of moral evil in the world with God's goodness is more difficult, since God evidently cannot directly cause moral evil without himself being responsible for moral evil. The presence of moral evil in the world challenges the very existence of a providential God in various ways. If God does not cause moral evil, how can he foreknow it? If he has the power to prevent it, why doesn't he? If he doesn't prevent things like the Holocaust, how can he be good? I shall consider Aquinas' views on these questions in connection with human freedom.

Reconciling the physical evil of human suffering with divine providence posed no problem for Aristotle, since the Prime Mover neither created the world nor preordained cosmic activities for the peculiar benefit of human beings. For Aristotle and Greek philosophers generally, the world of nature is indeed orderly, but the order results from the necessary effects of physical causes, with some effects good and some effects bad for particular human beings. This cosmocentric view contrasts sharply with the biblical view of a provident God creating and directing the universe for the benefit of human beings. In this regard, Greek religion to some extent compensated for what Greek philosophy lacked, since the Greeks invoked the favor of generally capricious gods to avert or remedy physical adversity.

The Human Soul and the Human Being

Contemporary philosophers are accustomed to speak of the mind-body problem. Does the human mind have activities irreducible to physical and sensory activities? If the mind's ability to universalize and to reflect on itself transcends physical and sensory powers, how is the mind united to the body? If we substitute the ultimate source of intellectual activity, the soul, for the proximate source of such activity, the mind, we shall be considering the problem from the perspective of medieval scholastic theologians.

Christianity promises the faithful everlasting life. This necessarily presupposes that each human being has an immortal soul that is united to a body in this life but is capable of surviving dissolution of the human composite. For Augustine, the leading Western patristic theologian, as for Nemesius, a leading nearly contemporaneous Greek patristic theologian (late fourth century A.D.), the soul was a spiritual *substance* united to the body.[11] Insofar as the unity of the human composite is concerned, this position echoed the Neoplatonist view that the human being *is* the soul, and that everything else in human beings is accidental,[12] although the union of the soul with the body is for Augustine and Nemesius natural and necessary. But insofar as the origin of the soul is concerned, Augustine rejected

---

[11]On Augustine and the soul as substance, see *City of God* XIII, 2. His position on the creation of the human soul with that of the angels before generation of the human composite also presupposes that the soul is a complete substance. See *On the Literal Meaning of Genesis* VII, 24–28 (PL 34:368–72). On Nemesius and the soul, see *On the Nature of Human Beings* 2 (PG 40:589, 592).

[12]E.g., see Plotinus, *Enneads* IV, tr. 7, c. 8. On Plotinus generally, see L. P. Gerson, *Plotinus* (London: Routledge, 1996).

the Neoplatonist doctrine of emanation and held the orthodox Christian doctrine of creation. The individual human soul, as purely spiritual, cannot be fashioned out of anything preexisting and so needs to be created de novo by God.

Aristotle held a different view of the human soul. For him, the soul is the substantial form of all living material things, whether animal or vegetable, whether human or nonhuman, that is, the intrinsic component that determines living material things to be what they specifically are. The human soul is the substantial form determining human beings to be specifically human and the ultimate source of all their vital activities, including those of the body. The human soul and the body comprise an integral human substance, but does such a view of the human soul as the form of the body entail the conclusion that the human soul, like all other souls and forms, ceases to exist when the composite dissolves? Such a conclusion would be clearly contrary to Christian doctrine.

Aristotle's view of the human soul as the form of the body was reintroduced into Christendom under the mantles of two influential interpreters. One was Avicenna. For him, an Aristotelian deeply influenced by Neoplatonism, the individual human soul emanates from a subsistent pure intelligence, itself the tenth successive emanation from the supreme intelligence. The human soul comes into existence with the body but is united with the body only temporarily. Because the soul is spiritual, its existence does not depend on the body, and so the human soul is immortal. This spiritual being is called a soul or form because of its relation to the body, not because of its essence.[13] This understanding of the human soul, however unacceptable to Christian thinkers the theory of its origin by emanation, was acceptable to them regarding its spiritual nature, and early 13th-century scholastics followed Avicenna in the latter regard. For Albert the Great, Aquinas' teacher, the spiritual soul was the perfection and actualization of the body without being a form in the strict sense, that is, limited by its reception in matter.[14] For Bonaventure, both the soul and the body were complete substances, although the two were naturally united to each other.[15]

---

[13]Avicenna, *De anima* I, 1.

[14]Albert wrote a treatise on the soul (*De anima*). On Albert generally, see A. de Libera, *Albert le Grand et la philosophie* (Paris: Vrin, 1990).

[15]On Bonaventure generally, see Etienne Gilson, *The Philosophy of Bonaventure* (Paterson, N.J.: St. Anthony's Guild, 1965) and J. G. Bougerol, *Introduction to the Works of Bonaventure*, trans. J. de Vinck (St. Anthony's Guild, 1964).

The other major interpreter of Aristotle was Averroes, and Aquinas regarded the latter as the authoritative commentator on the former. For Averroes, the human soul comes into existence by human generation and perishes with the dissolution of the human composite at death. Like other souls and forms, the human soul exists solely by reason of its composition with matter. The active and passive intellects (the intellect causing understanding and the intellect brought to understanding) are indeed spiritual, but they are common, collective powers of a separate substance, a pure intelligence, not intellects belonging to individual human beings. In short, the human soul is not essentially intellectual and so not essentially spiritual and immortal.

Aquinas distinguishes himself from the positions of both interpreters. As one would expect of any Christian thinker, Aquinas agrees with Avicenna that the individual human soul is spiritual and immortal. But he disagrees with Avicenna's (and Augustine's) view that the soul is a complete substance. Aquinas agrees with Averroes that the human soul is the form of the body in the proper sense, that is, the ultimate source of all the vital activities of human beings, including those of the body. But he disagrees vigorously and passionately with Averroes's view about the relation of the human soul to the powers of intellection. Contrary to Averroes, Aquinas holds that each human soul possesses its own active and passive powers of intellection, and so each human soul is spiritual and immortal. In short, the individual human soul, like other substantial forms, is only part, albeit the determinative part, of one human substance, but it is unlike other substantial forms by reason of its spiritual nature and so cannot perish.

Many of Aquinas' contemporaries, especially those unsympathetic to Aristotle, thought it theologically and philosophically impossible for the spiritual soul to be the form of the material body. If the human soul is the form of the body, they argued, then the soul would be incomplete without a body and so incapable of existing apart from the body. But Aquinas thought that analysis of experience justified his conclusions that the substance of human beings is a composite of body and soul, *and* that the soul engages in intellectual activities intrinsically independent of matter. However paradoxical it may be that something intrinsically subsistent can be part of something else, and that a part of something could be something intrinsically subsistent, he did not hesitate to follow where the evidence of experience and the analysis of reason led him. Moreover, his position supplies a rationale for Christian belief in the resurrection of the body, since the soul united to the glorified body will again be a human composite.

Earlier Christian theologians had disagreed about when human souls were or are created. Some said that each soul is created at the time of human generation.[16] Others said that all human souls were created with the angels and came to exist in particular human bodies at the time of human generation.[17] Aquinas, in common with other 13th-century theologians, holds that souls are created individually at the time of each human generation, not collectively with the angels before any human generation (ST I, Q. 90, A. 4). But Aquinas does not claim that the soul is created at the first moment of human generation. Rather, he holds that the human soul is created and infused into the body as its form about three months after conception.[18] Like Aristotle, he reasons that an embryo would not have developed sufficiently to be suitable to receive a rational soul. (This, incidentally, does not affect his position against earlier abortion, since the embryo is already part of the human life process, and human beings should not, in his opinion, directly contravene that process.[19])

The Human End and Human Action

The human soul's intellectual activity is not only cognitive, it is also affective, since human beings can and do desire things they understand, and they can and do will such things for themselves and others. The propriety of desiring and willing particular things depends on whether the things befit human nature and its end.

Aquinas, following Aristotle, identifies happiness as the ultimate goal of human life and understands happiness as the objective fulfillment and perfection of human nature, not a subjective state of euphoria (ST I–II, Q. 1, A. 7). And since human nature is specifically rational, human beings,

---

[16]E.g., Basil, *On the Six Days of Creation*, homily 2 (PG 29:29ff.); Ambrose, *On the Six Days of Creation* I, 7–8 (PL 14:135ff.); John Chrysostom, *On Genesis*, homily 2 (PG 53:31).

[17]E.g., Origen, *On First Principles* I, 6 (PG 11:165) and II, 9 (PG 11:225); Augustine, *On the Literal Meaning of Genesis*, n. 11, supra.

[18]Cf. Aquinas, SCG II, 89.

[19]Aquinas does not explicitly treat of the morality of abortion in the ST or the SCG. But it is evident that he would regard abortions after the infusion of the human soul, that is, during the second and third trimesters of pregnancy, as subject to the precept against direct killing of innocent human beings (cf. ST. II–II, Q. 64, A. 6), although the principle of double effect may be applicable when abortions are necessary to save the life of the mother. And he would regard abortions during the first trimester of pregnancy as subject to the precept against contraception (cf. ST II–II, Q. 154, A. 11, end of article).

in order to be happy, should engage in the cognitive and affective activities of reason itself and in all activities, both animal and rational, according to right reason. Concretely, every activity is either in accord with reason or contrary to it, and certain activities may be always contrary to reason because of their object (e.g., the direct killing of an innocent human being).[20] By good acts of the will, human beings develop good habits of action, moral virtues, the chief of which are justice, moderation, and courage, and the intellectual virtue of prudence, that is, practical wisdom, determines the appropriate means to achieve moral virtues and so governs them. (See Glossary, s.v. *Moral Virtues*, *Practical Wisdom*.)

Human beings enjoy the power of free choice. They can knowingly and willingly act in accord with right reason regarding particular goods. Aquinas devotes the entire second part of the *Summa Theologica* to considering moral good and evil in general and particular virtues and vices. In considering these topics, he reflects much of Aristotle's ethical theory, but he goes further, especially regarding the nature of moral obligation. As provident creator, God foreknows and foreordains human nature, its end, and the proper means to achieve the end. God in so doing commands that human beings act in ways befitting their nature as *rational* animals, and human beings through the use of their reason perceive his commands regarding their nature and apply the commands to their actions. God's commands that human actions befit human nature constitute his eternal law, and human beings' understanding that they should act in ways befitting their nature constitutes the natural law, that is, the law of *human* nature. The natural law is the law of God for human beings, and those who disobey it risk eternal damnation. (See Glossary, s.v. *Law*.)

Happiness in the life hereafter consists of the intellectual vision of God (cf. ST I–II, Q. 3, A. 8), a vision human beings are incapable of achieving by their natural power. The vision of God, however, is not superimposed on the natural end of human beings like a tower on a skyscraper. Rather, human beings have only a single end in the concrete salvific order: incomplete happiness in this life as they advance in intellectual and moral virtue, and complete happiness in the next life as they rest content in the vision of God. Indeed, since human beings naturally desire to know complete truth, they *naturally* desire to know God as he is in himself. Therefore, they cannot be completely happy without the vision of God, although no finite intellect can behold him without his assistance.

Aquinas focused his attention solely on the concrete end that God envi-

---

[20]On intrinsically evil acts generally, see ST I–II, Q. 18, A. 2. On the intrinsic evil of directly killing innocent human beings, see ST II–II, Q. 64, A. 6.

sioned for human beings in the plan of salvation. Later theologians posed a hypothetical, a "what if," question about the possibility of a purely natural end: If God had not chosen to bestow the vision of himself on those who cooperate with his grace, what would have been the human end? Complete happiness in the vision of God, something evidently not possessed in this life, would also have been impossible in the next life. In Thomist terms, although absolutely complete happiness would be impossible without the vision of God, relatively complete happiness would be possible, that is, as much happiness as could be achieved by acquiring theoretical and practical wisdom in this life and by enjoying theoretical wisdom in the next.

How the vision of God complements and fulfills human nature is a theoretical question. But how Christians should integrate their dual membership in earthly and ecclesial societies is preeminently a practical problem. Much of medieval history revolved around conflicts between church and state, and much of medieval political theory revolved around attempts to distinguish and integrate the respective roles of these institutions.

Aquinas distinguishes the two roles. He calls the earthly society secular, its end the secular common good, and its structure of authority the secular power. And he calls the ecclesial society spiritual, its end the spiritual common good, and its structure of authority the spiritual power. In his view, the pope is the supreme ruler in medieval Christendom and the church, but he ordinarily exercises secular power only in the Papal States. Secular rulers exercise secular power elsewhere, and they should exercise that power to assist the spiritual power, even to the point of putting persistent public heretics to death (ST II–II, Q. 11, A. 3). They should also defer to the spiritual power of the church in cases of conflict regarding religion and morals.

Aquinas' subordination of secular society to the church is, of course, inconsistent with the democratic principle of personal religious freedom. The secular-spiritual terminology may have contributed to the inadequate distinction of the two societies, since secular matters can involve spiritual matters (e.g., public policies may have moral dimensions), and spiritual matters can involve secular matters (e.g., safety regulations applied to religious schools). Liberal thinkers made a conceptually sharper and more functionally useful distinction. They distinguished the secular order from the *sacral* order, not the spiritual, and they explicitly denied to the state any competence in sacral matters as such and to the church any competence in secular matters as such. This distinction is now normative in the Western world.

The presence of moral evil in the world singularly challenges the idea of a provident God. Its presence supposes that human beings freely choose to desire and act contrary to God's will, whether he communicates his will by reason or revelation. Reflection on human experience, in

Aquinas' opinion, fully justifies that supposition. And reflection on God's role as the first cause of everything finite leads Aquinas to the conclusion that God both knows and ordains the presence of moral evil in the world he creates. If so, how can God know what human beings will freely do, and how can he ordain the presence of moral evil without being its cause? Aquinas' answers to these questions largely follow the analysis of Augustine.

Moral evil, like physical evil, is not an entity. Rather it is the absence of the requisite conformity of human desires and actions to God's will. Thus God can cause human desires and actions as entities without causing their moral deficiencies.

But if human beings alone are responsible for the moral defects of their desires and actions, how can God know them from all eternity? Material things and human beings exist in time, and their internal and external acts succeed one another. From our perspective, therefore, there are past, present, and future events. From God's perspective, however, all of world history, both material and human, is equally present to him and known by him from all eternity, since his knowledge is identical with himself. Physical causes necessarily produce certain physical effects, given the proper conditions and the absence of outside intervention. But human beings freely produce acts of the will and external acts when they deliberately desire and do things. God knows both kinds of effects *in the way in which they exist*, namely, as necessarily or freely caused. And so God knows everything that human beings have desired and done, are desiring and doing, and will desire or do in the course of human history, just as he knows everything that physical causes have caused, are causing, or will cause in the course of cosmic history.

This means that God knows the morally good desires and deeds of human beings as well as their morally evil desires and deeds. But morally good desires and deeds cannot be salvific, that is, ordered to the vision of God, without his grace, nor can human beings, because of original sin, achieve consistent natural moral rectitude without his grace. There is an asymmetry between the purely human potential for, and reward merited by, natural moral virtue, on the one hand, and the purely human potential for, and punishment merited by, natural moral vice. Consistent natural moral virtue is not possible without grace, nor can natural moral virtue merit salvation, but natural moral vice is due solely to the human will and can merit damnation. This poses the paradox of predestination: some human beings with the help of God's efficacious grace are predestined to heavenly blessedness, albeit with their free cooperation, and other human beings without that help can be predestined to eternal damnation, albeit by their own free choice.

Catholic theologians of the 16th and 17th centuries, principally members of the Dominican and Jesuit religious orders, did not think the Augustinian–Thomist explanation completely sufficient, especially in the context of Protestant theories of predestination.[21] How can God know with certainty what human beings will do? Without further explanation, does not the Augustinian-analysis render the course of human history independent of God's providence?

To remedy this perceived inadequacy, Dominican theologians postulated that God causes the predestined to choose moral good and reject moral evil, although human beings freely cooperate with his grace, and that the damned receive no like predetermination to choose moral good and reject moral evil. The Dominican explanation seemed to Jesuit theologians to vindicate divine omnipotence at the price of human freedom. For their part, Jesuit theologians postulated that God, in creating human beings, not only foresaw what human beings will do freely in the actual world, but also what human beings *would* do freely in a world God chose not to create. The Jesuit explanation seemed to Dominican theologians to vindicate human freedom at the price of divine omnipotence. How, they asked, can God know that human beings will be morally good in the actual world, or would be morally good in a hypothetical world, without predetermining their actions to be such?

In my opinion, these "further explanations" are unnecessary. Aquinas' analysis, derived from Augustine, links God's knowledge of free human acts to their reality as such, and that may be as much as we can say about God's knowledge and power regarding human freedom.

It is interesting to contrast the Reformation and Counter-Reformation concern about how to reconcile human freedom with God's power, and contemporary concern about how to reconcile moral evil and its consequences with his justice. How can a just and provident God tolerate moral evil and injustice? Is it just for God to create human beings who he knows will be damned (assuming there be any such)? Is it just for God to allow human beings to be subject to injustices, often monstrous, by other human beings? In Aquinas' view, human freedom itself involves the possibility of moral evil and its consequences, and God could not create human beings without them possessing the power of free choice. Moreover, regarding actual moral evil and its unjust consequences, God ultimately vindicates justice by punishing the sinner, perhaps in this world but certainly in the next.

---

[21]For a general description of the controversy, especially as Roman authorities became involved, see James Broderick, *Robert Bellarmine* (Westminster, Md.: Newman, 1961), pp. 189–216.

1

God

The ST begins with questions about God. This chapter deals with many of these questions and strictly follows the order in the Summa. *The order is precise. After defending theology as necessary and, in the Aristotelian sense, scientific (ST I, Q. 1), Thomas quite logically begins with questions about God's existence. Second, he deals with his so-called attributes, that is, characteristics we predicate of God considered in himself apart from considering his activity. Third, he explains our knowledge of God and assesses our predications about him. Fourth, he examines characteristics we predicate about God regarding his immanent activity (knowing and willing). Lastly, he analyzes aspects of his transitive activity regarding creatures, especially human beings (providence, predestination, power).*

Existence

Thomas here asks and answers three questions: Is God's existence self-evident, that is, known when we understand what the term God *means? If not, can we demonstrate his existence? If we can, how? The answer to the first question makes clear that God's existence, although self-evident in itself because the predicate* exists *necessarily belongs to the subject* God, *is not self-evident to us because we do not in this life know God's essence in itself. In response to an objection, he explicitly rejects Anselm's so-called ontological argument, namely, that God's existence is self-evident from the definition of God as the greatest conceivable being. Thomas rejects the argument's implicit transition from existing conceptually to existing outside the mind. The answer to the second question claims that we can demonstrate from known things that God exists as their cause, although we have no knowledge of what God is in himself. The answer to the third question proposes five ways to demonstrate his existence.*

The ways presuppose the principle of intelligibility or sufficient reason, namely, that things need to have a sufficient reason that explains why they exist or happen. Because we immediately recognize the truth of this principle, and of the related principle of causality (things happen because other things cause them to happen), when we understand the terms of the principles, philosophers commonly call the principles analytic, that is, self-evident.

The first way focuses on the observed locomotion and alterations that happen to material things. These changes are only intelligible if something else causes the changes, and there cannot be an infinite regress of caused causes, causes that themselves need to be moved or changed from inactivity to activity. Therefore, there exists an uncaused cause that is pure actuality.

The second way focuses on the same fact of accidental changes in the world from the perspective of the causes of the changes and reaches the same conclusion.

The third way is difficult to interpret, and many scholars, including some generally sympathetic to Thomas, find the argument flawed. The central problem concerns interpretation of the temporal references. Is Thomas assuming hypothetically that the world always existed, that is, that the world had no first moment? (Or conversely, is he assuming the biblical view that the world had a beginning?) Is he claiming that if the world has existed eternally, and if only substantially changeable things have existed, then everything would have ceased to exist by now? Is he assuming the possibility of time before things come to be and pass away?

But the temporal references need not be interpreted in a strictly temporal sense. When Thomas says that intrinsically contingent things, that is, substantially changeable things, at one time did not exist, he may simply mean that such things are things that come to be, and that something necessary needs to cause the intrinsically contingent things' coming to be. And when he says that if every existing thing is intrinsically contingent, there was a time when there was nothing, he may simply mean that nothing at all would exist because there would be nothing to cause the intrinsically contingent things to come to be.

If the argument is so interpreted, it can be summarized as follows. We observe that material things do not exist necessarily but come to be and pass away, that is, that material things are intrinsically contingent. But such things cannot exist by their own power and can do so only by the power of something else that does not come to be and pass away, that is, such things exist by the power of something intrinsically necessary. Therefore, if everything were intrinsically contingent, nothing would exist. But this is contrary to fact. Therefore, there needs to exist a necessary being that causes the existence of intrinsically contingent things, and ultimately an absolutely necessary being, one that is not only intrinsically necessary like angels but also does not depend extrinsically on any other necessary being. In short, intrinsically contingent beings can neither severally nor collectively account for their coming to exist, and only an absolutely necessary being, God, can. This interpretation of the third way is logically consistent and compatible with the similar arguments that Thomas advances in SCG I, 15, and CT I, 6.

The fourth way begins with the observed gradations of existing and perfection in the world. But we call things more or less excellent insofar as they ap-

proximate something most excellent, and being in the highest degree. And as the most in the transcendental genus of being, this most excellent thing causes the being and excellence of everything else. This way argues from the perfection of observed things to the existence of an absolutely perfect exemplar, but the exemplar is a concrete reality, not an abstract idea, and the efficient cause, not merely the exemplar, of everything else.

The fifth way begins with the observed regularity of the activities of natural material things in the world. The regularity indicates that the things act purposively, and yet they lack the intelligence prerequisite for purposeful activity. Therefore, there needs to be an intelligent being that orders the things of nature to their ends. Alone of the five ways, the fifth explicitly argues to the existence of an intelligent *source that ordains the activities of material things. The fifth way is also unique in not explicitly concluding to the existence of God as the efficient cause of the world's existence and processes of change. Thomas's argument is not the design argument of William Paley (1743–1805). Thomas here argues from the fact that particular things act in a regular way, not from the fact that the cumulative activities of particular things produce an ordered universe, a cosmos, although he indeed holds that to be true.*

1. Is the existence of God self-evident?[1]

I answer that a proposition is self-evident because its predicate is contained in its subject's essence. Therefore, if all know the proposition's predicate and its subject's essence, the proposition will be self-evident to all. But if some should not know the predicate and the subject's essence, the proposition will be self-evident in itself but not to those persons.

The proposition that God exists is in itself self-evident, since the predicate *(existing)* is the same as the subject *(God)*.[2] But we do not know what God is. Therefore, the proposition is not self-evident to us and needs to be demonstrated by things more known to us and less distinguished as to their nature, namely, by effects.

Objection. Propositions are self-evident if we know their truth as soon as we understand the terms, and we know that God exists as soon as we understand the term *God*. For God exists in the intellect as soon as we understand the term *God,* and the term *God* means that than which nothing greater can be conceived. But what exists in fact is greater than what exists in the intellect alone. Therefore, the existence of God is self-evident.

---

[1]ST I, Q. 2, A. 1.

[2]That God's essence is his existing, see below, pp. 6–7.

Reply Obj. Some believe that God is a material substance and so do not understand that the term *God* means that than which nothing greater can be conceived. Even supposing that one understands that the term *God* means that than which no greater can be conceived, it only follows that such a one would understand that the meaning of the term exists conceptually, not that it would exist actually. Nor can one prove that God really exists unless one admits that something than which no greater can be conceived really exists, a proposition that those who deny the existence of God do not admit.

2. Can we demonstrate the existence of God?[3]

I answer that we demonstrate in two ways. One way is by means of a cause, and this is to demonstrate why something is so. The other is by means of an effect, and this is to demonstrate that something exists. But we can demonstrate the existence of a cause from any of its effects if the latter are more known to us, since effects depend on their causes, and so causes necessarily preexist their effects. Therefore, we can demonstrate God's existence through the effects known to us.

3. Does God exist?[4]

I answer that we can demonstrate God's existence in five ways:

(1) The first and more evident way is the one from motion. Everything moved is moved by something else, for an object is only moved insofar as it has potentiality for that to which it is moved, while something produces motion only insofar as it is actual. To move something is only to bring it from potentiality to actuality, and only an actual being can do so. But the same object cannot at the same time be actual and potential in the same respect. Therefore, nothing can produce and undergo motion in the same respect and in the same way. Therefore, everything moved needs to be moved by something else. And if the cause of motion is moved, the cause itself needs to be moved by another, and that other by another. But this regress ought not to be endless, since there would then be no first cause of motion and so no other cause of motion. For example, a stick causes motion only because a hand moves it. Therefore, we need to arrive at a first cause of motion, one moved by nothing else, and all understand this first cause of motion to be God.

(2) The second way considers efficient causes. There is an order of efficient causes regarding objects of sense experience. But nothing is the

---

[3]ST I, Q. 2, A. 2. [4]ST I, Q. 2, A. 3.

efficient cause of itself. Nor can there be an infinite regress in the matter of efficient causes, since in all subordinated efficient causes, something first causes something intermediate, and something intermediate causes something last, whether the intermediate things be several or only one. And if a cause is taken away, its effect is taken away. Therefore, there will be no intermediate causes or final effect if there be no first cause. Therefore, an infinite regress regarding efficient causes is impossible. Therefore, we need to posit a first efficient cause, and we call this cause God.

(3) We take the third way from the possible and the necessary. There are kinds of things that can exist and can not-exist, since the things come to be and pass away. But it is impossible that all such things always exist, since what can not-exist, at some point of time does not exist. Therefore, if everything can not-exist, there was a time when nothing really existed. But if this is so, nothing would also now exist, since something nonexistent begins to exist only through the agency of something that does exist. Therefore, if nothing existed, nothing could begin to exist, and so nothing would now exist, and this conclusion is obviously false. Therefore, not every being is something that can not-exist, and there needs to be some necessary reality. But everything necessary either has or does not have the ground of its necessity from another source. And there cannot be an infinite regress regarding necessary things that have the ground of their necessity in another source. Therefore, we need to posit something intrinsically necessary, something that does not have the ground of its necessity from another source. And all call this intrinsically necessary being God.

(4) We take the fourth way from the gradations that we find in reality. We find things that are more good or less good, more true or less true, more excellent or less excellent, and so forth. But we predicate *more* or *less* of different things as they in various ways approximate what is most. Therefore, there is something that is most true and most good and most excellent and so being in the highest degree. But what we call most in any genus causes everything belonging to that genus. Therefore, there exists something that causes the existing and goodness and perfections of everything else, and we call this cause God.

(5) We take the fifth way from the governance of things. Certain things lacking knowledge, namely, natural material substances, act frequently in the same way in order to achieve what is best, and so they evidently achieve their goal by striving for it, not by chance. But things lacking knowledge strive for goals only if a being with knowledge and intelligence directs them, as, for example, an archer aims an arrow. Therefore, there is a being with intelligence that orders all the things of nature to their ends, and we call this being God.

Objection. If God were to exist, nothing evil would exist. But evil things do exist. Therefore, God does not exist.

Reply Obj. Because God is the highest good, it belongs to his infinite goodness to permit evil things and bring forth good things from them.

Simplicity

Thomas in this and immediately succeeding sections considers things we predicate of God essentially, that is, of God considered in himself apart from his activity. People frequently refer to these predicates as his attributes. But God, strictly speaking, has no attributes. He is the fullness of being and pure actuality and so does not "have" anything over and above his substance.

1. Is God identical with his essence or nature?[5]

I answer that in things composed of matter and form, particular matter is not included in the definition of things. For example, particular flesh and bones are not included in the definition of human being, although they are included in what human beings are. And so human beings and human being are not identical.

But in things not composed of matter and form, things in which there is no individuation by particular matter, the very forms are subsistent, individually existing substances. Therefore, individual substance and nature do not differ in them. Therefore, God is necessarily his divinity, his life, and anything else we predicate of him in this way.

Objection. Causes and their effects are similar. But existing created substances are not identical with their nature. For example, human beings are not identical with their humanity. Therefore, God is not identical with his divinity.

Reply Obj. God's effects imitate him insofar as they can. But God's effects can represent him only in limited ways. Therefore, God's effects are composite, and their individual substance and their nature are not identical in them, as God's individual substance and his nature are in him.

2. Are God's essence and his existing identical in him?[6]

I answer that God is both his essence and his existing, for three reasons. First, were this not so, God's existence would need to be caused by the sources of his essence or by an external cause. But nothing suffices to cause its own existence if it has a caused existence, and so such a thing's

---

[5]ST I, Q. 3, A. 3. [6]ST I, Q. 3, A. 4.

existence cannot be caused only by the sources of the thing's essence. Therefore, God's existence, were it not identical with his essence, would need to be caused by another. But we cannot say this about God, since he is the cause of every effect. Therefore, God's essence and existing are identical.

Second, existing is related to an essence distinct from it as actuality is related to potentiality. But there is nothing potential in God. Therefore, his essence is identical with his existing.

Third, what possesses existing and is not identical with existing shares in being. But if God's essence not be identical with his existing, he will share in being and not be such by his essence. Therefore, he will not be the first being, which is absurd. Therefore, God is his existing as well as his essence.

Perfection

1. Is God perfect?[7]

I answer that matter as such is potential, and the first material source the most potential. And so the first material source is most imperfect. But God is the first source as efficient cause, not as something material, and such a source is necessarily the most perfect. For things are perfect insofar as they are actual, and efficient causes as such are actual. Therefore, the first efficient cause is necessarily most actual and so most perfect.

2. Does God possess the perfections of all things?[8]

I answer that the perfections of all things exist in God. We can consider this from two perspectives. First, any perfection in an effect needs to be found in its efficient cause either in the same respect if the cause is univocal (e.g., human beings beget human beings) or in a more outstanding way if the cause is nonunivocal (e.g., the likeness of the sun and what the sun produces). Effects preexist in the power of their efficient causes, and efficient causes are perfect, although preexisting in the power of a natural cause is to preexist in a less perfect way. But God is the first efficient cause of things. Therefore, the perfections of all things necessarily preexist in him in a more outstanding way.

Second, God is intrinsically subsistent existing itself, and so he necessarily contains in himself the whole perfection of existing. But the perfections of everything belong to the perfection of existing, since things are

---

[7]ST I, Q. 4, A. 1.   [8]ST I, Q. 4, A. 2.

perfect insofar as they possess existence in some way. Therefore, God does not lack the perfection of anything.

3. Can creatures be like God?[9]

I answer that there are as many kinds of likeness as there are many ways of sharing in a form. Things sharing in the same form in the same respect and in the same measure are perfectly alike. Things sharing in the same form in the same respect but not in the same measure are imperfectly alike. Things sharing in the same form but in different respects, as in the case of nonunivocal causes and effects, are even more imperfectly alike. Therefore, if an efficient cause does not belong to a genus, its effects remotely approach a likeness to the form of the cause, although not in the same specific or generic respect. They share likeness by an analogy, as existing itself is common to all things. And the things made by God, insofar as they are beings, are likened to him as the first and universal source of all existing.

Objection 1. Things agreeing in form are similar. But nothing is one with God in form, since only God's essence is existing itself. Therefore, no creature is like God.

Reply Obj. 1. We do not say that there is a likeness of creatures to God because God and creatures share a form in the same generic or specific respect. Rather, we say that there is a likeness only by analogy, namely, as God is a being by his essence, and other things are beings by participation.

Obj. 2. There is mutual likeness in like things, since something like is like something like. Therefore, if a creature is like God, God will also be like the creature. But this is contrary to Is. 40:18: "To whom have you made God like?"

Reply Obj. 2. Although we may in one respect concede that creatures are like God, we can in no respect grant that God is like creatures, since there is no mutual likeness in causes and effects of different orders. For example, a portrait is like a human being, but not vice versa, and we likewise can in one respect say that creatures are like God, but not vice versa.

Goodness

1. Is God the highest good?[10]

I answer that God is the highest good without qualification and not only in some genus or order of things. For we attribute goodness to God inas-

---

[9]ST I, Q. 4, A. 3. [10]ST I, Q. 6, A. 2.

much as all desired perfections flow from him as first cause. But they flow from him as an efficient cause that is not one with its effects in specific or generic respects. And we find the likeness of effects in such a nonunivocal cause in a more excellent way. Since good is in God as the first, nonunivocal cause of all things, good is necessarily in him in the most excellent way. And so we call him the highest good.

Objection. Highest signifies comparison. But things not belonging to the same genus are not comparable. For example, sweetness is not greater or lesser than a line. Therefore, since God does not belong to the same genus as other things, we cannot call God the highest good in relation to other things.

Reply Obj. Things not belonging to the same genus are in no way comparable if they belong to different genera. But God does not belong to the same genus with other things because he is outside genus and is the source of every genus, not because he belongs to another genus. And so we compare him to other things by superfluity, and the highest good signifies such a comparison.

Infinity

1. Is God unlimited?[11]

I answer that matter does not perfect form. Rather, matter restricts the fullness of form. And so the infinite, as possessed by a form that matter does not limit, has the nature of something perfect. But the most formal of all things is existing itself. Therefore, since God is his subsistent existing, and his existing is not received in something, he is infinite and perfect.

Immutability

1. Is God altogether immutable?[12]

I answer that God is altogether immutable for three reasons. First, God is the first being, and such a being needs to be pure actuality without admixture of any potentiality. But everything in any way changed is in some way potential. Therefore, God cannot change in any way.

Second, everything changed remains partially and passes away partially. For example, something changed from white to black remains the

[11]ST I, Q. 7, A. 1. [12]ST I, Q. 9, A. 1.

same substantially. And so there is composition in everything changed. But there is no composition in God. Therefore, God cannot change.

Third, everything changed acquires something it did not have before. But God includes the entire full perfection of the whole of existing and cannot acquire anything he did not have before. And so God cannot change in any way.

Eternity

1. Is God eternal?[13]

I answer that the aspect of eternity is a logical consequence of immutability just as the aspect of time is a logical consequence of motion. And so being eternal is most proper to God, since he is most immutable. And God is such just as he is his essence.

Only One

1. Is there only one God?[14]

I answer that three arguments demonstrate that there is only one God. First, the simplicity of God demonstrates his uniqueness. For the source whereby an individual thing is this particular thing can in no way be communicated to many things. For example, the source whereby Socrates is human can be communicated to many things, but the source whereby Socrates is this particular human being can be communicated to only one thing. Therefore, if Socrates were human by the source whereby he is this human being, there could not be many human beings, just as there could not be many Socrates. But God is his nature and so God by the source whereby he is this God. Therefore, being God and being this God are identical. Therefore, there cannot be several Gods.

Second, the infinity of God's perfection demonstrates that there is only one God. God includes within himself the whole perfection of existing. Therefore, if there were several Gods, they would need to differ. Therefore, something would be proper to one that was not proper to another. But if such a thing were a privation, the one deprived would not be absolutely perfect, and if such a thing were a perfection, the other would lack it. And so there is only one infinite source.

---

[13]ST I, Q. 10, A. 2. [14]ST I, Q. 11, A. 3.

Third, the uniqueness of the world demonstrates the uniqueness of God. All existing things are related to one another insofar as some are subordinate to others. But different things would not be integrated in one orderly set of relations unless one thing disposed them. For one thing intrinsically causes one thing, and many things cause one thing only accidentally. And so one thing brings many things into an orderly set of relations better than many things would. But what is first is most perfect, and such intrinsically, not accidentally. Therefore, there is necessarily only one first being that brings everything into an orderly set of relations, and this first being is God.

Our Knowledge of God

Thomas here considers our knowledge of God. He affirms that the human intellect has a potentiality to know God as he is in himself, but that natural reason knows him in this life only through his effects.

1. Can a created intellect behold the essence of God?[15]

I answer that everything is knowable insofar as it is actual. But God is pure actuality without any admixture of potentiality. Therefore, he is most knowable as he is in himself.

Some thinkers have held that no created intellect can behold God's essence because that object, knowable in itself, surpasses such an intellect. But the intellectual activity of human beings is their highest activity, in which their happiness consists. If no created intellect can ever behold God's essence, either the created intellect will never attain happiness, or its happiness will consist of something other than God.

But faith contradicts this position. For everything is perfect insofar as it attains its source, and so a rational creature's ultimate perfection rests in the very thing that is the source of the rational creature's existing. Reason also contradicts the position. For human beings, when they see an effect, have a desire from nature to know the effect's cause. But if the intellect of a rational creature could not attain the first cause of all things, this desire from nature will remain unfulfilled. And so we need to admit without qualification that the blessed behold God's essence.

2. Can we know God in this life by natural reason?[16]

I answer that our natural knowledge originates with the senses, and so our natural knowledge can reach only as far as sensible objects can lead it.

---

[15]ST I, Q. 12, A. 1. [16]ST I, Q. 12, A. 12.

But sensible creatures are effects of God unequal to the power of their cause. Therefore, we cannot know the entire power of God from our knowledge of sensible objects, nor can we perceive his essence. But we can be led by God's effects to know that he exists, and to know about him what necessarily befits him as the first cause of everything, one who surpasses everything he has caused. And so we know the relationship of God to creatures, namely, that he causes everything, and the difference of creatures from him, namely, that he is not part of what he has caused, and his effects are apart from him because he surpasses them superabundantly, not because he lacks anything.

Objection. The good and the wicked obtain knowledge by natural reason. But only the good have knowledge of God, since only the virtue of faith can purify human understanding. Therefore, we cannot know God by natural reason.

Reply Obj. Knowledge of God by his essence is by grace and so belongs only to the good, but knowledge of him by natural reason can belong to the good and the wicked.

Our Predicates about God

Thomas here considers the truth value of our predications about God. He can easily defend the truth value of negative predications, predications that deny imperfections of God (e.g., God is not material). But affirmative predications pose a serious problem, since our intellect is dependent on sense images and so cannot know God in himself. He claims that we can affirm pure perfections, that is, perfections that as such do not imply imperfections (e.g., goodness, knowing, willing). Since effects are like their causes, we can analogously predicate of God the pure perfections found in finite ways in sensible things, that is, we can predicate those pure perfections of God in a sense partly the same and yet completely different insofar as he infinitely transcends creatures. Thomas thus proposes a via media between what he deems excessive rationalism and excessive agnosticism. This is an important contribution to the problem of what philosophers sometimes call God-talk.

1. Is any predicate appropriate for God?[17]

I answer that expressions are the signs of what we understand, and what we understand are the likenesses of things. And so expressions are related to signifying objects by means of what the intellect conceives. Therefore,

---

[17] ST I, Q. 13, A. 1.

we can apply a predicate to something insofar as we can know the thing intellectually. But we cannot perceive God by his essence. Rather, we know him from creatures by his causal relationship to them and by way of eminence and elimination. Therefore, we can apply predicates to him from creatures, although not in such a way that the predicates signifying him express his essence as it is, as, for example, the term *human being* by its meaning expresses the human essence as it is. For *human being* signifies the definition of human being, and the definition declares its essence.

Objection 1. Every predicate is either abstract or concrete. But concrete predicates are not proper to God because he is simple, and abstract predicates are not proper to him because they do not signify a complete and subsistent being.[18] Therefore, we can apply no predicate to God.

Reply Obj. 1. We know God from creatures, and we apply predicates to him from them. Therefore, the predicates signify in the way proper to material creatures, which we know connaturally. But what is complete and subsistent in such creatures is composite, and the forms of creatures are not complete subsistent things. Therefore, the predicates we apply to signify complete subsisting things signify things in their materiality, since materiality belongs to composite things. And the predicates we apply to signify simple forms signify the sources whereby things are such and such (e.g., whiteness signifies the source whereby something is white). Therefore, because God is both simple and subsistent, we attribute to him both abstract predicates to signify his simplicity and concrete predicates to signify his subsistence and completeness. But both such predicates fall short of his way, since our intellect in this life does not know him as he is.

Obj. 2. Nouns signify substances qualitatively, verbs and participles signify substances temporally, and pronouns signify substances demonstratively or relatively. And none of these is proper to God, since he lacks qualities, every accident, and time, and we cannot perceive him sensibly so as to point him out. Nor can we signify him relatively, since relative pronouns record the aforementioned nouns or particles or demonstrative pronouns. Therefore, we can in no way apply a predicate to God.

Reply Obj. 2. To signify a substance qualitatively is to signify an individually existing subject with the determined nature or form in which it subsists. And so, as we give predicates to God in their materiality in order to signify his subsistence and completeness, so do we give him predicates

---

[18]Abstract predicates (e.g., *wisdom*) signify forms apart from subjects, and concrete predicates (e.g., *wise*) signify forms in subjects. Therefore, the objection argues, the proposition *God is wisdom* fails to signify God's subsistence, and the proposition *God is wise* fails to signify his simplicity.

that signify his substance qualitatively. And we predicate of him verbs and participles connoting time because eternity includes all time. But we can understand subsistent things absolutely and signify them absolutely only by way of composite things. And so we can understand absolute eternity and give expression to it only by way of temporal things and because of the connaturality of our intellect for composite and temporal things. And we predicate demonstrative pronouns of God insofar as they point to what we understand, not to what we sensibly perceive. For things fall within demonstration insofar as we understand them. And so also we can signify God by relative pronouns in the way in which we predicate nouns and participles and demonstrative pronouns of him.

2. Do we apply any predicates to God substantially?[19]

I answer that predicates that we apply to God negatively, or that signify his relation to creatures, in no way signify his substance but signify the elimination of something from him, or the relation of something to him. And other predicates signify the divine substance, and we apply these predicates substantially, although such predicates deficiently represent him. Predicates signify God in the way in which our intellect knows him, and our intellect knows him in the way in which creatures represent him. But God, as absolutely and completely perfect, possesses in himself beforehand all the perfections of creatures. And so every creature is like him insofar as he has some perfection, so that creatures represent him as the preeminent source of creatures' perfections, not as something belonging to the same species or genus. And creatures' perfections fall short of his form even though they attain a certain likeness to him. The aforementioned predicates thus signify the divine substance, albeit imperfectly, just as creatures represent him imperfectly.

Therefore, when we say that God is good, we do not mean that God causes goodness, or that God is not bad, but we mean that the goodness in creatures preexists in God and in a higher way. And so it does not follow that good belongs to God because he causes goodness, but rather the converse, that he pours out goodness to things because he is good.

Objection. We apply a predicate in the way we understand the predicate. But we do not in this life understand God substantially. Therefore, we do not apply any predicate to him substantially.

Reply Obj. We cannot in this life know the essence of God as it is in itself, but we know his essence as represented in the perfections of creatures. And so the predicates we apply to him signify his essence.

---

[19]ST I, Q. 13, A. 2.

3. Do we apply any predicate to God in a proper sense?[20]

I answer that we know God from the perfections that come from him to creatures, and these perfections are in God in a more excellent way. But our intellect understands them in the way they are in creatures, and it signifies them by predicates in the way in which it understands them. Therefore, there are two things to consider in the predicates we apply to God, namely, the signified perfections themselves (e.g., goodness, life, and the like) and the way of signifying them. Therefore, such predicates, as to what they signify, belong to God in the proper sense and more properly than they belong to creatures, and we apply the predicates to him in the primary sense. But as to the predicates' way of signifying, we do not apply the predicates to God in the proper sense, since they have a way of signifying that belongs to creatures.

Objection. We take from creatures every predicate we apply to God. But we apply creatures' predicates to God metaphorically, as when we say that God is stone or lion or any such thing. Therefore, we apply every predicate to God metaphorically.

Reply Obj. Some predicates signify perfections that come from God to creatures in such a way that the imperfect way itself whereby a creature shares a divine perfection is included in the very meaning of the predicate. For example, stone signifies something that exists in a material way, and we can apply such predicates to God only metaphorically. But some predicates signify the perfections themselves absolutely, without any mode of sharing being included in their meaning (e.g., being, good, living, and the like), and we apply such predicates to God in the proper sense.

4. Are predicates of God synonyms?[21]

I answer that predicates of God are not synonyms. This would be easy to see if we were to say that such predicates were introduced to eliminate something or to designate a causal relationship regarding creatures. But such predicates signify the divine substance, albeit imperfectly, and the predicates have different aspects, since the considerations the predicates signify are conceptions of the intellect about the reality the predicates signify. And our intellect, knowing God from creatures, forms concepts proportioned to the perfections of creatures in order to understand him. And these perfections preexist in God as one and without composition, although they are received in creatures separately and diversely. Therefore, as the one simple source that these different perfections of creatures diversely represent corresponds to these perfections, so the one entirely

---

[20]ST I, Q. 13, A. 3. [21]ST I, Q. 13, A. 4.

simple being that we by different concepts imperfectly understand corresponds to such concepts. And so the predicates we apply to God, although they signify only one reality, are not synonyms, since they signify that reality under many different aspects.

5. Do we univocally apply predicates to God and creatures?[22]

I answer that we can predicate nothing of God and creatures univocally. For every effect unequal to its efficient cause receives a likeness of the cause in a different way. All the perfections of things, which exist in creatures separately and diversely, preexist in God as one. When we apply a perfection of creatures to creatures, the predicate signifies the perfection as distinct from other perfections by reason of its definition. For example, when we apply the predicate *wise* to human beings, we signify a perfection distinct from the essence of human beings, and from their power and their existing and the like. But when we apply the predicate *wise* to God, we do not intend to signify anything distinct from his essence or his power or his existing. And so the predicate *wise*, when predicated of human beings, somehow circumscribes and comprehends the thing signified, but the predicate, when predicated of God, leaves the thing signified as not grasped and surpassing the meaning of the predicate. And so we do not apply the predicate *wise* to God and human beings by the same consideration. And so also with other predicates. And so we do not apply any predicate to God and creatures univocally.

But neither do we apply any predicate to God purely equivocally, since we know God and demonstrate many things about him. Therefore, we need to say that we apply predicates to God and creatures analogously, that is, relationally. Such predications result in two ways. They result in one way because many things have a relation to one thing. For example, we predicate *healthy* of medicine and urine insofar as each has an order and relation to the health of animals, of which urine is the sign and medicine the cause. Such predications result in a second way because one thing has a relation to another thing. For example, we predicate *healthy* of medicine and animals insofar as medicine causes the health of animals. And we apply predicates to God in the latter way, not purely equivocally or univocally. And so whatever we predicate of God and creatures, we predicate insofar as there is a relation of creatures to God, as the source and cause in which all the perfections of things eminently preexist.

And that way of commonality is a mean between pure equivocation and absolute univocity. For there is neither one consideration in things predi-

---

[22]ST I, Q. 13, A. 5.

cated analogically nor totally different considerations. But words so predicated in different ways signify different relations to one thing. For example, the word *healthy*, when predicated of urine, signifies as the sign of animals' health, but when predicated of medicine, signifies as the cause of their health.

6. Do we temporally apply to God predicates signifying a relation to creatures?[23]

I answer that we temporally, not eternally, apply to God predicates that signify a relation to creatures. Some relations are real regarding one terminus and purely conceptual regarding the other, and this happens whenever the two termini do not belong to the same order. For example, sense perception and knowledge are related to sensible and knowable objects, and the latter, as real objects, exist outside the order of sensible and intelligible objects. And so there is a real relation in knowledge and sense perception as the latter are ordered to knowing or perceiving objects, but those very objects, considered in themselves, exist outside such an order. And so the objects have a purely conceptual relation to knowledge and sense perception as the intellect conceives the objects as termini of the relations of knowledge and sense perception. And so we predicate the objects of knowledge and sense perception relationally because acts of knowledge and sense perception are related to the objects, not because the objects are related to other things.

Therefore, since God exists outside the whole order of creatures, and all creatures are ordered to him, and not vice versa, creatures are really related to God himself, although there is only a conceptual relation of him to creatures insofar as creatures are related to him. And so nothing prevents us from applying such predicates of God temporally because of changes in creatures, not because of changes in him.

Objection. If we apply some predicates to God temporally because they signify a relation to creatures, then the same is true about any predicate that signifies a relation to creatures. But we apply to God from eternity some predicates that signify a relation to creatures. For example, Jer. 31:3 says that God knew and loved creatures from eternity. Therefore, we also apply to God from eternity other predicates signifying a relation to creatures, such predicates as *Lord* and *creator*.

Reply Obj. Operations of intellect and will are in the one who knows and wills, and so we apply to God from eternity predicates signifying rela-

---

[23]ST I, Q. 13, A. 7.

tions that result from the activity of his intellect and will. But we apply to God temporally predicates that result from his activity going out (according to our way of understanding) to external effects, such as the predicates *savior*, *creator*, and the like.

7. Do we apply the predicate *God* to God by participation, nature, and opinion?[24]

I answer that we understand the three aforementioned meanings analogically, not univocally or equivocally. This is clear because the meaning of univocal terms is entirely the same, the meaning of equivocal terms entirely different, but we in the case of analogical terms need to posit a term understood by one meaning in the definition of the same term understood by other meanings. For example, we posit the being predicated of substances in the definition of the being predicated of accidents. And we posit the healthy predicated of animals in the definition of the healthy predicated of urine and medicine, since urine is the sign, and medicine the cause, of what is healthy in animals.

And the same is true about the question at issue. For we understand the word *God*, as understood to mean the true God, to include the meaning of God predicated by opinion or participation. For when we call a being God by participation, we understand by the word *God* something that has a likeness to the true God. Likewise, when we call an idol God, we understand by the word *God* something that human beings think to be God. And so the meaning of the word is sometimes this and sometimes that, but one of those meanings is included in the other meanings. And so we evidently predicate the word *God* analogically.

8. Can we formulate affirmative propositions about God?[25]

I answer that we can form true affirmative propositions about God. The predicate and subject in a true affirmative proposition need to signify something really the same in one respect and something conceptually different. This is evident both in the case of propositions with accidental predicates and propositions with substantial predicates. For example, being human and being white are identical in their subject, but they differ conceptually, since the aspect of being white and the aspect of being human are different things. And the same is true when we say that human beings are animals. For the very thing that is human is truly animal, since both the sensory nature, by reason of which we call human beings animal,

---

[24]ST I, Q. 13, A. 10. [25]ST I, Q. 13, A. 12.

and the rational nature, by reason of which we call human beings human, exist in the same individually existing subjects. And so also the predicate and subject in propositions with substantial predicates are identical in the individually existing subject, although in different respects.

And this is true in one respect even in the case of propositions in which we predicate the same thing of itself. For the intellect ascribes to the individually existing thing what it posits of the subject, and to the nature of the form existing in the individual thing what it posits of the predicate. That is, we understand predicates as forms, and subjects as the matter. The plurality of subject and predicate corresponds to this conceptual diversity, and the intellect signifies the identity of the thing by the very composition of predicate and subject.

And God, considered in himself, is entirely one and simple, although our intellect knows him by different conceptions, since it cannot perceive him as he is in himself. But our intellect nonetheless knows that something absolutely one and the same corresponds to this conceptual diversity. Therefore, the intellect represents this conceptual plurality by the plurality of predicate and subject, and it represents the oneness of God by their composition.

Objection. Every act of the intellect that understands an object otherwise than the object exists is false. But God exists without any composition, and every affirmative act of the intellect understands an object as composite. Therefore, we cannot formulate true affirmative propositions about God.

Reply Obj. The proposition *An act of the intellect that understands an object otherwise than the object exists is false* is ambiguous, since the adverb *otherwise* can modify the verb *understands* as regards what is understood, or as regards the one who understands.

If the adverb modifies the verb as regards what is understood, then the proposition is true, and it means that any act of the intellect that understands something to be otherwise than it is is false. But this is irrelevant, since our intellect in formulating a proposition about God asserts that he is simple, not that he is composite.

If, however, the adverb *otherwise* modifies the verb *understands* as regards the one who understands, then the proposition is false, since the intellect's way in understanding differs from the object's way in existing. For example, our intellect understands in an immaterial way material objects inferior to itself without understanding the objects to be immaterial. And similarly when our intellect understands noncomposite beings superior to itself, it understands them in its own way, namely, a composite way. And so the acts of our intellect are not false when they formulate composite propositions about God.

Knowledge

Thomas here considers God's knowledge. Understanding is immaterial. For example, in understanding stone, the knower possesses the form of stone but not the concrete, individual matter of a stone. Because this is so, and because God is most immaterial, he is most knowing. He knows himself comprehensively, and his understanding is identical with his substance. In knowing himself, he knows other things as his essence contains the likeness of other things. For example, he knows what human beings are by knowing how they share in his perfection and imitate him in a limited way. His knowledge, in conjunction with his will, causes the things he makes, just as a craftsman's knowledge causes the things he crafts. God's knowledge of actual things extends across the whole spectrum of time and to everything that exists at any time. He knows possible things that he could create (e.g., a different kind of plant or animal) or a creature could "create" (e.g., the Mona Lisa). By pure understanding (i.e., understanding without any need to use deductive reasoning), he knows both the universal and the particular. He knows contingent things both in their proximate causes and in their actuality (i.e., in their individual condition). Although contingent things become actual successively and are future in relation to proximate causes, he knows all of them at once, like someone on a rooftop watching a stream of traffic on the street below.

1. Does God have knowledge?[26]

I answer that knowing beings are by nature constituted to possess the forms of other things as well as their own form, since the likeness of known objects exists in knowing subjects. But form is limited by matter. And so forms come closer to a kind of infinity as they are more immaterial, and the immateriality of things is the reason they are knowing beings, and the way of knowledge is by way of immateriality. But God is most immaterial. Therefore, he is most knowing.

2. Does God comprehend himself?[27]

I answer that to comprehend things is to know things as perfectly as they are knowable, and things are knowable insofar as they are actual. But God's power to know is as great as his actuality, since he knows because he is actual and without any matter or potentiality. And so he knows himself as much as he is knowable. And so he perfectly comprehends himself.

---

[26]ST I, Q. 14, A. 1. [27]ST I, Q. 14, A. 3.

3. Is God's understanding identical with his substance?[28]

I answer that God's understanding is his substance. Were that not the case, something else would be the actuality and perfection of the divine substance, to which the divine substance would be related as potentiality to actuality, since understanding is the perfection and actuality of one who understands. But this is completely impossible.

We need to consider how God's understanding is his substance. Understanding is not an activity that goes out to external things but an actuality and perfection that remains in the knower, just as existing perfects existing things. For intelligible forms give rise to understanding just as forms give rise to existing. But there is no form in God other than his existing, and his essence is also his intelligible form. And so his very understanding is his essence and his existing. And so the intellect and the object understood and the intelligible form and the understanding itself are entirely one and the same thing in God. And so we posit no multiplicity in God's substance by saying that he is a being that understands.

4. Does God know things other than himself?[29]

I answer that God understands himself perfectly. Otherwise, his existence would not be perfect, since his existing is his understanding. And if something is perfectly known, its power is necessarily known perfectly, which will be true only if one knows the things to which the power extends. But God's power as the first efficient cause extends to other things. And so God necessarily knows things other than himself.

And the very existing of the first efficient cause, God, is his understanding. And so it is necessary that all the effects preexisting in him as their first cause be in his very understanding, and that all things be in him in an intelligible way, since everything that exists in something else is such in the way of the other in which it exists.

To know how God knows things other than himself, we need to consider that we know something in two ways: in one way, in itself; in the second way, in another. We know something in itself when we know it by a special form equivalent to the knowable object itself, as, for example, when the eye sees a human being by the form of a human being. And we see in another what we see by the form of something surrounding it, as, for example, when we see a human being in a mirror by the mirror's form.

---

[28]ST I, Q. 14, A. 4. [29]ST I, Q. 14, A. 5.

God sees himself in himself because he sees himself by his essence. And he sees things other than himself insofar as his essence contains the likeness of things other than himself.

5. Does God's knowledge cause things?[30]

I answer that God's knowledge causes things. His knowledge is related to all created things as a craftsman's knowledge causes the things he crafts. But a craftsman's knowledge causes the things he crafts. And so a form in the intellect necessarily causes action. But intelligible forms are sources of action only in conjunction with an inclination to produce effects, and such an inclination results from the will. For intelligible forms are disposed toward contraries, since to know one contrary is to know the other, and so produce no fixed effects unless the will were to determine them to produce particular effects. But God's existing is his understanding. And so his knowledge necessarily causes things insofar as his knowledge is linked to his will. And so we call God's knowledge, insofar as it causes things, a knowledge of assent.

Objection. In positing a cause, we posit its effect. But God's knowledge is eternal. Therefore, creatures exist from eternity if God's knowledge causes created things.

Reply Obj. God's knowledge causes things as things are part of his knowledge. But it was not part of his knowledge that things would exist from eternity. And so, although God's knowledge is eternal, it does not follow that creatures would exist from eternity.

6. Does God know nonbeings?[31]

I answer that God knows all things, whatever they are, in whatever way they exist. But nothing prevents things that do not exist absolutely from existing in a way. And things that are not actual exist in the power of God himself or the power of a creature, whether in a creature's active or passive power or in a creature's power to conjecture or imagine or signify in any way. Therefore, whatever a creature can cause or think or say, and also whatever God himself can cause, all these things God knows even if they are not actual. And God knows even nonbeings to this extent.

We need to note that some things not now actual have existed or will exist, and God knows these things by a knowledge of vision. Eternity, which exists without succession and includes the whole of time, measures God's understanding, which is his existing. Therefore, his present contemplation is borne to all time and to everything that exists in any time, as

---

[30]ST I, Q. 14, A. 8. [31]ST I, Q. 14, A. 9.

things presently subject to him. But there are some things in the power of God or a creature that neither exist nor will exist nor have existed. And regarding these things, we speak of God having a knowledge of pure understanding, not one of vision. We make this distinction because the things we see around us have separate existence outside the seer.

7. Does God know individual things?[32]

I answer that all the perfections in creatures preexist in God in a higher way. But to know individual things belongs to our perfection. And so God necessarily knows individual things. But the separate perfections in lesser things exist in God without composition and as one. And so, although we by one power know what is universal and immaterial, and by another power know what is individual and material, God knows both by his pure understanding.

God causes things by his knowledge. Therefore, his knowledge reaches as far as his causality. But the causal power of God extends both to the forms of a common nature and to matter.[33] And so God's knowledge necessarily extends even to individual things, which matter individuates. For he knows things other than himself by his own essence, since he is the likeness of these things as their efficient cause. And so his essence is necessarily the sufficient source for him to know all the things he has made, both in general and in particular.

8. Does God know future contingent things?[34]

I answer that God knows all things, including things that exist in his power or the power of creatures. But some of the latter things are future things contingent on us. Therefore, God knows future contingent things.

We can regard things as contingent in two ways: in one way as actually existing; in the second way as existing in their causes. In the first way, we regard contingent things as present, not future, and as determined to one outcome, not contingent to one of several outcomes. And so we can know them with certitude. But in the second way, we regard contingent things as future and not yet determined to one outcome. And so we cannot know them with certitude, since whoever knows a contingent effect only in its cause has only probable knowledge about it. But God knows all contingent things both in their causes and in their actual existence.

And although contingent things become actual successively, God knows them at once. This is so because eternity measures his knowledge as

---

[32]ST I, Q. 14, A. 11. [33]That God's power extends to matter, see below, pp. 39–40. [34]ST I, Q. 14, A. 13.

well as his existing, and eternity, which exists simultaneously whole, embraces the whole of time. And so everything in time is present to God from eternity, both because he has the natures of things present with him, and because his sight is borne from eternity over all things as they exist in their presence to him.

And so God knows contingent things unerringly, since they are subject to his inspection by their presence, and yet they are future contingent things in relation to their own causes.

Objection. Everything we know exists necessarily, and God's knowledge is more certain than ours. Therefore, everything God knows exists necessarily. But no future contingent thing necessarily exists. And so God does not know any future contingent thing.

Reply Obj. We know successively things brought into actuality in time, but God knows such things in eternity, which transcends time. And so we cannot be certain of future contingent things, since we know them as contingent, but God and only God, whose understanding transcends time, can be certain of them. For example, travelers on a road do not see travelers behind them, but one with a view of the whole road from a height sees at once all the travelers on the road. We cannot know future contingent things as such, and so the things we know need to be necessary, as they are in themselves. But the things God knows need to be necessary in the way in which they are subject to his knowing but not absolutely in relation to their particular causes.

And so also we distinguish the proposition *Everything God knows exists necessarily*. The proposition can be about the thing or the statement. If we understand the proposition to be about the thing, the proposition is a simple proposition and false, and its meaning is: Everything God knows is necessary. If we understand the proposition to be about the statement, the proposition is a compound proposition and true, and its meaning is: The statement *The things God knows exist* is necessary.

Ideas

God's so-called ideas, his knowledge of the forms of things, is a theory with roots in Plato and especially Augustine. Since God, in creating, acts with understanding, he knows the forms of the things he creates. He intends the good order of the universe and so has an idea of that order. And one cannot contemplate the whole without contemplating the particular natures of the things out of which the whole is constituted. And he also knows the natures of things he does not make. See Glossary, s.v. Ideas.

1. Are there ideas in the divine mind?[35]

I answer that the Greek word *idea* is called *forma* in Latin, and so we understand by ideas the forms of different things, forms that exist in addition to the things themselves. But the form of a thing, the form that exists in addition to the thing itself, can serve two purposes, either to be the exemplar of the object of which it is the form, or to be the source of knowing the object itself. And we need to posit ideas in the divine mind to serve both purposes.

In everything not coming to be by chance, a form is necessarily the end of each thing's coming to be. But an efficient cause would only act for the sake of a form inasmuch as a likeness of the form exists in the efficient cause. In some efficient causes, things that act by nature, the form of the thing to be made preexists in the cause's nature. But in other efficient causes, things that act by means of their understanding, the form of the thing to be made preexists in the cause's understanding. For example, the likeness of a house preexists in the mind of its builder, and we call that likeness an idea of the house, since the builder intends the house to be like the form he conceives in his mind.

The world was not made by chance but by God acting by means of his understanding.[36] Therefore, there necessarily is a form in his mind to the likeness of which he made the world.

2. Are there several ideas in the divine mind?[37]

I answer that the chief efficient cause of any effect strives in the strict sense for what is the final end. For example, the commander of an army aims to deploy it. But what is best in the world is the good order of the universe. Therefore, God intends the universe's order in the strict sense and not as something that is the result of chance from successive efficient causes.

But if God created and intended the universe's very order, he necessarily has an idea of that order. And one cannot contemplate the nature of any whole without considering the peculiar natures of the things out of which the whole is constituted. For example, a builder could not conceive the form of a house unless he were to have in his mind the proper nature of each of its parts. Therefore, there needs to exist in the divine mind the proper natures of everything. And so several ideas exist in the divine mind.

---

[35]ST I, Q. 15, A. 1. [36]That God created the world intelligently, see below, pp. 31, 38–9. [37]ST I, Q. 15, A. 2.

The idea of a product exists in the producer's mind as the object the producer understands, not as the form by which the producer understands. For example, the form of a house in the mind of a builder is something the builder understands, and the builder fashions the house in the likeness of the form. But it is not contrary to the simplicity of God's intellect that it understand many things, although it would be contrary to its simplicity if it were informed by several forms. And so there are several ideas in God's mind as objects of his understanding.

We can understand this as follows. God knows his essence perfectly, and so he knows it in every way in which it is knowable, including ways in which it can be shared by creatures by any kind of likeness. But every kind of creature has its own form as it shares a likeness to the divine essence in some way. Therefore, God knows his essence as the proper nature and idea of each particular kind of creature, since he knows his essence as imitable in this way by such a creature. And so God understands the several proper natures of the several kinds of things, and these several natures are several ideas.

3. Does God have ideas of everything he knows?[38]

I answer that an idea is an exemplar insofar as an idea is the source in producing things, and ideas as exemplars belong to practical knowledge. And an idea as a source of knowledge is a nature in the strict sense, and ideas as natures can belong to theoretical knowledge as well. Therefore, the ideas as exemplars are related to everything that God makes in any period of time. But the ideas as sources of knowledge are related to everything God knows, even if the things at no time come to be, and to everything that God knows in its own nature, and as he knows it in a theoretical way.

Objection. God has no idea of evil, since, if he did, there would be evil in him. But God knows evil things. Therefore, God does not have ideas of everything he knows.

Reply Obj. God does not know evil by its own nature but by the nature of good. And so God has no idea of evil, either as an exemplar or as a nature.

Life

Thomas here distinguishes the immanent activity of plants, irrational animals, and human beings. Plants activate themselves only in executing their activities

---

[38]ST I, Q. 15, A. 3.

of nutrition, growth, and reproduction. Irrational animals activate themselves not only in executing the activities of nutrition, growth, and reproduction but also by forms acquired through the senses, forms that cause the animals to act (e.g., cats to chase mice). Intellectual beings activate themselves regarding chosen ends (e.g., to cook dinner), but the human intellect needs to be activated by first principles of theoretical understanding (e.g., the principle of contradiction) and the final end of practical activity (happiness). Since God's nature is his understanding, nothing is needed to activate his intellect, and so he has the highest degree of immanent activity. See Glossary, s.v. Action.

1. Is life proper to God?[39]

I answer that life is more perfectly in things the more perfectly they move themselves. And there are three related things in the causes of motion and the things they move. First, an end moves an efficient cause. Second, the chief efficient cause acts by its own form. Third, the chief efficient cause sometimes does so through an instrumental cause, which only executes the action of the chief cause.

Nature determines for some things the form by which they act and the end for the sake of which they act, but they move themselves in executing movement. These things are plants, and they move themselves to increase or decrease by the form implanted in them by nature.

Some things move themselves both in executing motion and regarding the self-acquired form that is the source of their motion. These things are animals, the source of whose motion is a form received through the senses. And the more perfect their senses, the more perfectly do they move themselves. For example, things with only the sense of touch (e.g., oysters) move themselves only by movements of expansion and contraction, and they hardly surpass the movements of plants. But things with complete powers of sense perception move themselves forward to perceive connected or separate objects.

Although animals receive by their senses the forms that are the sources of their movements, they do not intrinsically prescribe for themselves the end of their activity, which end nature has implanted in them. And so superior to animals are things that move themselves even regarding ends that they prescribe for themselves. This happens only through reason and intellect, to which belongs knowing the relation of means to ends. And so the more perfect way of life belongs to intellectual things. For example, in the same human being, the intellect moves sense powers, sense powers at

---

[39]ST I, Q. 18, A. 3.

the intellect's command move bodily organs, and bodily organs execute movements.

But nature prescribes some things for our intellect (e.g., first principles, which cannot be otherwise, and our final end, which our intellect cannot not will). And so our intellect needs to be moved by something else regarding those things. But the thing whose own nature is its very understanding, and for whom another thing does not determine what it by nature possesses, has the highest degree of life. And this is God.

Objection. Living things move themselves. But being moved does not belong to God. Therefore, neither does life.

Reply Obj. There are two kinds of action. One kind passes into external matter (e.g., heating or sawing); the other kind remains in the cause (e.g., understanding, sense perception, willing). But the first kind perfects the object, and the second kind the cause. And so, because motion is the actuality of a movable object, we call the second kind of action, as the actuality of the cause, the motion of the cause by this analogy: as motion is the actuality of something imperfect, so the second kind of action is the actuality of the cause. Although motion is the actuality of something incomplete, that is, something with potentiality, the second kind of action is the actuality of something complete, that is, something that has actuality. Therefore, what understands itself moves itself in the way understanding is motion. And God moves himself in this way, not in the way of something incomplete.

Will

Since anything that understands has a disposition to will the understood good, and God understands, he needs to will the understood good, and his willing is identical with his existing. He wills himself as the end, and he wills other things as means to that end in order that other things share in his goodness. His will is necessarily related to his goodness, and so he necessarily wills his goodness, but he wills other things only insofar as they are related to his goodness as their end. And it is only hypothetically necessary that he will other things than himself, that is, necessary to will them only if he should happen to do so. Everything happens that he wills absolutely, but anything he wills conditionally need not happen (e.g., he wills that human beings obey his laws, but that is conditioned on human beings' freely willing to do so). His will cannot vary, but he can will that things change. He wills some things to come to be necessarily (e.g., effects of the law of gravity) and other things to come to be contingently (e.g., observance of the moral law). He in no way wills sin, which he permits, but he does incidentally will natural deficiencies in connection with willing order in the universe (e.g., that this thing passes away when something else comes to be), and punishment of sin in connection with willing justice.

1. Is there a will in God?[40]

I answer that as things of nature have actual existing by their form, so the intellect actually understands by its intelligible form. And everything has such a disposition toward its natural form that it strives for the form when it does not possess the form, and it is at rest when it possesses its form. And the same is true about every natural perfection, which is the good of nature. And this disposition toward good in beings lacking knowledge is an appetite of nature. And so also an intellectual nature has a like disposition toward the good understood by an intelligible form, namely, that the intellect be at rest in such a good when possessed and seek after such a good when not possessed. And both resting in the good possessed, and seeking after the good not possessed belong to the will. And so there is a will in everything that has an intellect, just as there are animal appetites in everything that has senses. But there is an intellect in God. And so there needs to be a will in God. And as his understanding is his existing, so is his will.

2. Does God will things other than himself?[41]

I answer that things of nature have an inclination from nature both regarding their own good and to pour out their good into other things as much as possible. And so efficient causes, inasmuch as they are actual and perfect, produce things like themselves. And so also it belongs to the nature of the will that it as much as possible communicate to others the good it possesses. And this belongs most to the divine will, from which every perfection is derived by some likeness. And so if things of nature, insofar as they are perfect, communicate their good to other things, much more does it belong to the divine will as far as possible to communicate its good to other beings by likeness. Therefore, God wills both himself and other things to exist. But he wills himself as the end, and he wills other things as means to that end, since it befits his goodness that other things share in his goodness.

Objection. Desirable objects move appetites. Therefore, willed objects move the will. Therefore, if God should will anything other than himself, something else will move his will. But this conclusion is impossible.

Reply Obj. Human beings can will things both for the sake of something else and for their own sake. But God wills other things than himself only for the sake of his goodness. Therefore, it does not follow that anything

---

[40]ST I, Q. 19, A. 1. [41]ST I, Q. 19, A. 2.

other than his goodness moves his will. And so just as he understands other things than himself by understanding his own essence, so he wills other things than himself by willing his own goodness.

3. Does God necessarily will everything he wills?[42]

I answer that propositions are necessary in two ways: absolutely and hypothetically. We judge propositions to be absolutely necessary by the way subject and predicate terms are related to one another, as when the predicate term is contained in the subject term (e.g., human beings are animals), or when the subject term belongs essentially to the predicate term (e.g., numbers are odd or even). But it is not necessary that Socrates be sitting. And so the latter is not absolutely necessary. But if Socrates happens to be sitting, it is necessarily the case that he is sitting as long as he is. Therefore, it is hypothetically necessary that Socrates is sitting as long as he is.

With respect to what God wills, it is absolutely necessary that God will one thing but not everything. His will has a necessary relationship to his goodness. And so God necessarily wills that his goodness exist, just as our will necessarily wills our happiness.

But God wills other things than himself inasmuch as they are related to his goodness as their end. And when one wills an end, one does not necessarily will things that are means to that end unless the things be such that the end cannot be attained without them. But God's goodness is perfect and can exist without other things, since no perfection accrues to him from anything else. And so it is not absolutely necessary that he will other things than himself. But if he should will something other than himself, he cannot not will it. Therefore, it is hypothetically necessary that he do so.

Objection. God necessarily knows everything he knows. But God's will, like his knowledge, is his essence. Therefore, God necessarily wills everything he wills.

Reply Obj. As God's existing is intrinsically necessary, so also are his willing and knowing. But God's knowing has a necessary relationship to the objects he knows, and God's willing does not have such a relationship to the objects he wills. And this is so because knowledge concerns things as they exist in the knower, and the will is related to things as they exist in themselves. But all other things than himself have a necessary existence as they exist in God, and they have no absolute necessity as they exist in themselves. Therefore, God necessarily knows everything that he knows, and he does not necessarily will everything he wills.

---

[42]ST I, Q. 19, A. 3.

4. Does God's will cause things?[43]

I answer that God causes by his will but not by a necessity of nature. We can demonstrate this in three ways. First, both intellect and nature act for the sake of an end. Therefore, an intellect needs to predetermine the end and the necessary means to the end for causes that act by nature. For example, an archer predetermines the target and path of an arrow. And so a cause acting by intellect and will necessarily precedes a cause acting by nature. But God is the first efficient cause. Therefore, he needs to cause by his intellect and will.

Second, efficient causes, unless prevented, cause things insofar as the causes are of such and such a kind, and so natural efficient causes produce only one kind of effect. For causes act insofar as they are of such a kind, and so they as particular causes cause only particular effects. But God's existing is not limited. Therefore, he cannot act by a necessity of nature unless he were to cause something unlimited in existing. But this is impossible. Therefore, he does not cause by a necessity of nature. Rather, limited effects come from the unlimited perfection of himself as his intellect and will determine.

Third, efficient causes produce effects like themselves. Therefore, effects come from an efficient cause in the way in which they preexist in it. And effects preexist in their cause in the manner of the cause. But God's existing is his very understanding. And so effects preexist in him in an intelligible way. And so also they come from him in the same way. But his inclination to produce what his intellect has conceived belongs to his will. And so effects come from him by his will. Therefore, God's will causes things.

5. Is God's will always fulfilled?[44]

I answer that things can fall short of a particular form but not of the universal form. For example, something can be nonhuman or nonliving, but it cannot be nonbeing. Just so, something can happen outside the order of a particular cause but not outside the order of the universal cause. For the failure of a particular cause is due to hindrance by another particular cause, and the other particular cause is included in the order of the universal cause. And so effects can in no way depart from the order of the universal cause.

God's will is the universal cause of everything. Therefore, his will cannot not achieve its effect. And so what seems to recede from the divine will in one respect slips back under the divine will in another. For example, the sinner, who by sinning retreats from the divine will insofar as this lies

---

[43]ST I, Q. 19, A. 4. [44]ST I, Q. 19, A. 6.

within the sinner's power, falls under the order of God's will when God's justice punishes the sinner.

Objection. The Apostle says in 1 Tim. 2:4 that God wills that every human being be saved. But this does not turn out to be so. Therefore, God's will is not always fulfilled.

Reply Obj. First, we can understand the words of the Apostle to mean that God wills every one of the saved to be saved.

Second, we can understand the words to mean that God wills that human beings of every condition be saved, men and women, Jews and Gentiles, little and big, but not everyone of every condition.

Third, we can understand the words to be about God's antecedent will, not about his consequent will. And we understand this distinction to be on the part of the things that God wills, not on the part of the divine will itself. And to understand this, we need to consider that God wills everything insofar as it is good. Moreover, things can be good or evil in their primary aspect, as we consider them absolutely, and yet they have the contrary character as we consider them with something added, which is a secondary aspect. For example, it is good, absolutely considered, that human beings live, and it is evil that they be killed, but if we add about a particular human being that he is a murderer or one who is a threat to the community as long as he lives, it is good that such a one be killed, and it is evil that he live. And so a just judge wills antecedently that every human being live, but consequently that a murderer be hanged. Similarly, God wills antecedently that every human being be saved, but consequently, by what his justice requires, that some individuals be damned.

And yet we will in one respect, not absolutely, what we will antecedently. This is because the will relates to things as they exist in themselves, and they exist in themselves in particular ways. And so we will things absolutely as we will them with all their particular circumstances taken into consideration, and this is to will consequently. And so a just judge wills absolutely that a murderer be hanged, but he would in one respect will that the murderer live, namely, insofar as the murderer is a human being. And so such a qualified willing is a wish rather than an absolute will.

And so everything God wills absolutely occurs, even if what he wills antecedently does not occur.

6. Can God's will vary?[45]

I answer that it is one thing to change one's will, and another to will that some things change. For example, one can with the same unalterably per-

[45]ST I, Q. 19, A. 7.

sisting will will that something be done now, and that its contrary be done later. But if one were to begin to will what one has not previously willed, or if one were to cease to will what one has willed, one's will would then be changed. And this can happen only if we presuppose a change on the part of one's knowledge or with respect to the substantial disposition of the one willing. For one can in two ways begin anew to will something. One can begin to will something in one way as the thing begins to be good for someone, and this does not exist without the person's condition being altered. For example, when the cold of winter arrives, it begins to be good to sit by a fire, something that was not previously good. One can begin to will something in the second way as one newly recognizes that the thing is good for oneself. But both God's substance and his knowing cannot change at all. And so his will is altogether invariable.

Objection. Jer. 17:8 speaks of God being willing, if the people repent, to repent of the evil he had planned against Israel. Therefore, God's will varies.

Reply Obj. God's will as the first and universal cause does not exclude intermediary causes, which have the power to produce some effects. But intermediate causes have less power than the first cause. And so there are many things in God's power, knowledge, and will that are not included in the order of inferior causes. And so in the case of Lazarus, one who regards inferior causes could say: "Lazarus will not rise again." And one who regards the divine cause could say: "Lazarus will rise again." God wills both that things will at times come to be by inferior causes, and that things by the superior cause will at times not be, or the converse. Thus God sometimes declares that something will come to be insofar as the thing is included in the order of inferior causes, as, for example, nature or merits so dispose, and yet the thing does not come to be, since it is otherwise regarding the superior cause.

Therefore, we understand the statement of Jeremiah in a metaphorical way, since human beings seem to repent when they do not carry out what they have threatened to do.

7. Does God's will impose necessity on the things he willed?[46]

I answer that when a cause causes an effect, the effect results from the cause both as to what comes to be and as to its way of coming to be or existing. For example, a child may be born dissimilar to its father in accidental characteristics because the causal power in the father's semen is weak. But God's will is most efficacious. Therefore, the things he wills both

[46]ST I, Q. 19, A. 8.

come to be and come to be in the way he wills them to come to be. But God wills some things to come to be necessarily and other things to come to be contingently. And so he has prepared necessary and unfailing causes for some effects, and such effects result necessarily from such causes, and he has prepared fallible, contingent causes for other effects, and such effects result contingently from such causes. Therefore, effects willed by God do not contingently come to be because their proximate causes are contingent. Rather, he prepared contingent causes for contingent effects because he willed that the effects contingently come to be.

8. Does God will evils?[47]

I answer that the good and the desirable are essentially the same, and evil is the contrary of good. And so no natural appetite or animal appetite or intellectual appetite (i.e., the will) can seek anything evil as such. But evil things are incidentally sought inasmuch as they result from good things. For example, a natural efficient cause strives for one form that involves the deprivation of another form, and for the coming-to-be of one thing that involves the passing away of another, not for the privation and passing away. And when a lion kills a stag, the lion aims to feed itself, and this involves killing the stag. And a fornicator intends his pleasure, which involves the deformity of sin.

The evil accompanying a particular good is the deprivation of another good. Therefore, evil would never be sought, not even incidentally, unless the good involving evil were to be sought more than the good evil takes away. But God wills no good more than his own goodness, although he wills one particular good more than another. And so God in no way wills the evil of sin, which takes away the proper order to the divine good. But he wills the evil of a natural deficiency or of punishment when he wills a particular good involving such an evil. For example, he wills punishment when he wills justice, and he wills that some things pass away when he wills that the order of nature be observed.

Objection. The proposition *Evils exist* and the proposition *Evils do not exist* are contradictories. But evils exist, and so God, whose will is always fulfilled, does not will that evils not exist. Therefore, God wills that evils exist.

Reply Obj. The propositions *Evils exist* and *Evils do not exist* are contradictories. But the propositions *God wills evils to exist* and *God wills evils not to exist* are not, since both propositions are affirmative. God neither wills

---

[47]ST I, Q. 19, A. 9.

that evils exist, nor that they not exist. Rather, he wills to permit evils to exist. And this is good.

9. Does God have free choice?[48]

I answer that God necessarily wills his own goodness, but he does not will other things necessarily. Therefore, he has free choice with respect to those things.

Love

Since acts of the will tend toward good, and love concerns good in general, love is by nature the first act of the will. And since God wills, he loves. And since his will causes every other existing thing, which as such is good, he wills some good for everything. And so he loves everything, but not equally. Moreover, his love pours out the very goodness of things.

1. Does God love?[49]

I answer that the first movement of the will and every appetite is love. For acts of the will and every appetite tend toward good as their object principally and intrinsically, and toward evil as their object secondarily and by reason of something else, namely, as contrary to good. And so acts of the will and appetite regarding good are by nature necessarily prior to acts regarding evil. For what intrinsically exists is always prior to what exists by reason of something else.

Things more general are by nature prior. There are some acts of the will and appetite that regard good under a special condition. For example, joy and pleasure concern a good that is present and possessed, and desire and hope concern a good not yet possessed. But love concerns good in general, whether possessed or not. And so love is by nature the first act of the will and appetite.

And so all other appetitive movements presuppose love as their first source. For no one desires, or rejoices in, anything except as a good that is loved. And so love needs to exist in everything in which there is will and appetite. But God has a will. Therefore, God loves.

Objection. Love is a unifying and binding force. But there cannot be such in God, since he is uncomposed. Therefore, God does not love.

Reply Obj. An act of love tends toward two things: the good that one

---

[48]ST I, Q. 19, A. 10. [49]ST I, Q. 20, A. 1.

wills for someone, and the one for whom one wills the good. To will good for someone is in the proper sense to love that one. And so persons, insofar as they love themselves, will good for themselves. And so they seek to unite that good to themselves as much as they can. And so love is a unifying force even in the case of God. But the good he wills for himself is only himself, who is by his essence good. Therefore, his love implies no composition in him.

In loving another, one wills good for the other. But one rejoices in the other as if in oneself, judging the good for the other as the good for oneself. And so love is a binding force, since love, being disposed toward the other as toward oneself, unites the other to oneself. But God wills good for others. And so God's love for others is a binding force without any composition in him.

2. Does God love everything?[50]

I answer that every existing thing as such is good. But God's will causes everything. And so things necessarily have as much existing and perfection as God wills. And so God wills some good for everything that exists. But loving is willing good for something. And so God loves everything that exists.

But he does not love in the same way that we do. For our will does not cause the goodness of things. Rather, the goodness of things moves our will. Therefore, our love, whereby we will good for things, does not cause the goodness of the things, and the things' goodness, whether real or putative, evokes the love whereby we will for the things both the preservation of goods possessed and the addition of goods not possessed. And we act to achieve this. But God's love pours out and creates the goodness in things.

Objection. There are two kinds of love, namely, the love of desire and the love of friendship. But God does not love irrational creatures by a love of desire, since he needs nothing outside of himself. Nor does he love them by a love of friendship, since one cannot have the love of friendship toward irrational creatures. Therefore, God does not love everything.

Reply Obj. One can only have friendship toward rational creatures, among whom there can be mutual love and life's shared activities, and for whom things may by good or bad fortune turn out well or ill, just as there is benevolence in the proper sense toward such creatures. But irrational creatures cannot attain to loving God or sharing the intellectual and blessed life he enjoys. Therefore, God, properly speaking, does not love them with a love of friendship. But he does love them with a love of desire inasmuch as

---

[50]ST I, Q. 20, A. 2.

he ordains them for rational creatures and even for himself. He loves them because of his goodness and their benefit to us, not because he needs them. Similarly, we desire some things both for ourselves and for others.

3. Does God love everything equally?[51]

I answer that things can be loved more or less in two ways. They can be loved more or less in one way regarding the very act of the will, which can be more or less intense. And God does not love some things more or less in this way, since he loves everything by an act of the will that is one and uncomposed and always disposed in the same way. Things can be loved more or less in a second way regarding the good itself that one wills for the object of one's love. And this is the way in which we love more than another one for whom we will a greater good. But God's goodness causes the goodness of things. And so nothing would be better than something else if he were not to will a greater good for one thing than for another. And so he loves some things more than others in this way.

Justice and Mercy

God's justice consists in his creating things with due order and proportion. But creatures are ultimately due anything only because of the mercy of his goodness, and he dispenses to creatures more than anything proportional.

1. Are there justice and mercy in all his works?[52]

I answer that divine justice renders either what is due to God or what is due to creatures. But God does everything as befits his wisdom and goodness, and things are due to God in this way. And he does everything regarding created things with befitting order and proportion, and the nature of justice consists in this. And so there needs to be justice in every work of God.

And the work of God's justice presupposes the work of his mercy and is based on it. For creatures are not due anything except because of something in them that exists or is weighed beforehand. And to avoid infinite regression in prior things, we need to arrive at something that depends only on the goodness of the divine will. This is like saying that having hands is due to human beings because human beings have rational souls, and having souls is due to human beings because human beings are human, and being human is due to human beings because of God's goodness.

---

[51]ST I, Q. 20, A. 3. [52]ST I, Q. 21, A. 4.

And so there is mercy in every work of God as to the action's first source. And the power of his mercy is preserved in everything that results, and works more strongly, since the primary cause influences effects more than secondary causes do. And so God, out of the richness of his goodness, dispenses even the things owed to creatures more abundantly than anything proportional to creatures' demands. For what would suffice to preserve the order of justice is less than what God's goodness brings. And his goodness surpasses every proportion to creatures.

Providence

God causes the good in creatures by his intellect in conjunction with his will, and so his plan ordering things to their ends needs to preexist in his mind. This plan is providence in the strict sense. His causality reaches to all things as to their specific and individual causes and as to both destructible things (i.e., material things) and indestructible things (i.e., the human soul, angels). And so he necessarily orders everything to its end, and every existing thing is subject to his providence. Rational creatures exercise free choice, but the very acts of free choice are traceable to God as their first efficient cause. He directly provides for everything but communicates his causal power to creatures to execute his order. His goodness is the chief end of his providence, but the secondary end is the perfection of the universe. And his providence has prepared necessary causes to produce effects that necessarily come to be, and contingent causes to produce effects that contingently come to be.

1. Is God provident?[53]

I answer that God created everything good in the world. But things are good both regarding their substance and regarding their order to ends and especially to their final end, which is God's goodness. Therefore, God created the good in creatures regarding their order to ends. But the nature of every one of his effects needs to preexist in him, since God causes things by his intellect. And so the plan ordering things to their ends needs to preexist in his mind. And the plan ordering things to ends is providence in the proper sense. For providence is the chief part of practical wisdom, toward which the other two parts, namely, remembering the past and understanding the present, are ordered, since we draw conclusions about the future from remembering the past and understanding the present.

---

[53]ST I, Q. 22, A. 1.

And it belongs to practical wisdom to order other things to ends, either regarding oneself, as, for example, wise human beings rightly order their actions to the goal of their life, or regarding others subject to oneself, as in the case of families or cities or kingdoms. And practical wisdom or providence can in the latter way be proper for God. The very plan ordering things to ends constitutes his providence. And both the plan ordering things to ends and the plan integrating parts into the whole are dispositions.

2. Is everything subject to God's providence?[54]

I answer that every efficient cause acts for the sake of an end. Therefore, the order of effects to ends reaches as far as the causality of the primary efficient cause reaches. Regarding the activity of particular efficient causes, things not ordered for the things for which they strive may result from the activity of other particular causes. But the causality of God, the first efficient cause, reaches to all beings as to both their specific and their individual causes, as to both destructible and indestructible things. And so God necessarily orders everything, in whatever way it exists, to its end. But God's providence is his plan ordering things to ends. Therefore, everything is necessarily subject to his providence as much as it shares existing.

Similarly, God knows everything, both the universal and the particular. But his knowledge is ordered to things as knowledge of a craft is ordered to the product of the craft. And so everything needs to be subject to his order as every product of a craft is subject to the order of the craft.

Objection 1. Nothing foreseen is fortuitous. Therefore, if God has foreseen everything, nothing will be fortuitous, and so there will be no chance or luck. But this is contrary to the general opinion.

Reply Obj. 1. The universal cause and particular causes differ. Things can depart from the order of particular causes, since things are taken away from the order of particular causes by other particular causes preventing the order. For example, the action of water prevents wood from burning. But all particular causes are included under the universal cause. Therefore, no effect can escape the order of the universal cause. Therefore, there are effects by chance or luck with respect to particular causes but not with respect to the universal cause. For example, the meeting of two slaves, although by chance on their part, is nonetheless foreseen by their master, who knowingly sends them to the same place without one knowing about the other.

Obj. 2. Things left to themselves are not subject to the providence of one who directs things. But God leaves human beings, especially the

---

[54]ST I, Q. 22, A. 2.

wicked, to themselves. Therefore, some things are not subject to divine providence.

Reply Obj. 2. Rational creatures by free choice move themselves to action. But we need to trace the very acts of free choice back to God as their cause. Therefore, deeds done by free choice need to be subject to his providence. But God does not allow anything to happen that would definitively prevent the salvation of the just. Therefore, he provides for the just in a more excellent way than for the wicked. But God does not entirely exclude the wicked from his providence; otherwise, they would fall into nothingness if his providence were not to preserve them.

3. Does God directly provide for everything?[55]

I answer that two things belong to providence: the plan ordering foreseen things to ends, and the execution of this order, which execution is governance. With respect to the first, God has a plan for everything, even the least, in his mind, and he gave to all the causes he appointed for particular effects the power to produce those effects. And so he needs to have considered beforehand in his plan the order of those effects. And so God directly provides for everything.

With respect to the second, the execution of the order, he governs lower things by higher things because of the richness of his goodness, so that he communicates the excellence of his causal power to creatures. And so there are intermediaries of God's providence in the execution of his order.

4. Does providence impose necessity on foreseen things?[56]

I answer that providence orders things to ends. But next after God's goodness, the chief end, which exists in things themselves, is the perfection of the universe, and that perfection would not exist if there were not to be in the world every grade of existing. And so God's providence has prepared necessary causes for some effects, so that the latter necessarily come to be, and his providence has prepared contingent causes for other effects, so that the latter contingently come to be.

Predestination

Part of God's providence is to convey human beings to himself, their final end, which they cannot attain by their own power. This part of providence is predes-

---

[55]ST I, Q. 22, A. 3. [56]ST I, Q. 22, A. 4.

tination. And as predestination is the part of providence regarding those he orders to eternal life, so damnation is the part of providence regarding those who fall away from their end. Damnation includes his will to allow some to fall into sin in this life and to cause them to be punished for their sins by damnation in the next life. Human beings cannot cause the effect of predestination in general, but a particular effect of predestination (merit) can by God's ordering be the cause and reason of another particular effect of predestination (glory). Why God chose some and damned others has no reason other than the fact that God so willed it.

1. Does God predestine human beings?[57]

I answer that everything is subject to God's providence. And his providence orders things to ends. And there are two ends to which he orders creatures. One end surpasses the proportion and ability of created nature, and this end is eternal life, which consists in the vision of God. The other end is proportioned to a created nature, namely, the end that a created nature can attain by its own natural power.

But another needs to convey things to a destination that the things cannot attain by their own natural power. For example, an archer conveys an arrow to its target. And so, properly speaking, rational creatures, creatures capable of eternal life, are brought to that life conveyed, as it were, by God. But the plan for this transmission preexists in God, as the plan ordering everything to ends exists in him, and this plan is providence. And to destine is to send someone, and so God's plan for the conveyance of human beings to their end of eternal life is predestination. And so predestination, as regards its objects, is one part of providence.

2. Does God damn any human being?[58]

I answer that predestination to eternal life is part of God's providence. But it belongs to providence to allow deficiencies in things subject to providence. And so it belongs to God's providence to allow some human beings to fail to attain eternal life. And this is to damn them.

As predestination is part of providence regarding those whom God ordains to eternal life, so damnation is part of providence regarding those who fall away from this end. And so damnation both denotes foreknowledge and adds something conceptually. As predestination includes the will to confer grace and glory, so damnation includes the will to allow some to fall into sin and to cause their punishment of damnation for sin.

---

[57]ST I, Q. 23, A. 1. [58]ST I, Q. 23, A. 3.

Objection. Damnation would need to be related to the damned in the same way that predestination is related to the predestined. But predestination causes the salvation of the predestined. Therefore, condemnation will cause the destruction of the damned. But this is false. Therefore, God does not damn anyone.

Reply Obj. Damnation causes in a different way than predestination does. Predestination causes both what the predestined hope for in the future life, namely, glory, and what exists in the present life, namely, grace. But damnation does not cause what exists in the present life, namely, sin, although damnation causes abandonment by God. Sin results from the free choice of those damned and bereft of grace, but damnation causes what is rendered the damned in the future life, namely, eternal punishment.

3. Does God's foreknowledge of merits cause predestination?[59]

I answer that predestination includes willing. But we cannot ascribe a cause to God's willing as regards the act. Therefore, we cannot say that merits cause God's predestination as regards the act. But we can ascribe a reason for God's willing as regards the things willed. And so one can ask whether predestination has any cause regarding its effects, that is, whether God preordained to bestow the effect of predestination on some because of their merits.

We can consider the effect of predestination in two ways. We can consider the effect in one way in particular. And so nothing prevents one effect of predestination from being the cause and reason of another effect, a subsequent effect being the cause of a prior effect by way of a final cause, and a prior effect being the cause of a subsequent effect by way of a meritorious cause, which we trace back to the disposition of the matter. This is like saying that God preordained to give glory to some because of their merits, and that he preordained to give grace to some in order that they merit glory.

In the second way, we can consider the effect of predestination in general, and then the entire effect of predestination cannot have any cause on our part. This is because everything in human beings ordering them to salvation is included in the effect of predestination, even the very preparation for grace, and this effect of predestination happens only by God's help. And the effect of predestination in general has God's goodness for its reason, and the whole effect is ordered to his goodness as its end, and it proceeds from his goodness as its first efficient cause.

---

[59]ST I, Q. 23, A. 5.

Objection. It seems unfair to give unequal benefits to those who are equal. But all human beings are equal as regards both their nature and original sin, and human beings are unequal as regards the merits or demerits of their own acts. Therefore, God prepares unequal rewards for human beings by predestining some and damning others only because he foreknows their diverse merits.

Reply Obj. We can understand from God's goodness why he predestines some and damns others. God made everything to manifest his goodness. But his goodness needs to be manifested in things in many ways, since created things cannot attain his simplicity. And so different grades of things are required to fill up the universe, and some things in the universe have high rank, and other things low rank. And to preserve the multiplicity of grades in things, God allows some evils to occur.

Consider the whole human race as the entire universe. God willed to manifest his goodness in some human beings, those he predestines, by his mercy, by sparing them, and in others, those he damns, by his justice, by punishing them. And this is the reason why God chooses some and damns others.

But why he chose some and damned others has no reason except God willing it so. Similarly, we can ascribe the reason why God established parts of prime matter under different forms, namely, that there be a diversity of species in things of nature. But why this particular part of matter is under this particular form depends on God's absolute will, as it depends on the absolute will of a craftsman that this particular stone is in this particular part of a wall.

Still, there is no unfairness in God if he prepares unequal benefits for equal things. For regarding things bestowed as a favor, one can at one's pleasure, without detriment to justice, give more or less to whomever one wishes, provided one does not take away from another what is due to the other.

Power

As pure actuality, God has active power in the highest degree. He can do anything that is absolutely possible. Only nonbeing, something simultaneously signifying existing and nonexisting, is absolutely impossible and beyond his power. Since his will causes anything created, and his will is not determined by nature and necessity to create the things created, he can make other things than those he does (e.g., a different kind of plant or animal). With respect to the goodness that belongs to a thing's essence, he cannot make anything better than he has (e.g., an essentially better human being). But with respect to the goodness over and above a thing's essence, he can make better the things he has made (e.g., a better human digestive system). And he can make something else better than anything he has made (e.g., human beings with higher IQs).

1. Does God have power?[60]

I answer that there are two kinds of power, namely, passive power and active power. Things cause other things insofar as they are actual and perfect, and things are acted upon insofar as they lack something and are imperfect. But God is pure actuality and absolutely perfect. And so he is most properly an active source and not acted upon in any way. But efficient causality belongs to active power. Therefore, God has active power in the highest degree.

2. Is God all-powerful?[61]

I answer that things are possible in two ways. They are possible in one way with respect to some power. For example, we call things subject to human power possible for human beings. But God's power extends to more things than the things creatures can do. Therefore, we cannot say that God is all-powerful because he can do everything creatures can do. Nor should we say that he is all-powerful because he can do everything he can do, since that is circular reasoning. Therefore, we should say that God is all-powerful because he can do everything that is absolutely possible, and this is the second way of things being possible. And things are absolutely possible or impossible by reason of the compatibility or incompatibility of the terms of a proposition.

Every efficient cause produces effects like itself. And so possible things correspond to active powers as the powers' proper object by reason of the actuality on which active powers are based. But God's existing, on which his power is based, is unlimited, possessing in itself beforehand the perfection of all existing. And so everything that can have being is included in the class of things absolutely possible. And God is all-powerful with respect to these things.

Only nonbeing is contrary to being. Therefore, only things signifying existing and nonexisting at the same time are absolutely impossible and not subject to God's omnipotence. Everything else is absolutely possible and so included in his power. And so we can more appropriately say that contradictory things cannot be made rather than that God cannot make them.

---

[60]ST I, Q. 25, A. 1. [61]ST I, Q. 25, A. 3.

3. Can God make things he does not make?[62]

I answer that God's will causes everything, and his will is not determined by nature and necessity to the things he created. Nor is God's power limited to the present course of things because of his wisdom and justice. We appropriately say that God has no power apart from the order of his wisdom, since his wisdom includes the total capacity of his power, but his wisdom is not limited to the order that it implants in things, in which order the aspect of justice consists. For although wise human beings take from the end the whole plan of the order that they impose on the things they have made, God's wisdom is an end that surpasses created things beyond any proportion. And so his wisdom is not limited to a fixed order of things such that no other course of things could flow from his wisdom. And so God can make other things than those he makes.

4. Can God make better the things he makes?[63]

I answer that there are two kinds of goodness. One kind belongs to a thing's essence. For example, being rational belongs to the essence of human beings. And with respect to this kind of goodness, God cannot make anything better than it is. The second kind of goodness is over and above a thing's essence. For example, being virtuous or wise is good for human beings. And with respect to this kind of goodness, God can make better the things he makes. And absolutely speaking, he can make something else better than anything he has made.

Objection. What is best cannot be made better. But all things made by God are collectively best, since the beauty of the universe consists of them all. Therefore, God cannot make a better universe.

Reply Obj. God assigned the most becoming order to the things he made, and the good of the universe consists of that order. Therefore, presupposing the things God made, the universe cannot be better. But God could make other things or add other things to those he made, and so such a universe would be better.

---

[62]ST I, Q. 25, A. 5. [63]ST I, Q. 25, A. 6.

2

Creation and Governance

Creation concerns how and why God causes things in the universe to come to exist. Governance concerns how and why he governs the universe. Thomas considers creation under five topics: the cause; the mode; the origin; the diversity; the problem of evil.

God the First Cause

God is the first efficient cause of every existing thing, since the first being, intrinsically subsistent existing, needs to cause everything that shares in different ways of existing. The cause of things as beings needs to cause whatever belongs in any way to their existing, and so the universal cause of beings also causes the substratum of material things, prime matter. And exemplars (models) are necessary to produce things with definite forms as his essence is imitable in different ways. Efficient causes, since they act to produce particular effects, act to achieve ends. The first efficient cause, God, acts to communicate his goodness, and the goodness of creatures is a likeness of his goodness. And so his goodness is the final cause of all things.

1. Does every being need to be created by God?[1]

I answer that every perfection that exists in things by sharing, needs to be caused in them by something to which the perfection belongs essentially (e.g., iron is heated by fire). But God is intrinsically subsisting existence itself, and there can be only one such. Therefore, everything other than God is not existence but shares in existence. Therefore, one first being, which exists most perfectly, needs to cause all the other things that are differentiated by various sharings in existence and so exist more or less perfectly.

2. Does God create prime matter?[2]

I answer that ancient philosophers considered being in a particular aspect, either as this particular being or as such a kind of being. And so they

---

[1]ST I, Q. 44, A. 1. [2]ST I, Q. 44, A. 2.

ascribed particular efficient causes to things. Some went further to consider being as such, and the causes of things as beings and not only as individual things and things of such a kind. But the cause of things as beings necessarily causes things both as to being such by accidental and substantial forms and as to whatever belongs in any way to their existing. And so the universal cause of beings also creates their prime matter.

3. Is anything but God the exemplary cause of things?[3]

I answer that exemplars are necessary to produce things so that the things produced attain definite form. But things of nature attain definite forms. And so the determination of forms is necessarily traceable to God's wisdom as their first cause, and his wisdom planned the order of the universe, which consists of different things. And so there exists in God's wisdom the essences of all things, the ideas, that is, exemplary forms in the divine mind. And although these ideas are multiple with respect to things, they are in fact nothing other than God's essence, since different things share his likeness in different ways. Thus God himself is the exemplar of everything.

Creatures are also exemplars of other creatures insofar as some are like others either specifically or by imitation.

4. Is God the final cause of all things?[4]

I answer that every efficient cause acts for the sake of an end. Otherwise, the action of an efficient cause would not produce this particular effect rather than that one except by chance. Moreover, the end of the active thing and the end of the thing acted upon, as such, are the same. Some things are simultaneously active and acted upon, and these are imperfect efficient causes that even in acting strive to acquire something.

But the first efficient cause, which is only active, does not act to acquire an end. Rather, the first efficient cause acts to communicate his perfection, that is, his goodness. And every creature strives to gain its own perfection and goodness, which is a likeness of God's. And so God's goodness is the end of all things.

Manner

The emanation of the whole of being from the universal cause does not presuppose comings-to-be by particular emanations, and so the emanation of the

---

[3]ST I, Q. 44, A. 3. [4]ST I, Q. 44, A. 4.

whole of being in general from the first cause cannot presuppose any beings, that is, the emanation comes "out of" nothing. God's proper effect in creating is existence without qualification, and so nothing else can act dependently and instrumentally to produce that effect.

1. Is creation the making of things out of nothing?[5]

I answer that we need to consider not only the emanation of a particular being from a particular efficient cause but also the emanation of the whole of being from the universal cause, that is, God. But emanation from the universal cause does not presuppose coming-to-be by a particular emanation (e.g., begetting human beings out of something nonhuman). And so the emanation of the whole of being in general from the first cause cannot presuppose any being. But nothing is the same as no being. Therefore, as human beings are begotten out of the nonbeing that is nonhuman, so creation, that is, the emanation of the totality of being, is out of the nonbeing that is nothing.

2. Is creation proper only to God?[6]

I answer that we need to trace more universal effects to more universal and prior causes. But the most universal effect is existing itself. And so that effect needs to be the proper effect of the first and most universal cause, that is, God. But it belongs to the nature of creation to produce existence absolutely, not inasmuch as this particular thing or such a kind of thing exists. And so creation is the proper action of God himself.

Nor can anything else be an instrumental cause in the action of creating. For a secondary, instrumental cause shares in the action of a higher cause only to the extent that it dispositively acts by something proper to itself to produce the effect of the chief cause. For example, an ax used to cut wood, which power the ax possesses by a property of its form, produces the form of a footstool, which form is the proper effect of the chief cause. Therefore, if a secondary cause were to do nothing by what is proper to itself, in vain would it be employed in the action, nor would specific instruments be needed for specific actions.

But God's proper effect in creating is what all other effects presuppose, namely, existence without qualification, and creation is not by anything presupposed, something that could be disposed by the action of an instrumental cause. And so nothing can act dispositively and instrumentally to produce the effect of existence without qualification. Thus no creature can create, whether by its own power or instrumentally.

---

[5]ST I, Q. 45, A. 1. [6]ST I, Q. 45, A. 5.

Beginning

Since God does not need to will that anything other than himself exist, the world need exist only as long as he wills it to exist. Although God has revealed that the world had a beginning, we cannot demonstrate the impossibility of the world having always existed.

1. Did the created universe always exist?[7]

I answer that God's will causes things, and things need to exist as long as God wills them. But absolutely speaking, God does not need to will anything other than himself. Therefore, God does not need to will that the world should always have existed. But the world exists as long as God wills it to exist, since the existence of the world depends on God's will as its cause. Therefore, it is neither necessary nor demonstrable that the world always exists.

2. Is it an article of faith that the world had a beginning?[8]

I answer that we hold only by faith and cannot demonstrate that the world has not always existed. We cannot demonstrate by the world itself how the world originates. For the principle of demonstration is something's essence, and everything regarding a specific essence abstracts from particular places and times. Nor can we demonstrate by the world's efficient cause, who produces creatures by his will, how the world originates. For reason can investigate God's will only regarding what he absolutely needs to will, and he does not absolutely need to will what he wills regarding creatures. But revelation can reveal God's will to human beings. And so we can believe that the world had a beginning, although we cannot demonstrate or have theoretical knowledge of this truth.

Diversity

The multiplicity and diversity of things comes from the intention of the first cause, God. The goodness that exists simply and uniformly in God exists in many ways and separately in creatures. And the world is one by reason of its integrated order.

---

[7]ST I, Q. 46, A. 1. [8]ST I, Q. 46, A. 2.

1. Do the multiplicity and diversity of things come from God?[9]

I answer that some thinkers have ascribed the cause of things' diversity wholly or partially to matter. But such opinions are untenable for two reasons. First, God created even matter itself, and so we need to trace things' diversity, even if it comes partly from matter, to a higher cause. Second, matter is for the sake of form, and particular forms distinguish different things. Therefore, things do not have diversity because of matter, but created matter lacks form in order that matter may be adapted to different forms.

And some thinkers ascribed things' diversity to secondary efficient causes [pure intelligences]. But such an opinion is untenable for two reasons. First, creating belongs to God alone, and things not subject to coming to be and passing away [the intelligences] need to be created. Second, were the opinion true, the whole universe would result from the conjunction of many efficient causes (i.e., by chance), not from the aim of the first efficient cause, which is impossible.

And so the multiplicity and diversity of things comes from the intention of the first efficient cause, God. For he brought things into existence in order that his goodness be communicated to creatures and be represented by them. And since one kind of creature cannot adequately represent his goodness, he produced many diverse creatures, and so one creature supplies what another lacks in representing his goodness. For the goodness that exists simply and uniformly in God, exists in creatures in many ways and separately. And so the whole universe shares and represents his goodness more completely than any single kind of creature would.

2. Is there only one world?[10]

I answer that the world is one by reason of its integrated order as some things are ordered to other things. But all things from God are related to one another and God. And so everything necessarily belongs to one world.

Evil

Thomas devotes considerable attention to the problem of evil. Following Augustine, he defines evil as a privation, not the mere absence, of good and holds

---

[9]ST I, Q. 47, A. 1. [10]ST I, Q. 47, A. 3.

that evil as such is not an existing thing. But some things can and do pass away and so fall short of goodness, and the nature of evil consists of falling short of goodness. And so there is evil, that is, privation of good, in things, and good things are subjects of the privations (e.g., blindness is the privation of sight in a human being, who as such is something good). Good things cause evil, since causes are beings, and beings are good. But good things cause evil incidentally (i.e., incidentally to seeking some good), not intrinsically (i.e., as the object striven for). Evil results from the deficiency of a cause (e.g., Down's syndrome in offspring from the recessive genes of parents) or from the indisposition of matter (e.g., poor soil results in poor plants). Since there is no defect in God, the evil resulting from particular deficient causes is not traceable to him. But the evil in things' passing away is traceable to him insofar as he intends the good order of the universe, in which some things can and do pass away (e.g., plants pass away when animals eat them, and this is evil for the plants but good for the animals). He does not cause the evil of sin, but the order of justice requires that sinners be punished. There is no first cause of evil comparable to the first cause of good.

1. Is evil a nature?[11]

I answer that we know one contrary by the other, and so we need to understand evil by the nature of good. But good is something desirable, and every nature desires its own existence and perfection. Therefore, the existence and perfection of every nature possesses the nature of goodness. And so evil cannot signify a way of existing or a form or a nature. And so we conclude that evil signifies the absence of good, and, since being as such is good, that evil is neither anything existing nor anything good, and the absence of one is the absence of the other.

Objection. Every constitutive difference is a nature. But evil is a constitutive difference in moral matters, for evil habits differ specifically from good habits. Therefore, evil signifies a nature.

Reply Obj. Moral matters take their species from their ends, that is, the object of the will. But good has the nature of end. And so good and evil are uniquely specific differences in moral matters, good as such and evil as taking away a due end. But taking away a due end constitutes a species in moral matters only insofar as the taking away is connected to an undue end. And so the evil that constitutes the specific difference in moral matters is a good linked to the privation of another good. For example, an intemperate person aims to gain a sensibly perceptible good apart from the order of reason, not to be deprived of the good of reason. And so evil by

---

[11]ST I, Q. 48, A. 1.

reason of a connected good, not evil as such, constitutes a specific difference in moral matters.

2. Is there evil in things?[12]

I answer that the perfection of the universe requires dissimilarity in things, so that every grade of goodness be realized. But there are grades of good that can fall short of good, and these grades of goodness are in existing itself. For there are some things (e.g., immaterial things) that cannot lose their existence, and other things (e.g., material things) that can. Therefore, as the perfection of the universe requires that there be both things that cannot pass away and things that can, so the perfection of the universe requires that there be some things that can fall short of goodness. And so such things sometimes do fall short. But the nature of evil consists in the fact that things fall short of good. And so there is evil in things, just as things pass away, which is itself an evil.

Objection. Being and *thing* are convertible terms. Therefore, if evil is a being in things, then evil is a thing. But this is contrary to what was said in the preceding article.

Reply Obj. We speak of being in two ways. Being in one way signifies the reality of something, and being in this sense is convertible with thing. But no privation is a being in this sense, and so no evil is either. Being in the second way signifies the truth of a proposition. And the word *is* indicates composition, in which the truth of a proposition consists. And being in this sense answers the question: Is it? And we say in this sense that there is evil.

3. Is something good the subject of evil?[13]

I answer that not every taking away of good is evil. Taking away good by way of negation does not have the nature of evil, since then things that in no way exist would be evil, and everything that did not possess the good of something else would be evil. For example, human beings would be evil because they did not possess the swiftness of a deer or the strength of a lion.

But taking away good by way of privation is an evil. The subject of a privation and the subject of a form are the same thing, namely, a potential being, and the form by which a being is actual is a perfection and something good. And so every potential being as such is something good insofar as it is ordered to good. As something is a potential being, so also is it a potential good. Therefore, the subject of evil is something good.

---

[12]ST I, Q. 48, A. 2. [13]ST I, Q. 48, A. 3.

4. Can good cause evil?[14]

I answer that evil is the deficiency of a good that is produced by nature and ought to be possessed, and so every evil is in some way caused. And only a cause driving something away from a thing's natural and requisite disposition can bring it about that the thing lack its proper disposition. But only something good can cause, since causes are beings, and every being as such is good. As to particular kinds of causes, efficient causes, forms, and ends signify a perfection proper to the nature of good, and matter, as a potentiality for good, also has the nature of good.

Good is the subject of evil, and so good causes evil by way of a material cause. Evil, which consists of the deprivation of form, has no formal cause. Nor does evil, which consists of the deprivation of an order to a requisite end, have a final cause, since ends and useful means for ends have the nature of good. But evil does have a cause by way of an efficient cause, albeit incidentally and not intrinsically.

Evil is caused in one way in actions and in another way in effects. A deficiency in any cause of action, whether the chief or the instrumental cause, causes there to be evil in the action. For example, either weakness in the power of locomotion, as in the case of the young, or the incapacity of the means of locomotion, as in the case of the lame, can cause deficiency in an animal's movement.

And sometimes the power of an efficient cause, sometimes a deficiency of the cause or the matter, causes evil to result in something, although not in the cause's proper effect. The power or perfection of an efficient cause causes evil in something when the form striven for necessarily results in the deprivation of another form. For example, fire results in the deprivation of the forms of air and water, and so the more complete the power of fire, the more completely it imprints its form and destroys the forms of air and water. And this destruction is by accident, since fire strives to introduce its own form, not to cause the deprivation of water's form.

And there may be a deficiency in the proper effect of a cause because of an indisposition of the matter receiving the action. For example, fire may fail to heat because of an indisposition of the matter to receive the heating action.

Still, the deficient existing itself befalls something good, to which causal activity intrinsically belongs. And so evil is caused only incidentally. And so good causes evil in this way.

---

[14]ST I, Q. 49, A. 1.

5. Does God cause evil?[15]

I answer that the deficiency of an efficient cause always causes the evil in defective action. But there is no deficiency in God. And so the evil in defective action or the evil caused by a deficient cause is not traceable to God.

An efficient cause in producing a form whereby the destruction of another form results causes such destruction. And so the evil in things passing away is traceable to God. But the form that God chiefly strives for in created things is the good order of the universe, and the good order of the universe requires that some things can and do pass away. And in so doing, God consequently and incidentally, as it were, causes things to pass away.

And the order of justice, which requires that punishment be inflicted on sinners, also belongs to the order of the universe. And so he is the cause of the evil of punishment. But he does not cause the evil of sin.

6. Is there a supreme evil that causes every evil?[16]

I answer that there is no first cause of evil comparable to the first cause of good. Three arguments make this clear. First, every being as such is good, and there is evil only in a subject that is good. And so nothing can be evil by its essence. Second, evil, although it always diminishes good, can never completely destroy good. And so nothing wholly and completely evil can exist. Third, something good causes every evil, and evil can only cause something accidentally. But an accidental cause is secondary to an intrinsic cause. And so evil cannot be a first cause.

Governance

Two considerations show that the universe is governed: the fixed order of things toward ends, and the nature of God's goodness, which requires that he bring things to their ends. Since the universal end of all things is a universal good, which is intrinsically and essentially good, and the particular ends of particular things are only good by sharing in the universal good, the end of the universe needs to be extrinsic to the universe. And since the world's governance is intrinsically good, it needs to be the best, and the best governance is by one ruler.

Regarding the end, governance of the universe has only one effect, namely, to imitate the supreme good. Regarding means, governance of the universe has two general effects: the preservation of the goodness of created things, and the

---

[15]ST I, Q. 49, A. 2. [16]ST I, Q. 49, A. 3.

goodness of things that created things cause. And governance of the universe has countless particular effects.

God's providence governs everything directly, but he executes his providence by means of some created things causing other created things. Since he is the first, universal cause, nothing can happen outside the order of his governance, and nothing can resist his order.

God preserves all things intrinsically and directly, since every creature's existing depends on him. And created things preserve other created things indirectly and incidentally by removing destructive causes (e.g., salt preserves meat from putrefying) or directly and intrinsically as intermediate causes (e.g., the sun sustains life). His shared goodness is the end of every activity by creatures. He is the first efficient cause of every created efficient cause. And he gives created efficient causes the forms by which they act. He can do things outside the order of created things (i.e., he produces miracles) insofar as the latter depend on secondary causes.

1. Is the world governed?[17]

I answer that two considerations show that it is impossible that everything in the world happen by chance. First, things themselves evidence this. Something better either always or for the most part results regarding things of nature. But such would not be the case unless a providence were to direct things of nature toward a good end, and this is governance. And so the fixed order of things itself demonstrates the world's governance.

Second, it belongs to the best to produce the best, and so it is proper for the supreme goodness of God to bring the things he produces to a perfect state. But the final perfection of each thing consists in attaining its end. And so it belongs to God's goodness to bring things to their ends, just as his goodness brings them into existence, and doing this is governance.

2. Is the end of the world something extrinsic to the world?[18]

I answer that ends correspond to causes. And so we know the end of things when we know their cause. But the cause of things, namely, God, is extrinsic to the universe. Therefore, the end of things needs to be an extrinsic good.

For good possesses the nature of end. And so the particular end of a particular thing is a particular good, and the universal end of all things is a universal good. But the universal good is intrinsically and essentially good, and a particular good is good by sharing in good. And everything in

---

[17]ST I, Q. 103, A. 1.   [18]ST I, Q. 103, A. 2.

the created universe is good by sharing in good. And so the good that is the end of the whole universe needs to be extrinsic to the universe.

3. Does one ruler govern the world?[19]

I answer that the end of the world's governance is something intrinsically good, what is best. And so governance of the word needs to be the best.

Governance directs the governed to an end or good, and unity belongs to the nature of goodness. For all things desire the good of unity, without which they cannot exist, and so the end for which a ruler aims is unity or peace.

The cause of unity is intrinsically one. But what is intrinsically one can more suitably and more perfectly cause unity than many rulers in concert can. And so one ruler governs a multitude better than several rulers can.

Therefore, we conclude that the best governance of the world is one by a single ruler.

4. Does governance of the world produce only one effect?[20]

I answer that actions bring about attainment of ends. Therefore, we can assess the effects of actions by their ends. But the end of the world's governance is an intrinsic good that everything strives to share and assimilate.

We can understand the effect of the governance of the world in three ways. First, we can understand the effect regarding its very purpose, and then governance of the world has only one effect, namely, to imitate the supreme good. Second, we can consider the effect regarding the means whereby creatures are produced in the likeness of God. And so governance of the world, in general, has two effects. For creatures imitate God in two respects: one regarding God's goodness inasmuch as creatures are good; the other regarding the fact that God causes goodness for other things inasmuch as creatures cause the goodness of other creatures. And so the world's governance produces two effects, namely, the preservation of things in goodness and the movements of things to cause the goodness of other things. Third, we can consider the effect of governance of the world in particular, and then we cannot count their number.

5. Is everything subject to God's governance?[21]

I answer that it is proper to God to govern things and to cause things for the same reason, since it belongs to him to produce things and to give

---

[19]ST I, Q. 103, A. 3. [20]ST I, Q. 103, A. 4. [21]ST I, Q. 103, A. 5.

them their perfections. But God causes both particular kinds of things and every single being. And so, as nothing can exist that God does not create, so nothing can exist that is not subject to his governance.

Second, a ruler's governance reaches as far as the end of his governance can reach. But the end of God's governance is his very goodness. And so, since nothing can exist that is not ordered to his goodness as its end, nothing belonging to things can be withdrawn from his governance.

6. Does God govern everything without intermediaries?[22]

I answer that concerning the essence of governance, which is providence itself, God governs everything directly, but concerning the execution of governance, he governs some things by means of others.

We should attribute each thing to God according to what is most good in it, since God is the very essence of goodness. But the best in every way or plan or practical knowledge consists in knowing actual particular things. And so God possesses the essence of the governance of everything, even the least particular.

And since governance ought to bring the governed to perfection, the greater the perfection a ruler shares with his subjects, the better will be his governance. And it is a greater perfection that things cause goodness in others in addition to being intrinsically good. And so God governs things in such a way that he constitutes some things the causes of other things.

7. Can anything happen outside the order of God's governance?[23]

I answer that nothing comes about outside the disposition of a particular cause unless another cause impedes the latter, and we need to trace the other cause back to the first, universal cause. Therefore, effects can come about outside the disposition of particular causes but not outside the disposition of the universal cause. But God is the first, universal cause both of one kind of being and of every kind of being. Therefore, nothing can happen outside the order of his governance. But effects from one perspective seem to depart from the order of God's providence regarding particular causes. Therefore, effects need to be related to that order by other causes.

Objection. Nothing preordained exists by chance. Therefore, if nothing happens in the world outside the order of God's governance, then nothing in the world would exist by chance.

Reply Obj. Things exist in the world by chance in relation to particular causes, and such things happen outside the disposition of those causes.

---

[22] ST I, Q. 103, A. 6. [23] ST I, Q. 103, A. 7.

But nothing in the world happens by chance in relation to God's providence.

8. Can anything resist the order of God's governance?[24]

I answer that as the order of God's providence comes from him, nothing resists the order of his governance. There are two reasons why this is so. First, the order of his governance aims entirely for good, and everything in its activity and effort strives only for good. Second, every tendency, whether natural or voluntary, is an impulse from the first cause, and so everything, whether by nature or free will, arrives at the end to which God orders the thing.

9. Does God need to preserve creatures?[25]

I answer that God, by removing destructive causes, preserves some things indirectly and incidentally. But God preserves all things intrinsically and directly. For every creature's existing depends on God, so that no creature could exist even for a moment without being annihilated were the activity of God's power not to preserve it in existence.

Every creature is disposed toward God as air is disposed toward the sun illuminating it. The sun by its nature shines, and air becomes luminous by sharing in light from the sun, not by sharing in the nature of the sun. Just so, God alone is a being by his essence, since his essence is his existing. But every creature is a being by sharing, not a being such that its essence is its existing. And so the nature of created things would cease if the power of God were to cease.

10. Does God preserve every creature apart from intermediate causes?[26]

I answer that some created things preserve other created things indirectly and incidentally by removing destructive causes. For example, salt preserves meats from putrefying. But the existence of some effects depends directly and intrinsically on creatures. For effects produced by many subordinated causes, although they depend first and chiefly on the primary cause, depend secondarily on all the intermediate causes. And so, although the primary cause chiefly preserves the effects, the intermediate causes do so secondarily. And the higher the intermediate cause and the closer to the primary cause, the more the intermediate cause preserves the

---

[24]ST I, Q. 103, A. 8. [25]ST I, Q. 104, A. 1. [26]ST I, Q. 104, A. 2.

effects. And so we attribute the preservation and continued existence of things to their higher intermediate causes.

11. Does God act in every created efficient cause?[27]

I answer that some thinkers hold that God acts in every efficient cause in such a way that no created power would cause anything. But this position is impossible for several reasons. First, it would take the order of cause and effect away from things and imply lack of power on the part of the creator. For an efficient cause's power results in the cause imparting to its effect the power to act. Second, we would erroneously attribute to things the active powers they have if they were to do nothing by means of those powers. Every created thing would seem to be purposeless if it were to be deprived of its own activity, since everything exists for the purpose of its activity. Form, the first actuality, exists for the sake of its activity, the second actuality. And so activity is the end of created things.

Of the four kinds of causes, ends, efficient causes, and forms, but not matter, are disposed as causes of action, albeit in a certain order. The first cause of action is the end that moves an efficient cause to act. The second cause of action is the efficient cause. The third cause of action is the form of what an efficient cause brings to the thing to be made.

Thus God acts in three ways in everything that acts. First, God himself causes every action as its end, since every action is for a real or apparent good, and things are really or apparently good only insofar as they share a likeness to the highest good, God. Second, in subordinated efficient causes, the second cause acts in the power of the first, and so everything acts in the power of God, and he causes the action of every efficient cause. Third, God both moves things to act by applying their forms and powers to actions and gives created efficient causes their forms and preserves them in existence. And so he causes their actions insofar as he bestows the forms that are the sources of their actions.

12. Can God do anything outside the order he implants in things?[28]

I answer that as the order of things depends on their primary cause, God cannot do anything contrary to that order, since he would thereby do something contrary to his foreknowledge or his will or his goodness. But as the order of things depends on a secondary cause, God can do something outside that order. For he is not subject to the order of secondary

---

[27]ST I, Q. 105, A. 5. [28]ST I, Q. 105, A. 6.

causes. Rather, such order is subject to him, proceeding from him by the choice of his will, not by a necessity of nature. And so God can, when he has so willed, do things outside the order he has established, by producing the effects of secondary causes apart from those causes or by producing effects beyond the reach of secondary causes.

13. Is every deed of God outside the natural order of things a miracle?[29]

I answer that we derive the word *miracle* from wonderment. And wonderment arises when effects are apparent, and the cause is hidden. But miracles are wonder-full in that they have a cause absolutely hidden from absolutely everyone. And this cause is God. And so we call things produced by God outside causes known to us miracles.

[29]ST I, Q. 105, A. 7.

3

The Soul

Essence

Aristotle and Thomas call the primary source of life in living material things the soul. See Glossary, s.v. Soul. *The primary source of life is the actuality (i.e., the form) of a living material substance, not the material substance itself. See Glossary, s.v.* Actuality. *The human soul is the primary source of intellectual cognition, and the intellect, unlike the senses, can know every kind of material thing. Therefore, the human soul, unlike the souls of irrational animals, is intrinsically subsistent. The human being is a composite of soul and body, not the soul alone. The intrinsically subsistent human soul cannot pass away when the composite does.*

1. Is the soul of living things a material substance?[1]

I answer that not every source of vital activity is the soul. For example, were this so, the eye, the source of sight, would then be the soul, as would other instrumentalities of the soul. Rather, the soul is the *primary* source of life. No material substance can be the primary source of life. For being alive does not belong to a material substance as such, since then every material substance would be alive. Therefore, life belongs to a material substance because the matter is *a particular kind.* But the fact that things are actually such derives from a source that is the things' actuality. Therefore, the soul, the primary source of life, is the actuality of a material substance, not the material substance.

2. Is the human soul subsistent?[2]

I answer that human beings with their intellects can know the nature of every kind of material substance. Such knowers necessarily possess no part of the known material substance in the knowers' natural condition, since what would be part of the knower by nature would prevent knowledge of other kinds of material things. For example, a sick person's tongue, saturated with bile, cannot perceive anything sweet. Therefore, if

[1]ST I, Q. 75, A. 1. [2]ST I, Q. 75, A. 2.

the source of intellection were to have in itself the natural condition of a particular material substance, the source would be unable to know every material substance. But every kind of material substance has a fixed nature. Therefore, the source of intellectual activity cannot be a material substance. Nor can the source of intellectual activity understand by bodily organs, since the fixed nature of such organs would also prevent knowledge of every kind of material substance. For example, liquid poured into a colored vase appears to be of the same color.

Therefore, the source of intellection intrinsically has an activity in which the body does not share. But nothing can intrinsically act unless it intrinsically subsists, since things act in the same way that they exist. We conclude, therefore, that the human soul, which we call the intellect or mind, is something immaterial and subsistent.

3. Are the souls of irrational animals subsistent?[3]

I answer that bodily changes accompany sense perceptions and the resulting activities of sensory souls. And so sensory souls have no intrinsic activity of their own, and all of their activities belong to the composites of soul and matter. But everything has a way of existing like its way of acting. Therefore, the souls of irrational animals, since they do not act intrinsically, are not subsistent.

4. Is the human soul the human being?[4]

I answer that some thinkers held that the form alone belongs to the nature of the species, but the matter belongs to individuals. But this cannot be true. For the meaning of definitions belongs to species, and definitions of things of nature signify form and matter, not simply form. The matter signified is general matter, not particular matter. For example, as it belongs to the nature of a particular human being to be composed of a particular soul and particular flesh and bones, so it belongs to the nature of human being to be composed of soul and flesh and bones.

Nor is the particular human soul the particular human being. We could maintain this if we were to suppose that the activities of sensory souls are proper to such souls apart from bodies, since all the activities that we attribute to human beings would belong to the human soul. But sense perception is an activity of human beings, although not their proper activity, and sense perception is not an activity of the soul alone. Therefore, the human being is a composite of soul and body, not the soul alone.

---

[3]ST I, Q. 75, A. 3. [4]ST I, Q. 75, A. 4.

5. Is the human soul composed of matter and form?[5]

I answer that the human soul does not have matter. We can perceive this in one way from the nature of the soul in general. For it belongs to the nature of the soul to be the form of a body. Therefore, the soul is either entirely or partially a form. If entirely, no part of it can be matter, assuming we mean by matter purely potential being. This is because form as such is actuality, and something purely potential cannot be part of actuality, since potentiality, as distinguished from actuality, is incompatible with actuality. And if part of the soul be a form, that part is the soul, and the matter that the soul first actualizes is the first enlivened thing.

Second, we can from the nature of the human soul as intellectual specifically perceive that the human soul does not have matter. For everything received in something else is received in the recipient according to the recipient's condition, and each thing is known in the way in which its form is in the knower. But the intellectual soul completely knows things regarding their nature. For example, the intellectual soul completely knows stone as such. Therefore, the form of stone, regarding stone's own formal nature, is completely in the intellectual soul. Therefore, the intellectual soul is a pure form and not something composed of matter and form.

If the intellectual soul were composed of matter and form, the soul would receive in itself the forms of things as individual forms. And so it would know only singular things, as in the case of sensory powers, which receive the forms of things in bodily organs. This is because matter is the source that individuates forms.

Therefore, we conclude that the intellectual soul (and every intellectual substance) has no composition of form and matter.

6. Can the human soul pass away?[6]

I answer that things pass away in two ways: in one way intrinsically; in the other way incidentally. But nothing subsistent can come to be or pass away incidentally, that is, when something else has come to be or passed away. For coming-to-be and passing away belong to things in the same way that existing does, and existing is acquired by the coming-to-be and lost by the passing away. And so things that have existing intrinsically, can come to be or pass away only intrinsically, but nonsubsistent things (e.g., accidents and material forms) come to be and pass away by the coming-to-be and the passing away of composites. The souls of irrational animals are

---

[5]ST I, Q. 75, A. 5. [6]ST I, Q. 75, A. 6.

not intrinsically subsistent, and so those souls pass away when irrational animals' bodies pass away. But human souls are intrinsically subsistent, and so they could not pass away.

And it is altogether impossible for any subsistent form to do so. For what as such belongs to things cannot be separated from them. But existing belongs intrinsically to forms, which are actualities. And so matter acquires actual existing when it acquires form, and matter passes away when form is separated from it. But form cannot be separated from itself. And so subsistent form cannot cease to exist.

We can also take evidence of this matter from the fact that each thing by nature desires to exist in its own way, and knowing things desire as a result of knowledge. But the intellect, unlike the senses, understands existing unconditionally and regarding every point of time. And so everything with an intellect desires by nature to exist forever. But a desire from nature cannot be in vain. Therefore, no intellectual substance can pass away.

Union with the Body

Thomas here addresses a series of questions about the human soul. Is the soul the form of the human body and thereby the source of all the vital activities of human beings? Is there one intellectual soul, or intellect, in all human beings collectively? Do human beings have other souls than the intellectual soul? Do human beings have other substantial forms than the intellectual soul? Is the human soul in every part of the body? See Glossary, s.v., Form, Soul.

His answer to the first question is crucial and puts him at variance with Augustine and even his formative teacher, Albert the Great. (See Introduction.) Thomas forcefully defends the proposition that the intellectual soul is the primary source of all the vital activities of human beings. He thereby rejects every kind of substantial dualism regarding the source of human vital activities. This position aroused considerable opposition, since traditional theologians thought it entailed denial of the soul's immortality.

The answers to the succeeding questions derive from the answer to the first question. If the intellectual soul is the substantial form of human beings, then one and the same form cannot belong to several numerically different things, and so there cannot be one intellect in all human beings collectively. If the intellectual soul is the substantial form of the body, then there cannot be several essentially different souls informing one and the same body. Nor can there be any other substantial form, since then the intellectual soul would not confer existing on the body without qualification. And the intellectual soul, if it is the form of the body, actualizes the whole body and every part of the body, al-

though the soul is not in every part of the body regarding every one of the soul's powers (e.g., the power of sight is in the eyes, not the hands).

1. Is the source of intellection the body's form?[7]

I answer that the source of activity is the form of the thing to which we attribute the activity. This is because nothing acts except insofar as it is actual, and so things act by reason of the sources whereby they are actual. But the soul is the primary source whereby the body is alive. And since the different kinds of activities in different grades of living things manifest life, the source whereby we perform each of these vital activities is the soul. For the soul is the primary source whereby we nourish ourselves and sensibly perceive and move ourselves from place to place, as well as the primary source whereby we understand. Therefore, the primary source whereby we understand, whether called the intellect or the intellectual soul, is the form of the body.

If one should choose to deny that the intellectual soul is the form of the body, one would need to find a way in which the activity of understanding is the action of a particular human being, since all experience that they are the ones who understand. When we say that Socrates understands, we do not attribute understanding to him by accident, since we attribute to him as a human being what we predicate essentially of him. And we cannot say that Socrates understands by his whole self, that is, that human beings are intellectual souls. For the very same human beings perceive that they both understand and sense. But there is no sense perception apart from the body. And so the body is necessarily part of human beings. Therefore, we conclude that the intellect whereby Socrates understands is a part of Socrates in a way in which the intellect is somehow united to the body.

The connection or union of the potential intellect to a particular human body by intelligible forms in the potential intellect is not enough to explain why the activity of Socrates' intellect is the activity of Socrates. From the fact that there are [intelligible] forms of sense images in his potential intellect, it only follows that he or his sense images are understood, not that he is understanding.

Some have held that the intellect is united to the body as the efficient cause that moves the body, and so that the intellect and the body form a unit to which we can attribute the activity of the intellect. But this explanation is pointless for several reasons. First, the intellect moves the body

---

[7]ST I, Q. 76, A. 1.

only by the will, whose motion presupposes intellectual activity, and so the intellect moves Socrates because Socrates understands. Second, understanding is an activity that remains in its source, not a transitive activity, and so we cannot attribute understanding to Socrates because the intellect moves him. Third, we do not attribute activity to things moved except as a means to an end, and understanding is not the product of bodily organs. Fourth, we never attribute the activity of one part to another part except, perhaps, accidentally, and so we would be unable to attribute the activity of the intellect to Socrates. And if Socrates is a whole composed of the intellect and other things belonging to him, but the intellect is united to the other things only as the cause moving them, Socrates would not be one or a being unconditionally.

The nature of the human species manifests the same thing. For the activity of each thing reveals its nature. But the characteristic activity of human beings as such, the activity whereby they surpass all other animals, is understanding. Therefore, human beings need to share in their species by the form characteristic of the species. Therefore, the source of intellection is the specific form of human beings.

Objection 1. A form is the source whereby something exists, and so the very existing of a form does not belong to the form itself as such. Therefore, what intrinsically possesses existing is not united to a body as the body's form. But the source of intellection, as such, possesses existing and is subsistent. Therefore, the source of intellection is not united to the body as the body's form.

Reply Obj. 1. The soul communicates to corporeal matter the existing in which the soul itself subsists, and the corporeal matter and the intellectual soul form one thing in such a way that the existing belonging to the whole composite also belongs to the soul itself. And this does not happen in the case of other forms, forms that are not subsistent. And for this reason, the human soul abides in its own existing when the body is destroyed, and other forms do not.

Obj. 2. What belongs to something as such always belongs to it. But being united to matter belongs to forms as such. For form is by its essence, not accidentally, the actuality of matter; otherwise, matter and form would be one thing accidentally, not substantially. Therefore, forms cannot exist without their matter. But the source of intellection, since it cannot pass away, abides separate from the body after the body is dissolved. Therefore, the source of intellection is not united to the body as the body's form.

Reply Obj. 2. Being united to the body belongs to the soul as such, and the human soul, when separated from the body, abides in existence with a natural disposition and inclination for union with the body.

2. Is there one intellect in all human beings collectively?[8]

I answer that if we hold that the intellect is a power of the soul that is the form of human beings, it is impossible that there be one intellect in all human beings collectively. For one and the same form cannot belong to several numerically different things, just as one and the same existing cannot belong to them, since form is the source of existing.

And the intellect, howsoever it is united or joined to this or that human being, has primacy over other things that belong to human beings, since human beings' sensory powers obey and are at the service of the intellect. Therefore, if there is one intellect in all human beings collectively, however much all the other things that the intellect uses may differ, we could in no way speak of Socrates and Plato other than as one human being who understands.

And if no instrument other than the intellect itself causes the very act of understanding, that is, the intellect's understanding, it will further follow that there is but one efficient cause and one action, that is, that all human beings constitute one subject who understands and one act of understanding.

And if sense images themselves, as one image in me and another in you, were to be the form of the potential intellect, the diversity of sense images would be able to distinguish my intellectual activity from yours. But intelligible forms abstracted from sense images, not the sense images themselves, are the forms of the potential intellect, and in one intellect, only one intelligible form is abstracted from different sense images. For example, a single human being may have different sense images of stones but abstracts from those images only the one intelligible form of stone, by which the intellect of that human being understands the nature of stone. Therefore, if one intellect were to belong to all human beings collectively, different sense images in this and that human being could not cause the different intellectual activities of the human beings.

3. Do human beings have other souls besides the intellectual soul?[9]

I answer that if we hold that the soul is united to the body as the body's form, it seems completely impossible that there be several essentially different souls in one body, and we can demonstrate this by three arguments.

First, things are unconditionally one by one form, since things have being and oneness from the same source. Therefore, if human beings were

---

[8]ST I, Q. 76, A. 2. [9]ST I, Q. 76, A. 3.

to have life from one form, the vegetative soul, and animality by another form, the sensory soul, and humanity from another form, the rational soul, a human being would not be unconditionally one thing. And if there were several souls in human beings, what would unite them? We cannot say that the unity of the body unites several souls, since the soul contains the body and makes the body itself one thing, not the converse.

Second, we predicate animal of human beings intrinsically, not by accident, and we posit animal in the definition of human being, not the converse. Therefore, the form by which something is an animal, and the form by which it is a human being, are one and the same; otherwise, human beings would not truly be animals, such that we may predicate animal of human beings intrinsically.

Third, one kind of activity, when intense, hinders another kind of activity, and such could happen only if the source of the several kinds of activity were to be essentially one.

And we can consider how this can be by noting the differences in species and forms. For example, living things are more perfect than nonliving things, animals more perfect than plants, and human beings more perfect than irrational animals. And so species are like numbers, which differ by adding or subtracting units. Therefore, the intellectual soul in its power contains whatever the sensory soul of irrational animals and the nutritive soul of plants possess.

4. Is there any other form in human beings besides the intellectual soul?[10]

I answer that accidental forms bestow existing in a particular way, but substantial forms bestow existing without qualification. Therefore, if in addition to the intellectual soul, there were to preexist any other substantial form in matter, by means of which the soul's substratum would be an actual being, the soul would consequently not bestow existing without qualification. And so the soul would not be a substantial form.

And so we need to say that the only substantial form in human beings is the intellectual soul, that that soul by its power contains all the lower forms, as well as the nutritive and sensory souls, and that the intellectual soul alone does whatever less perfect forms do in other things. And we should say the same about the sensory soul in irrational animals, and about the nutritive soul in plants, and universally about all more perfect forms in relation to less perfect forms.

---

[10]ST I, Q. 76, A. 4.

5. Is the whole soul in every part of the body?[11]

I answer that because the soul is united to the body as the body's form, the soul needs to be in the whole body and in every part of the body. For the soul is a substantial form and so needs to be the form and actuality of the whole body and every part of the body.

The whole soul, regarding the totality of the soul's perfection and essence, is in every part of the body. But the whole soul, regarding the totality of its power, is not. For the soul is not in every part of the body regarding every one of the soul's powers. For example, the soul is in eyes only regarding the power of sight, and in ears only regarding the power of hearing.

And we should note that the soul needs the diversity in the body's parts, and so the soul is differently related to the whole body and to the body's parts. The soul is primarily and intrinsically related to the whole body as what the soul can properly and duly perfect, while the soul is secondarily related to parts of the body as the latter are ordered to the whole body.

Vegetative Powers

Three vegetative powers are necessary for a living body: nutrition, growth, and reproduction. The human soul, as the form of the body, has these powers.

1. What are the vegetative powers of the soul?[12]

I answer that vegetative power has for its object the very body that is a living body by means of the soul, and three activities of the soul are necessary for such a body. The living body acquires existing by one kind of activity, and the power of generation is ordered to that end. And the living body acquires its requisite size by a second kind of activity, and the power of growth is ordered to that end. And the body of a living thing is preserved in its existing and requisite size by a third kind of activity, and the power of nutrition is ordered to that end.

We should note a difference between these powers. For the powers of nutrition and growth produce effects in the things in which the powers exist, but the power of generation produces its effect in another body. And so the power of generation approaches the power of the sensory soul, which has activities in relation to external things. And so the power of generation is the ultimate and most important and most perfect of the three powers. And the powers of nutrition and growth assist the power of generation, and the power of nutrition assists the power of growth.

---

[11]ST I, Q. 76, A. 8. [12]ST I, Q. 78, A. 2.

Cognitive Sense Powers

Thomas distinguishes the five external senses by what properly and intrinsically belongs to each, the external things each sense perceives (e.g., sight perceives color). The senses require an immaterial change, which produces the representation of a perceptible form in a sense organ. In senses other than sight, there is also a natural change either on the part of the object or on the part of the sense organ. Several senses, in perceiving their own proper objects, also perceive quantitative forms like size and shape.

Human beings have four internal senses: the common sense, the power of imagination, the cogitative (in irrational animals, the estimative) power, and the power of memory. The common sense unifies the perceptions of different external senses. The power of imagination retains and preserves the forms of perceived things and composes and divides these forms to create new forms. The cogitative power, called particular reason, by a process of comparison perceives particular imports that things are beneficial or detrimental. The power of memory preserves and recalls particular imports about past things.

1. Are there five external sense powers?[13]

I answer that we should not understand the reason for numbering and distinguishing the external senses from the sense organs, in which one or another element predominates. For sense organs exist because of sense powers, and so nature constituted different sense organs to correspond to different sense powers. Nor should we understand the reason for numbering and distinguishing the external senses from the media by which the senses perceive. For nature assigned different media to different senses by what was suitable for the activities of the sense powers. Nor should we understand the reason for numbering and distinguishing the external senses from the different natures of perceptible properties as belonging to simple or complex material substances. For knowing the natures of perceptible properties belongs to the intellect, not to the senses.

Therefore, we should understand the reason for numbering and distinguishing the external senses by what properly and intrinsically belongs to each sense. But the senses are passive powers constituted to be affected by external perceptible things. Therefore, external perceptible things are what the senses intrinsically perceive, and we distinguish sense powers by the diversity of those things.

There are two kinds of change: one natural and the other immaterial. There is a natural change as the form of something causing change is re-

[13]ST I, Q. 78, A. 3.

ceived in the thing changed according to the form's natural existing. For example, heat is received in the thing heated. And there is an immaterial change as the form of something causing change is received in the thing changed according to the form's immaterial existing. For example, the form of color is received into an eye's pupil, but the pupil does not become colored. And an immaterial change, which produces the representation of a perceptible form in a sense organ, is required for activities of the senses. Otherwise, were a natural change alone to suffice for perceiving, every natural material substance would perceive when it is changed.

In some sense perceptions, as in the sense of sight, there are only immaterial changes. In other sense perceptions, there are both immaterial changes and natural changes, and the latter are only on the part of objects or on the part of sense organs as well. There is a natural change on the part of the object, one regarding place, in sound, which is the object of the sense of hearing, since percussion and disturbance of air cause sound. And there is a natural change on the part of the object by alteration in odor, which is the object of the sense of smell, since something hot needs to change a material substance in some way in order that the substance emit an odor. And there is a natural change on the part of sense organs in the senses of touch and taste, since the hand that touches hot things becomes hot, and the tongue becomes moistened by the moisture of flavors. But natural changes alter the organs of the senses of smell and hearing in the course of perception only incidentally.

The sense of sight, since it has no natural change of its organ or its object, is the most immaterial, the most perfect, and the most universal of the senses. The next most immaterial, most perfect, and most universal sense is the sense of hearing, and the next the sense of smell, both of which senses have natural changes on the part of their objects. And the senses of touch and taste are the most material. And so the senses of sight, hearing, and smell are not executed by conjoined media, and so no natural change affects their sense organs, as happens in the case of the senses of touch and taste.

Objection 1. Size and shape and other things we call things perceptible by several senses are not things accidentally perceptible. But the intrinsic differences of powers' objects distinguish powers, and size and shape differ more from color than sound differs from color. Therefore, it seems that there ought much more to be a different sense power cognitive of size and shape than there ought to be different sense powers cognitive of color and sound.

Reply Obj. 1. Things peculiarly perceptible by one sense primarily and intrinsically affect the senses, but we trace all the things perceptible by several senses to quantity. Size and number are forms of quantity, and shape is a property that concerns quantity, since the essence of shape consists of the limitation of size. And we perceive motion and rest as their subject is in one or several ways disposed regarding the subject's size (as to growth) or regarding the magnitude of the subject's spatial distance (as to locomotion) or regarding perceptible qualities (as in change). And so perceiving motion and rest is in a way to perceive one thing and many things. But quantity is the proximate subject of the qualities that cause change. For example, surfaces are the proximate subjects of color. And so things perceptible by several senses affect the senses by reason of the things' properly perceptible qualities, not primarily and intrinsically. For example, surfaces affect the sense of sight by reason of their color.

Nor are things perceptible by several senses things accidentally perceptible, since they produce different alterations of the senses. For example, large and small surfaces affect the senses in different ways, since we call whiteness large or small and so distinguish it by the subject to which it belongs.

Obj. 2. The object of each sense is one set of contraries. For example, the object of the sense of sight is white and black. But the sense of touch knows several sets of contraries, namely, hot and cold, wet and dry, and the like. Therefore, there are several senses of touch. Therefore, there are more than five senses.

Reply Obj. 2. The sense of touch is generically one sense and specifically many senses, and different sets of contraries are for this reason the object of the sense of touch. But different sets of contraries accompany one another throughout the body and are not separate from one another with respect to sense organs, and so there is no apparent distinction between them. (By contrast, the sense of taste accompanies the sense of touch in the tongue, not throughout the body, and so we easily distinguish the sense of taste from the sense of touch.)

We could say that each set of contraries of the sense of touch belongs to a proximate genus, and that all of them belong to a common genus, which in its common aspect is the object of the sense of touch. But there is no name for this common genus. Similarly, there is no common name for the proximate genus of hot and cold.

2. Are there four internal senses?[14]

I answer that the sensory soul of perfect animals needs to be capable of activities sufficient for their life as perfect animals. But powers of the soul are proximate sources of the soul's activities. Therefore, activities we cannot trace to the same source require different powers.

---

[14]ST I, Q. 78, A. 4.

The proper external senses and the common internal sense are ordered to receive perceptible forms. The proper senses judge about the perceptible things proper to them by distinguishing those things from other things that fall within the power of those senses. For example, the sense of sight distinguishes white from black or green. But neither the sense of sight nor the sense of taste can distinguish white from sweet, since a sense that distinguishes several perceptible things needs to know each of them. And so the judgment that distinguishes between several perceptible things needs to belong to the common sense, to which all perceptions of the external senses are related, and by which the imports of external sense perceptions are perceived, as when individuals perceive that they see. For the proper sense of sight, which knows only the form of the perceptible thing affecting it, cannot do this. And the act of seeing is completed in the alteration of the sense of sight, and from that alteration results another alteration in the common sense, which perceives the act of seeing.

Perfect animals need to perceive absent things. Otherwise, animals would not be moved to seek absent things, and perfect animals have forward motion to do so. Therefore, animals need both to receive the forms of perceptible things when those things are currently affecting the animals and to retain and preserve such forms. But we trace receiving and retaining to different sources. And so a separate power of imagination is ordered as a storehouse to retain and preserve perceptible forms. And the power of imagination in human beings but not in other animals composes and divides imaginary forms. For example, we compose the one form of a gold mountain, which we have never seen, from the imaginary forms of gold and mountain.

And animals need to seek after, or flee from, certain things to gain benefits or avoid detriments. Therefore, animals need to perceive such imports, imports that the external senses do not perceive. And there needs to be another source of such perceptions, since they do not derive from the changes that perceptible things cause. And so a separate estimative power is ordered to perceive imports that the external senses do not perceive.

And the power of memory, a storehouse of such imports, is ordered to preserve those imports. This is indicated by the fact that the source of remembering comes from such an import, for example, the import that something is harmful or suitable. And the very aspect of the past, which memory notes, is counted among such imports.

There is no difference between human beings and animals regarding perceptible forms, but there is a difference regarding the aforementioned imports, since nonhuman beings perceive such imports only by natural instinct, while human beings perceive the imports by a process of comparison. And the natural power of estimation in other animals is the cogitative power in human beings. And so we call the cogitative power particular reason, since the power compares the individual imports just as reason understands universal imports.

Moreover, human beings, in addition to having with other animals memory in the unanticipated recollection of past things, also have the power of recall regarding the particular imports of past things.

And so we need to posit four internal powers of the sensory part of the soul: the common sense, the power of imagination, the estimative power, and the power of memory.

Sense Appetites

Thomas and Aristotle distinguish two kinds of sense appetite: the concupiscible and the irascible. See Glossary, s.v. Appetite, Concupiscible, Irascible. *The concupiscible power seeks to acquire sensibly agreeable things and to flee from harmful things (e.g. the appetites of love and hate). The irascible power concerns useful things that can be obtained only with difficulty (e.g., the appetites of joy and sorrow). Acts of these appetites are subject to judgments of reason, to particular reason, reason in conjunction with the cogitative power (e.g., this apple is good for me) and ultimately to universal reason (e.g., I should eat the apple), and the acts are subject to commands of the will regarding execution (e.g., to eat the apple).*

1. Are there two distinct sense appetites, the irascible and the concupiscible?[15]

I answer that there is one generic sense appetite but two specific kinds of appetitive sense power. One power is the appetitive power whereby the soul unconditionally tends to gain sensibly agreeable things and to flee from harmful things, and we call this power the concupiscible power. And the second power is the appetitive power whereby animals resist hostile forces that attack suitable things and inflict harms, and we call this power the irascible power. And so the object of the irascible power is the difficult, since the power strives to conquer and overcome contrary things.

And we trace these two tendencies to two sources, since the soul, contrary to the tendency of the concupiscible power, sometimes imposes itself on harsh things, as the soul fights against contrary things. And emotions of the irascible power seem to be repugnant to emotions of the concupiscible power. For example, burning desire in most cases lessens anger, and

---

[15]ST I, Q. 81, A. 2.

burning anger in most cases lessens desire. And because the irascible power rises up against hindrances to suitable things that the concupiscible power seeks, and presses against harmful things from which the concupiscible power shrinks, all the emotions of the irascible power arise from the emotions of the concupiscible power and are terminated in them. For example, anger arises on the occasion of melancholy and ends in joy when it brings deliverance.

2. Do the irascible and concupiscible powers obey reason?[16]

I answer that the irascible and concupiscible powers obey the superior part of the soul in two ways: in one way regarding reason; in the second way regarding the will.

The irascible and concupiscible powers obey reason regarding their acts. In other animals, sense appetites are constituted to be moved by the estimative power. But human beings have in place of the estimative power the cogitative power, that is, particular reason. And so sense appetites in human beings are constituted to be moved by particular reason. But particular reason itself is constituted to be moved and directed by universal reason. And so it is clear that universal reason governs sense appetites, the concupiscible and irascible powers, and that sense appetites obey universal reason. (We say that the irascible and concupiscible powers obey reason because drawing conclusions from universal principles is the work of reason, not of simple understanding.) Everybody experiences this. For example, anger or fear is lessened or aroused by applying universal considerations.

Sense appetites are also subject to the will regarding their execution. Human beings, unlike other animals, await a command of the will, that is, the higher appetite, in order to act. For in all interrelated powers causing movement, the second cause moves only by the power of the first, and so lower appetites do not suffice to cause movement unless the higher appetite consents.

Objection. Nothing resists what it obeys. But the irascible and concupiscible powers resist reason. Therefore, the irascible and concupiscible powers do not obey reason.

Reply Obj. The principle of governance whereby a master rules slaves lacking the capacity to resist the orders of the master is despotic. But the principle of governance whereby a ruler rules free persons subject to the ruler but possessing things of their own to resist the orders of the ruler is political and kingly.

---

[16]ST I, Q. 81, A. 3.

The soul rules the body by a despotic principle of governance, and every member of the body subject to voluntary movement is immediately moved at the soul's will. But reason rules the irascible and concupiscible powers by a political principle of governance, since sense appetites have things of their own whereby they can resist the orders of reason. For sense appetites are constituted to be moved not only by the estimative power in the case of other animals, and by the cogitative power in the case of human beings, which universal reason directs, but also by the power of imagination and the external senses. We perceive or imagine things to be pleasant that reason forbids, or things to be harsh that reason commands, and so the irascible and concupiscible powers resist reason. And so the irascible and concupiscible powers are not precluded from obeying reason because they resist reason in some matters.

Cognitive Intellectual Powers

*The potential intellect is initially like a blank slate (*tabula rasa*) and brought to actual understanding. The active intellect makes universal things actually understood by abstracting forms from the particular conditions of matter. The active intellect belongs to each human soul, although a higher intellect, God, needs to help the soul to understand.*

The potential intellect retains intelligible forms (memory). The potential intellect can proceed from understanding some things to understanding other things (reason), and some understood things are self-evident (first principles, such as Every whole is greater than any of its parts*). See Glossary, s.v.* Principle. *As nature implants in human beings first principles about theoretical things, so it implants in them first principles about practical things (e.g., one should act in accord with right reason). See Glossary, s.v.* Synderesis. *Conscience is an act of the intellect whereby human beings judge that they have or have not done something, that they should or should not do something, or that they have or have not done something worthily. See Glossary, s.v.* Conscience.

1. Is the intellect a passive power?[17]

I answer that things are acted upon in a general sense simply by reason of the fact that they, without losing anything, receive something for which they had potentiality, and it is in this way that everything going from potentiality to actuality is acted upon, even when perfected, and that our intellect is acted upon.

---

[17]ST I, Q. 79, A. 2.

The intellect has activity regarding being in general. There is one intellect that is related to all being as the actuality of all being, and such is the divine intellect, that is, the essence of God, in the source of whose essence, as first cause, the totality of being preexists. And so the divine intellect is pure actuality and has no potentiality. But no created intellect can be related as actuality with respect to the totality of all being, since such an intellect would then be an infinite being. And so no created intellect by the fact of its existence is the actuality of all intelligible things but is related to them as potentiality to actuality.

And potentiality is related to actuality in two ways. There is one kind of potentiality that is always actualized and another kind that goes from potentiality to actuality. The angelic intellect is always actualized with regard to the things that it has the potentiality to understand, but the human intellect is potential with regard to the things that it can understand and is initially like an empty tablet. The fact that we are subsequently brought to understand actually what we initially understand only potentially demonstrates this.

And so our intellect is acted upon in a general sense and is a passive power.

2. Is there an active intellect?[18]

I answer that the forms of natural things subsist in matter, and forms existing in matter are not actually intelligible. Therefore, the natures or forms of perceptible things, which are the objects of our understanding, are not as such actually intelligible. But only actual beings bring things from potentiality to actuality. For example, actual perceptible things activate the senses. Therefore, we need to posit a power of the intellect that would make things actually intelligible by abstracting forms from material conditions. And this is why we need to posit an active intellect.

3. Does the active intellect belong to the soul?[19]

I answer that what shares in something and can change and is imperfect requires antecedent to itself something that is essentially such and unchangeable and perfect. But the human soul is intellectual by sharing intellectual power. For only one part of the soul is intellectual, the soul arrives at understanding discursively, and the soul has imperfect understanding. Therefore, there needs to be a higher intellect that helps the soul to understand.

---

[18]ST I, Q. 79, A. 3. [19]ST I, Q. 79, A. 4.

Although there is such a separate active intellect, we still need to posit in the human soul a power shared from the higher intellect, a power whereby the human soul makes things actually intelligible. In perfect natural things, each is endowed with its own power, and nothing on earth is more perfect than the human soul. And so the human soul has a power derived from a higher intellect that enables the soul to illumine sense images.

We know from experience that we have such a power when we realize that we abstract universal forms from conditions of particularity, that is, make things actually intelligible. But activity belongs to something only by reason of a source formally inhering in it. Therefore, a power that is the source of such activity needs to belong to the soul. And so Aristotle compared the active intellect to light.

But the separate intellect is God himself, who creates the soul, and in whom alone the soul is made happy. And so the human soul shares in intellectual light from him.

4. Is there memory in the intellectual part of the soul?[20]

I answer that the potential intellect becomes each thing as it receives the form of each thing. Therefore, the potential intellect, by reason of the fact that it receives intelligible forms, has the capacity to act whenever it chooses. But it does not have the power to be always active, since, even in possession of intelligible forms, it is potential in one way (although otherwise than before understanding), namely, in the way in which habitual knowledge is potential with respect to actual consideration.

Also, the intellect has a more stable and enduring nature than material substances do. Therefore, if material substances retain their forms after they have ceased to act by reason of the forms, much more firmly does the intellect retain intelligible forms without changing or losing them. Therefore, if we understand memory to mean only the power to preserve forms, there is memory in the intellectual part of the soul. But the sensory part of the soul perceives individual things. Therefore, there will be memory of past things as past only in the sensory part of the soul, since the past as past belongs to the condition of something individual.

5. Are reason and intellect different powers?[21]

I answer that understanding consists of comprehending truth without qualification. But reasoning consists of proceeding from one understood thing to another in order to know truth. Therefore, reasoning is related to understanding as being moved is related to being at rest, or as acquiring is

---

[20]ST I, Q. 79, A. 6. [21]ST I, Q. 79, A. 8.

related to possessing, and understanding belongs to something complete, and reasoning to something incomplete.

Human reasoning progresses by inquiry and discovery from some things understood absolutely, that is, from first principles. And human reasoning returns analytically to the first principles and considers the things discovered in relation to them.

Moreover, we trace being at rest and being moved to one and the same power even in the case of things of nature, since the same nature causes things to be moved to a place and to be at rest in that place. Therefore, much more do we understand and reason by the same power. And so reason and intellect in human beings are the same power.

6. Is *synderesis* a special intellectual power?[22]

I answer that human reasoning progresses from understanding some things, namely, things known by nature without inquiry by reason, and terminates in understanding, since we judge by naturally self-evident principles about things we discover by reasoning. But practical reason reasons about practical things in the same way that theoretical reason reasons about theoretical things. Therefore, as nature needs to implant in us the first principles about theoretical things, so also does nature need to implant in us the first principles about practical things.

But the first principles about theoretical things implanted in us by nature belong to a special characteristic disposition, not to a special power. And so also *synderesis* incites to good and complains about evil, since we by first principles progress to discovery and judge about the things we have discovered. Therefore, *synderesis* is a characteristic disposition, not a power.

7. Is conscience a power?[23]

I answer that conscience, according to the proper meaning of the word, signifies a relation of knowledge to something, since we define *con-science* as knowledge with something else. But acts connect knowledge to things. And so conscience is an act.

The same conclusion is evident from the things we attribute to conscience. For we say that conscience bears witness, binds or incites, and accuses or disquiets or reproves. And all these things result from connecting some knowledge of ours to what we do. In one way, we recognize that we have done or have not done something, and then we say that conscience bears witness. In the second way, we connect our knowledge to something

---

[22]ST I, Q. 79, A. 12. [23]ST I, Q. 79, A. 13.

as we judge that we should or should not do something, and then we say that conscience incites or binds. In the third way, we connect our knowledge to something as we judge that we have done or have not done something worthily, and then we say that conscience excuses or accuses or disquiets. All three of these ways result from the actual connection of knowledge to what we do. And so, properly speaking, conscience signifies an act.

How the Soul Understands Material Things

The intellect understands the forms of material substances in an immaterial, universal way. It does not do so by knowing its own essence. Nor are the forms of material things implanted by nature in the human soul. Nor do intelligible forms flow into the soul from separate forms. The human soul knows material things in their eternal natures only insofar as eternal natures are the sources of knowledge, not as known objects. The senses provide images that are the sources of human understanding, but the active intellect makes sense images actually intelligible. In this life, the intellect needs to have recourse to sense images to understand anything. And the intellect cannot form perfect judgments if the senses are restrained.

1. Does the soul know material substances intellectually?[24]

I answer that forms exist in sensibly perceptible things in different ways. For example, one thing is whiter than another, and some white things but not others are sweet. And so also sensibly perceptible forms exist in one way in things outside the soul, and in another way in the senses, which receive the forms of such things apart from the things' matter (e.g., the color of gold apart from gold). Likewise, the intellect receives in its way, an immaterial and unchangeable way, the forms of material substances, material and changeable substances, since things are received in the way of the recipients. Therefore, the soul intellectually knows material substances by a knowledge that is immaterial, universal, and necessary.

Objection. Things necessary and always disposed in the same way constitute the object of the intellect. But every material substance can undergo change and is disposed in different ways. Therefore, the soul cannot know material substances intellectually.

Reply Obj. Every change presupposes something constant, since substances remain constant when qualitative changes occur, and matter re-

---

[24]ST I, Q. 84, A. 1.

mains constant when changes of substantial form occur. Also, constant relationships belong to changeable things. For example, it is unalterably true that Socrates remains in one place while he is seated even though he is not always sitting. And this is why nothing prevents us from having inalterable knowledge about changeable things.

2. Does the soul know material things by reason of its essence?[25]

I answer that ancient philosophers held that the forms of known objects are in the knowing subject in the same way that the forms are in the things known. And since known things are corporeal and material, the philosophers held that known things need to exist in a material way in the souls that know them. And so they held that the soul has a common nature with everything. And since sources determine the nature of effects, they ascribed to the soul the nature of the effects. But this opinion is untenable for several reasons. First, only potential effects exist in material causes, and we know things only as actual. Therefore, unless the natures and forms of individual effects were to exist in the soul, ascription of the nature of things' causes to the soul would be insufficient for the soul to know all things. Second, there would be no reason why things subsisting in a material way outside the soul should lack knowledge if known things were necessarily known in a material way in knowing subjects.

Therefore, known material things need to exist in the knower in an immaterial way. Acts of knowledge extend to things that exist outside the knower, since we know such things. But matter limits the forms of things to individual things. And so things that receive forms only in a material way, such as plants, are in no way cognitive. But the more immaterially something receives the forms of the things it knows, the more perfectly it knows. And so the intellect, which abstracts forms both from matter and from the individuating conditions of matter, knows more perfectly than do the senses, which receive the forms of known things apart from matter but with the conditions of matter. And the more immaterial the intellect, the more perfect it is.

If an intellect knows all things by reason of its essence, its essence needs to possess all things in an immaterial way. But it belongs to God that his essence comprise all things in an immaterial way, since effects preexist in their cause by reason of its power. Therefore, God alone understands all things by his essence, and neither the human soul nor an angel does so by reason of its essence.

---

[25]ST I, Q. 84, A. 2.

3. Does the soul understand material things by forms implanted by nature?[26]

I answer that the actions of sensibly perceptible things on the senses bring human beings from potentiality to actuality, so that human beings perceive, and learning or discovery brings human beings from potentiality to actuality, so that they understand. And so the cognitive soul has potentiality both for the likenesses that are the sources of sense perception and for the likenesses that are the sources of understanding. And Aristotle for this reason held that the intellect initially has potentiality for all forms and does not possess any forms implanted by nature.[27]

Plato held that the human intellect is by nature replete with every intelligible form, and that union with the body prevents the intellect from being able to spring into action.[28] But this dictum is inappropriate for several reasons. First, it seems impossible that the soul with natural knowledge of all things should come to such a state of forgetfulness that it would not know that it has such knowledge, and especially so if we hold that it is natural for the soul to be united to the body. Second, persons lacking a particular sense power lack knowledge of things perceived by that sense. For example, a person born blind cannot have knowledge of colors, which would not be the case if the natures of all intelligible things were to be implanted by nature in the soul.

4. Do intelligible forms flow into the soul from separate forms?[29]

I answer that Plato held that the forms of sensibly perceptible things subsist as such apart from matter, and that both our souls and corporeal matter share in these forms.[30] But it is contrary to the nature of sensibly perceptible things that their forms subsist apart from matter.

Therefore, Avicenna held that the forms of sensibly perceptible things do not subsist apart from matter but preexist in an immaterial way in separate intellects.[31] But if intelligible forms flow into our soul from separate forms, we cannot ascribe a sufficient reason why our soul is united to the body. For if the soul were by its nature constituted fit to receive intelligible forms only by reason of the causal influence of separate sources and not to receive those forms from the senses, the soul would not need the body in order to understand, which is the soul's characteristic activity. And so there would be no purpose to the soul being united to the body.

26ST I, Q. 84, A. 3. 27*De anima* III, 4. 429b29–430a2.

28*Phaedo* 18 et seq.; 72E et seq. *Meno* 15; 81C. *Phaedrus* 30; 249D–250C.

29ST I, Q. 84, A. 4. 30*Timaeus* 18; 49-52.

31*De anima*, part 5, c. 5. *Metaphysics*, tr. 8, c. 6, and tr. 9, cc. 4–5.

Nor would it suffice to say that the soul needs the senses in order to be awakened to consider the things whose intelligible forms it receives from the separate sources. For such awakening seems necessary for the soul only insofar as the soul, because of its union with the body, is in some sort of stupor and forgetful. And so the senses would be of use to the intellectual soul only to take away the obstacle that comes to the soul as a result of its union with the body.

Nor would it suffice to say that the soul needs the senses because they rouse the soul to direct itself to the active intelligence from which it receives intelligible forms. For if it belongs to the soul's nature to understand by forms issuing from the active intelligence, then the soul by its natural inclination could sometimes direct itself to the active intelligence. Or it might be the case that the soul, when aroused by one sense power, would direct itself to the active intelligence in order to receive the forms of sensibly perceptible things that are the object of another sense power that a person lacks. And so a person born blind could have knowledge of colors, and this is not true.

And so we need to say that the intelligible forms by which our soul understands do not issue from separate forms.

5. Does the intellectual soul know material things in their eternal natures?[32]

I answer that something is known in something in one way as in a known object. For example, one sees in a mirror the things whose images are reflected in the mirror. And the soul in the condition of our present life cannot behold all things in their eternal natures, although the blessed, who behold God and all things in him, do so.

Something is known in something in a second way as in a source of knowledge. For example, we see in the sun the things we see by the sun. And so the human soul knows all things in their eternal natures, by sharing which we know all things. For the light of the intellect in us is but a shared likeness of the uncreated light, in which the eternal natures of things are contained.

But in order to have knowledge of material things, we need, in addition to the intellectual light in us, to receive intelligible forms from things. Therefore, we do not have knowledge of material things only by sharing in their eternal natures.

---

[32]ST I, Q. 84, A. 5.

6. Do we obtain intellectual knowledge from sensibly perceptible things?[33]

I answer that the body participates in the characteristic activities of the senses. But the intellect engages in its activity without the participation of the body, and nothing material can make an imprint on something immaterial. And so impressions made by sensibly perceptible things do not alone suffice to cause intellectual activity. But this does not mean that our intellectual knowledge is caused only by impressions made by higher things. Rather, the higher and more excellent efficient cause that we call the active intellect makes the images received by the senses actually intelligible by a process of abstraction.

The senses cause intellectual activity regarding sense images. But sense images do not suffice to affect the potential intellect, and the active intellect needs to make sense images actually intelligible. Therefore, sense knowledge is in a sense the cause's matter, not the entire and complete cause of intellectual knowledge.

7. Can the intellect without recourse to sense images actually understand by intelligible forms in its possession?[34]

I answer that two indications evidence that our intellect in the condition of our present life cannot understand anything without having recourse to sense images. First, injury to a bodily organ would in no way impede the activity of the intellect if the intellect's activity were not to need the act of a power that uses a bodily organ. But the external senses and the power of imagination and other powers belonging to the sensory part of the soul use bodily organs. And so our intellect, in order actually to understand, needs acts of the power of imagination and other powers both to acquire new knowledge and to use knowledge already possessed. For example, if injury to a bodily organ prevents acts of the power of imagination, as in the case of those afflicted with a brain disease, human beings are prevented from understanding even things of which they previously acquired knowledge. Similarly, if injury to a bodily organ prevents acts of the power of memory, as in the case of those afflicted with drowsiness, human beings are prevented from understanding such things.

Second, our intellect in the condition of our present life cannot actually understand without having recourse to sense images because we, in trying to understand things, form sense images to serve as examples, in which images we perceive what we are striving to understand. And so we, want-

[33]ST I, Q. 84, A. 6. [34]ST I, Q. 84, A. 7.

ing others to understand things, also propose examples by means of which they can form sense images for themselves in order to understand.

And the reason why our intellect in the condition of our present life cannot actually understand without having recourse to sense images is because the power to know is proportioned to the knowable object. But the proper objects of the human intellect, which is united to a body, are essences or natures existing in material substances, and the human intellect by means of those natures of visible things rises to some knowledge of invisible things. Moreover, it belongs essentially to such natures of visible things to exist in individual things, and there is no such existence apart from material substances. For example, it belongs essentially to the nature of stone to exist in particular stones, and to the nature of horse to exist in particular horses. And so we can completely and truly know the nature of stones or any material thing only insofar as we know that nature as it exists in a particular stone or material thing. But we know particular things through our senses and our power of imagination. And so, in order for the intellect actually to understand its proper objects, it needs to have recourse to sense images to spy out the universal natures existing in particular things.

Objection. No sense images belong to immaterial things, since the power of imagination does not transcend time and space. Therefore, if our intellect could not actually understand anything without recourse to sense images, it could not understand anything immaterial. But we understand truth and God and angels. Therefore, our intellect can actually understand things without recourse to sense images.

Reply Obj. We know immaterial things, of which we have no sense images, in relation to sensibly perceptible material substances, of which we do have sense images. For example, we understand truth by considering the things about which we spy out the truth, and we know God as their cause, and by what surpasses them, and by eliminating their defects. And we can in the condition of our present life know other immaterial substances only by eliminating defects from, and in relation to, material substances. And so when we understand things about immaterial substances, we need to have recourse to sense images, although we have no sense images of the immaterial substances themselves.

8. Does restraint of the senses prevent the intellect's judgment?[35]

I answer that the proper objects proportioned to our intellect are the natures of sensibly perceptible things, and we cannot form perfect judg-

[35]ST I, Q. 84, A. 8.

ments about things unless we know everything belonging to those things. The latter is especially true if we do not know the end of our judgments. For example, blacksmiths seek knowledge about knives only because of their work, and they could not form perfect judgments about knives if they did not know their work. Likewise, natural scientists seek to know the nature of stone and the nature of horse only in order to know the natures of sensibly perceptible things, and they cannot form perfect judgments about the things of nature if they are ignorant of sensibly perceptible things. But we know everything we understand in our present condition in relation to sensibly perceptible things of nature. And so our intellect cannot form perfect judgments when the senses, by which we know sensibly perceptible things, are restrained.

Manner and Process of Understanding

Material things are the proper object of the human intellect, since the intellect is a power of the soul, and the soul is the form of the body. Forms exist individually in matter, but the intellect knows the forms apart from individual matter. And so the intellect understands material things by abstracting their forms (e.g., human being) from individual sensible matter (e.g., this flesh and these bones) but not from common sensible matter (e.g., flesh and bones). And the intellect can abstract mathematical forms (i.e., numbers) from both individual and common sensible matter but not from common intelligible matter.

Material things, not the intelligible forms of things, are what the intellect first understands, although it can by reflection understand intelligible forms as the means whereby it understands the things. Our intellect has more general knowledge before it has more distinct knowledge. Different intelligible forms cannot at the same time actualize the same intellect to understand different things.

The senses cannot err about their proper objects (e.g., sight about color) except by reason of defective sense organs. Senses can be deceived about quantitative things like size and shape and about accidental characteristics of things. The intellect cannot misunderstand the essences of things but can err when it relates one understood thing to another by affirmation or negation (judgment). For example, some can, and many do, err if they judge that the human intellect is intrinsically dependent on matter. The human intellect cannot err regarding the definition of simple things (e.g., plants, animals, human beings) or regarding first principles (propositions immediately recognized as true when the terms are understood). Understanding is the same for all, but the power of understanding is greater in some than in others.

1. Does the intellect understand material things by abstracting from sense images?[36]

I answer that there are three grades of cognitive powers. One kind, that of the senses, is the actuality of bodily organs, and so the object of every sense power is a form as it exists in corporeal matter. A second kind, that of the angelic intellect, is neither the actuality of a bodily organ nor in any way joined to corporeal matter. A third kind, the human intellect, is disposed in a middle way, for the human intellect is a power of the soul, that is, the form of a body. And so its proper object is to know forms that exist individually in matter but not as they exist in such matter. But to know what exists in individual matter in a way other than it exists in such matter is to abstract a form from individual matter, which sense images represent. And so the human intellect understands material things by abstracting from sense images and comes by means of material things so considered to some knowledge of immaterial things.

Objection 1. An intellect that understands a thing otherwise than the thing is errs. But the forms of material things are not taken away from individual things, whose likenesses are sense images. Therefore, if we should understand material things by taking forms away from sense images of things, our intellect will err.

Reply Obj. 1. The statement, *an intellect that understands a thing otherwise than the thing is errs,* is true if the word *otherwise* refers to the thing understood. For the intellect errs when it understands a thing to be otherwise than the thing is. And so the intellect would err if it were to take the form stone away from matter in such a way as to understand that the form does not exist in matter.

But the statement is false if the word *otherwise* be understood to refer to the one who understands. For things understood exist in an immaterial, not a material, way in the intellect of those who understand. And so it is true to say that the way of those who understand, in understanding, differs from the material way of things in existing.

Obj. 2. Material things are things of nature, and matter is included in the definition of such things. But we cannot understand anything apart from what is included in its definition. Therefore, we cannot understand things apart from matter. But matter is the source of individuation. Therefore, we cannot understand material things by abstracting universals from individual things, that is, by abstracting intelligible forms from sense images.

---

[36]ST I, Q. 85, A. 1.

Reply Obj. 2. We posit matter in the definitions of things of nature. But there are two kinds of [sensible] matter: common matter (e.g., flesh and bones) and particularized or individual matter (e.g., this flesh and these bones). And so the intellect abstracts the forms of things of nature from individual matter but not from common matter. Therefore, the intellect abstracts the forms of things of nature from individual sensible matter but not from common sensible matter. For example, the intellect abstracts the forms of things of nature from this particular flesh and these particular bones, which do not belong to the nature of the human species but are parts of the individual human being. And so the intellect can consider the form of human being apart from this flesh and these bones. But the intellect cannot abstract the form of human being from flesh and bones.

And our intellect can abstract mathematical forms from both individual and common sensible matter but only from individual and not common intelligible matter. Intelligible matter is a substance insofar as matter is the subject of extension, and a material substance has extension before it has sensible properties. And so we can consider quantities as numbers, which are limitations of extension, apart from sensible properties, and this is to abstract quantities from sensible matter. But we cannot consider quantities without understanding a substance that is the subject of extension, that is, we cannot abstract quantities from common intelligible matter, although we can consider quantities apart from this or that particular substance.

Obj. 3. Sense images are to the intellectual soul what colors are to sight. But colors produce vision by imprinting themselves on the power of sight. Therefore, sense images produce understanding by imprinting themselves on the intellect, not because anything is abstracted from them.

Reply Obj. 3. Colors have the same way of existing that the power of sight has, and so they can imprint their likenesses on the power of sight. But sense images, since they are the likenesses of individual things and in bodily organs, do not have the same way of existing that the human intellect has. And so sense images cannot by their own power imprint themselves on the potential intellect. But the power of the active intellect by its recourse to sense images produces likenesses in the potential intellect. And these likenesses, regarding only the nature of species, represent the things of which we have sense images. And it is in this way that we abstract intelligible forms from sense images, not that the numerically identical forms previously present in sense images later come to be in the potential intellect, as material substances are taken from one place and transported to another.

2. Are the abstracted intelligible forms the things the intellect understands?[37]

I answer that some thinkers held that our intellect understands only its potentiality being acted upon, that is, the intelligible forms it receives. Two considerations show this opinion to be false. First, if the forms in the soul were to be the only things we understood, it would follow that things outside the soul would not be the objects of science. Second, if a cognitive power should know only its potentiality being acted upon, it would judge only about that, and so every opinion would be equally true.

And so we need to say that intelligible forms are the means by which the intellect understands. And the following argument makes this evident. Forms produce action. But forms that produce immanent actions are likenesses of the objects of those actions. And so the likenesses of visible things are the means by which the power of sight sees, and the likenesses of things understood, that is, the intelligible forms, are the forms by which the intellect understands.

But the intellect, by reflex consciousness of itself, understands its acts of understanding and the forms whereby it understands. And so the things of which the intelligible forms are likenesses are the things it understands first, but it secondarily understands the intelligible forms.

3. Do we intellectually know more extensive universals first?[38]

I answer that our intellectual knowledge originates in the same way from sense knowledge. And because the objects of the senses are individual things, and objects of the intellect universals, our knowledge of individual things is necessarily prior to our knowledge of universals.

Second, our intellect goes from potentiality to actuality, and everything going from potentiality to actuality comes first to an incomplete actuality in between potentiality and actuality. But the intellect's incomplete actuality consists of incomplete knowledge, knowledge whereby the intellect knows things in an indistinct way and a way subject to some confusion. And so the things first evident to us and certain are rather confused, and we later know them by distinguishing their sources and elements in a distinct way. We can know universal wholes with potential parts and integrated wholes in a somewhat confused way without knowing the parts distinctly. For example, to know animal in an indistinct way is to know animal as such, and to know animal in a distinct way is to know animal as rational or irrational, that is, to know human being and lion. Therefore, our

---

[37]ST I, Q. 85, A. 2. [38]ST I, Q. 85, A. 3.

intellect knows animal before it knows human being, and the explanation is the same whenever we relate the more universal to the less universal.

The reason for this is evident. One who knows something indistinctly still has potentiality to know sources of distinction. For example, one who knows a genus has potentiality to know specific differences. And so indistinct knowledge is in between potentiality and actuality.

And so our knowledge of individual things is prior to our knowledge of universals, since sense knowledge is prior to intellectual knowledge, but more general knowledge is prior to less general knowledge.

4. Can we understand many things at the same time?[39]

I answer that the intellect can understand at the same time whatever it can understand under one form. But specifically different forms of the same genus cannot at the same time perfect the same subject, and all intelligible forms belong to the same genus, since they perfect the same intellectual power, although the things of which they are the forms belong to different genera. Therefore, different intelligible forms cannot at the same time perfect the same intellect actually to understand different things.

5. Does our intellect understand by affirmative and negative judgments?[40]

I answer that the human intellect in its first understanding understands something about things, for example, their essences, which are the first and proper object of the intellect. And then the intellect understands the properties and accidents and dispositions that accompany the things' essences. And then the intellect needs to compose one understood thing with, or divide one understood thing from, another, and to advance from one composition or division to another, and this is to reason. And so the human intellect, unlike the intellect of God and the angels, knows by affirmative and negative judgments, and by reasoning.

6. Can the intellect be false?[41]

I answer that the intellect is like the senses regarding the possibility of error. The senses are not deceived about their proper objects (e.g., sight about color), except, perhaps, by accident, by impediments related to sense organs (e.g., the taste of persons with a fever judges sweet things to be bitter, since their tongues are replete with harmful juices). And the senses are deceived about things perceptible by more than one sense, such

---

[39]ST I, Q. 85, A. 4. [40]ST I, Q. 85, A. 5. [41]ST I, Q. 85, A. 6.

as size or shape (e.g., sight, contrary to fact, judges that the sun is a foot in diameter). And much more are the senses deceived about the accidental characteristics of perceptible things (e.g., sight judging that vinegar is honey because of their like color). But as long as sense powers remain intact, their judgments about their proper objects do not fail, since every power is intrinsically ordered to its proper object.

And the essences of things are the proper object of the intellect. And so, properly speaking, the intellect cannot err regarding the essences of things. But the intellect can err regarding things that accompany the essences or quiddities of things when the intellect relates one thing to another, whether by affirmative or negative judgment or by reasoning. And this is also why the intellect cannot err about those propositions immediately known when the essences of their terms are known, as in the case of first principles. And unerring truth about conclusions arises from such principles by way of scientific certitude.

But the intellect may by accident be deceived in judging about what something is. This happens regarding extraneous judgments that concern definitions, either when the definition of one thing is false about another (e.g., the definition of a circle about a triangle), or when a definition as such is false because it involves a contradiction (e.g., the definition of something as a winged rational animal). And so we cannot be deceived regarding simple things, in the definition of which there is no extraneous judgment. Rather, in cases of deception about simple things, we fail to attain any knowledge of them at all.

7. Can one person understand the very same thing better than another person can?[42]

I answer that we can in one way understand the word *better* to modify the act of understanding with respect to the thing understood. And then one person cannot understand the same thing more than another, since one would err and not understand if one were to understand the thing otherwise than it is. And we can in a second way understand the word *better* to modify the act of understanding with respect to those who understand. And then one person can understand the same thing better than another, since one person has greater power of understanding than another, just as those with more powerful and more accurate vision see things better than others do.

There may be greater power of understanding in two ways. First, there may be greater power regarding the more perfect intellect itself. It is evi-

---

[42]ST I, Q. 85, A. 7.

dent regarding things of different species that the better disposed the material substance, the more excellent the soul allotted to it. And so also some human beings, because they have better disposed bodies, are allotted souls with greater power of understanding. Second, there may be greater power of understanding regarding the lower powers that the intellect needs for its activity. For those with better disposed power of imagination, better disposed cogitative power, and better disposed power of memory are better disposed to understand.

What the Intellect Knows about Material Things

The intellect directly knows universals but can know individual things indirectly and reflexively. It understands one thing after another. Since we could only know infinite things if we were to have considered all of them, which we cannot do, the intellect can know infinite things only potentially. It knows the universal and necessary natures of things directly and individual contingent things, things that can be or not be, indirectly. It can know future things only insofar as they certainly or probably result from given causes, not in themselves.

1. Does our intellect know individual things?[43]

I answer that our intellect understands by abstracting intelligible forms from individual matter. But what is abstracted from individual matter is something universal. And so the intellect directly knows only universals.

But the intellect can know individual things indirectly and reflexively. This is because the intellect, after it has abstracted intelligible forms, can by means of them actually understand only when it has recourse to the sense images in which it understands the intelligible forms. Therefore, the intellect directly understands universals themselves by intelligible forms and indirectly understands the individual things of which there are sense images.

Objection. Our intellect understands itself. But the intellect is something individual; otherwise, it would have no acts, since acts belong to individual things. Therefore, our intellect knows individual things.

Reply Obj. Individual things as such can be understood, but individual things as material cannot, since we understand only in an immaterial way. And so something immaterial like the intellect can be understood.

---

[43]ST I, Q. 86, A. 1.

2. Can our intellect know infinite things?[44]

I answer that powers are proportioned to their object. Therefore, the intellect needs to be related to the infinite in the same way that its object, the essence of something material, is related to the infinite. But material things are only potentially infinite, as one thing comes after another. And so there is something potentially infinite in our intellect, namely, understanding one thing after another, since our intellect never understands so many things that it could not understand more things.

Our intellect can at the same time actually know only what it knows by one form, and nothing infinite has only one form. And so our intellect can know something infinite only by understanding one part after another. And so we could actually know something infinite only if we were to count all of its parts, which is impossible. And we cannot have habitual knowledge of the infinite, since habitual knowledge is the product of actual knowledge. And so we would only be able to have habitual knowledge of infinite things as distinct knowledge if we were to have considered all of the infinite things, by counting them as we know them successively, which is impossible. And so our intellect can know infinite things only potentially.

3. Does our intellect know contingent things?[45]

I answer that matter causes things to be contingent, since contingent things can exist or not exist, and potentiality belongs to matter. But necessity results from form, since the things resulting from form are necessarily present in things. We understand universal natures by abstracting forms from particular matter, and universals are intrinsically and directly the object of the intellect. Individual things, of which matter is the source of their individuation, are the object of the senses and indirectly the object of the intellect.

Therefore, the intellect knows the universal and necessary natures of things directly and contingent things as such indirectly. And so, if we look to the universal nature of knowable things, necessary things are the object of every science. But if we look to the knowable things themselves, then necessary things are the objects of certain sciences, and contingent things the objects of other sciences.

4. Does our intellect know future things?[46]

I answer that future things can be known in two ways, in themselves and in their causes. Only God can know future things in themselves, and they

---

[44]ST I, Q. 86, A. 2. [45]ST I, Q. 86, A. 3. [46]ST I, Q. 86, A. 4.

are present to him even when future in relation to the course of history, since his eternal vision is borne at once over the whole course of time. But we too can know future things as they exist in their causes. And we know future things with scientific certitude if they exist in their causes as causes from which they necessarily result. And if future things exist in their causes in such a way that they result from the causes in most cases, then we can know them by an inference more or less certain as the causes are more or less inclined to produce such effects.

How the Soul Knows Itself, Its Innate Dispositions, and Its Acts

The natures of material things are the first object of our intellect, but the intellect also understands itself as it is actualized by the intelligible forms of material things. It does so in particular as one is conscious that one is understanding. It does so in general as one contemplates the intellect's nature by considering its activity. And it understands habits of the soul and acts of the will in the same two ways.

1. Does the intellectual soul know itself by its essence?[47]

I answer that everything is knowable insofar as it is actual and unknowable insofar as it is potential. And so each immaterial substance is disposed by its essence to be intelligible insofar as it is disposed by its essence to be actual. But the human intellect belongs to the genus of intelligible things as a purely potential reality. Therefore, the human intellect, considered essentially, is potentially understanding. And so it by itself does not have the power to be understood except insofar as it becomes actual.

It is inborn to our intellect, in the condition of our present life, to have material and sensible things as its object. Therefore, our intellect understands itself as it is actualized by the forms that the light of the active intellect abstracts from such things. And the active intellect actualizes intelligible things, and the potential intellect by those intelligible things. Therefore, our intellect knows itself by its acts, not by its essence.

And our intellect does so in two ways. It does so in particular, as one perceives that one has an intellectual soul by reason of the fact that one perceives that one is understanding. It does so in general, as we contemplate the nature of the human mind by considering the intellect's activity.

---

[47]ST I, Q. 87, A. 1.

The mind's presence, the source of the acts whereby the mind perceives itself, suffices for it to have the first kind of knowledge of itself. But a painstaking and discriminating inquiry is required for the mind to have the second kind of knowledge of itself. And so many do not know the nature of the soul.

2. Does our intellect know the characteristic dispositions of the soul by their essences?[48]

I answer that we know nothing except insofar as it is actual. But characteristic dispositions are in between pure potentiality and pure actuality. Therefore, insofar as characteristic dispositions fall short of complete actuality, they fall short of being knowable in themselves and need to be known by their acts. We know the dispositions either when we perceive that we have them by perceiving that we produce the acts belonging to them, or when we inquire into their natures or essences by considering their acts. And the presence of a characteristic disposition of the soul produces the first way of knowing the disposition, since its presence causes the acts in which we immediately perceive it. And keen inquiry produces the second way of knowing a characteristic disposition of the soul.

3. Does the intellect know its acts?[49]

I answer that everything is known as it is actual. But the ultimate perfection of the intellect is its action, which abides in the knower as the knower's perfection and actuality. Therefore, the intellect's action, namely, the act of understanding, is the first thing that is understood about the intellect.

The first object of the human intellect's understanding is something external, namely, the nature of a material thing, not the intellect's essence. And so what the human intellect primarily knows is such an object. But the human intellect secondarily knows the acts by which it knows such objects and knows the intellect itself, whose perfection is the act of understanding, by the acts. And so the human intellect knows its objects before its acts and its acts before its powers.

Objection. It is by acts that we know everything that we know. Therefore, if the intellect knows its act, it knows its act by an act, and, again, it knows the latter act by another act. Therefore, there will be an infinite regress, and this seems impossible.

Reply Obj. The act of understanding is not the actuality and perfection of an understood material nature in such a way that we could by the same

---

[48]ST I, Q. 87, A. 2. [49]ST I, Q. 87, A. 3.

act understand the nature of the material thing and the act of understanding. And so there is one act by which the intellect understands stone and another act by which the intellect understands that it understands stone, and so forth. Nor is it improper that the intellect have unlimited potentiality.

4. Does the intellect understand acts of the will?[50]

I answer that intelligent things, as sources and proper subjects, have intellectual inclinations, that is, acts of the will, by way of intellectual knowledge. Therefore, intelligent things understand what is in them by way of intellectual knowledge. And so the intellect understands acts of the will both insofar as persons perceive that they are willing, and insofar as persons know the nature of such acts. And so the intellect understands the nature of the acts' source, which is a characteristic disposition or the power of the intellect.

How the Soul Knows Superior Things

In the present life, the intellect is by nature ordered to understand the essences of material things, and so we cannot primarily and intrinsically understand immaterial substances as such. And so, much less can God be the first thing that we know.

1. Can the human soul in the present life understand immaterial substances precisely as such?[51]

I answer that our intellect in our present life is by nature ordered to the essences of material things, and so our intellect understands only by recourse to sense images. And so we cannot primarily and intrinsically understand immaterial substances, which do not fall within the power of the senses and imagination.

Averroes held that human beings in this life can finally arrive at understanding of separate substances by their connection to a separate substance he called the active intellect.[52] Because the active intellect is a separate substance, it by its nature understands separate substances, and when it has been perfectly united to us, we too shall understand separate substances.

---

[50]ST I, Q. 87, A. 4. [51]ST I, Q. 88, A. 1.

[52]*Commentary on the De anima* III, in the digression of comm. 36.

And he held that the active intellect is united to us as follows. The potential intellect receives understood observed things and the active intellect at the same time. And the greater the number of understood observed things we receive, the closer we come to the active intellect being perfectly united to us. Therefore, when we shall know every kind of understood observed thing, the active intellect will be perfectly united to us, and we shall be able to know every kind of material and immaterial thing by means of it.

But this opinion cannot be true for many reasons. One reason is because the active intellect is not a separate substance but a power of the soul that reaches to the same things that the potential intellect does. Every human intellect in our present life, therefore, extends only to material things, which the active intellect makes actually intelligible, and which the potential intellect receives. And so we in our present life cannot understand immaterial substances, whether by means of the potential intellect or by means of the active intellect.

2. Can our intellect by its knowledge of material things come to understand immaterial substances?[53]

I answer that since we hold that immaterial substances are altogether of a different nature than the essences of material things, our intellect will never arrive at anything like an immaterial substance, howsoever much the intellect abstracts the essences of material things from matter. And so we cannot perfectly understand immaterial substances by means of material substances.

Objection. The human soul belongs to the genus of immaterial substances. But we can understand the human soul by its own activity, the activity whereby it understands material things. Therefore, we can also understand other immaterial substances by their effects in material things.

Reply Obj. The human soul understands itself by reason of its understanding, that is, by reason of its characteristic activity, which perfectly manifests its power and nature. But we cannot know perfectly the power and nature of immaterial substances by such activity, or by anything else in material things, since material things are not commensurate with the powers of immaterial substances.

3. Is God the first thing that the human mind knows?[54]

I answer that the human intellect in our present life cannot understand created immaterial substances. Therefore, much less can it understand the

---

[53] ST I, Q. 88, A. 2. [54] ST I, Q. 88, A. 3.

essence of the uncreated substance. And so God is not the first thing that we know. Rather, we arrive at knowledge of God through creatures, and the first things that we understand in our present life are the essences of material things, which essences are the object of our intellect.

Appetitive Intellectual Power, the Will

The necessity of coercion is completely contrary to the will, but there is a natural necessity that the will adhere to the ultimate human end, happiness. Although the goods whereby human beings adhere to God have a necessary connection to happiness, the will does not necessarily adhere to them before the vision of God evidences the necessity of such a connection.

The intellect as such and absolutely is higher than the will, but the will inclines to a higher good than the intellect insofar as the will inclines to a good more excellent than the soul itself, namely, God.

The intellect activates the will insofar as the intellect presents understood goods to the will as objects (ends) to be desired, and the will as efficient cause activates all the powers of the soul except the vegetative to their particular acts. Human beings can be borne to desire contrary things, and so they have free choice regarding particular things. The source of free choice is the will. Intellect and will work together to produce election. Regarding the intellect, there needs to be deliberation, whereby we judge something to be preferred to something else. Regarding the will, there needs to be acceptance of what we judge by deliberation. And election is an act of the will because it chooses means to happiness, and this object has the nature of a useful good.

1. Does the will desire anything necessarily?[55]

I answer that things are necessary by reason of an external efficient cause when the cause so compels someone that the person cannot do the contrary. This is the necessity of coercion, and this necessity is altogether repugnant to the will. It is impossible that something be coerced and voluntary, absolutely speaking.

But the necessity of an end is not repugnant to the will if the will can arrive at its end in only one way. Nor is natural necessity repugnant to the will. As the intellect necessarily adheres to first principles, so the will necessarily adheres to our ultimate end, happiness. For what by nature and immutably belongs to things needs to be the foundation and source of everything else belonging to them.

---

[55]ST I, Q. 82, A. 1.

2. Does the will necessarily will everything that it wills?[56]

I answer that one can be happy without some goods. Therefore, such goods have no necessary connection to happiness, and the will does not of necessity adhere to them. And although goods whereby human beings adhere to God, in whom alone true happiness consists, have a necessary connection to happiness, the will does not adhere necessarily to them before the vision of God shows the necessity of such a connection. Therefore, the will does not necessarily will whatever it wills.

Objection. The will tends toward good, not evil. Therefore, the will tends necessarily toward the good proposed to it.

Reply Obj. The will can tend toward things only under the aspect of good. But there are many kinds of good. Therefore, the will is not determined necessarily to one of them.

3. Is the will a higher power than the intellect? [57]

I answer that the object of the intellect is the nature of a desirable good, and the object of the will is the desirable good whose nature the intellect possesses. But the simpler and more abstract something is, the more excellent and superior it is. And so the object of the intellect is superior to the object of the will. But a power's nature is in relation to its object. Therefore, the intellect as such and absolutely is higher and more excellent than the will.

But the will is sometimes higher than the intellect in one respect and in relation to something else, namely, in that an object of the will regards something higher than an object of the intellect regards. For intellectual activity consists in the nature of an understood thing being in the one who understands, and activity of the will consists in the will being inclined to the very thing as it is in itself. Therefore, the will is superior to the intellect regarding a good more excellent than the soul itself, and the intellect is superior to the will regarding a good inferior to the soul. And so love of God is better than knowledge about him, and, conversely, knowledge of material things is better than love of them. Still, absolutely speaking, the intellect is more excellent than the will.

4. Does the will move the intellect?[58]

I answer that things cause movement in one way as ends, and this is the way that the intellect moves the will, since understood goods are the ob-

[56]ST I, Q. 82, A. 2. [57]ST I, Q. 82, A. 3. [58]ST I, Q. 82, A. 4.

ject of the will and move the will as ends.

Things cause movement in a second way as efficient causes, and this is the way that the will moves the intellect and every power of the soul. This is because, in all cases of subordinated active powers, the power whose object is a general end moves the powers whose objects are particular ends. And the object of the will is the good in general. And so the will as efficient cause moves to their special acts all the powers of the soul except the natural powers of the vegetative part of the soul.

5. Do human beings have free choice?[59]

I answer that some things act without judgment. For example, stones move downward without judgment. And other things, irrational animals, act by judgment but not free judgment. For example, sheep on seeing a wolf judge by a natural but not free judgment that they should flee from the wolf. They so judge by an instinct from nature, not by a comparison.

And human beings act by judgment, since they by their cognitive power judge that they should flee from, or seek to gain, something. But such judgments about prospective actions are by a comparison of reason, not by natural instinct. Therefore, human beings act by free judgment, capable of being borne to contrary things. For reason about contingent matters leads to contrary conclusions, as is evident in the syllogisms of logicians and the arguments of rhetoricians. But prospective actions are contingent things, and so judgments of reason about them are disposed to different things and not determined to one thing. And so human beings necessarily have free choice, since they are rational.

Objection 1. To be free is to cause oneself to act. Therefore, whatever is moved by something else is not free. But God moves the will. Therefore, human beings do not have free choice.

Reply Obj. 1. Human beings by free choice move themselves to act. But it does not of necessity belong to freedom that what is free be its own first cause, nor is it required for something to cause something else that the former be the first cause of the latter. Therefore, God is the first cause that moves both natural and voluntary causes. And as God by causing the movement of natural causes does not take away the fact that their actions are from nature, so God by causing the movement of voluntary causes does not take away the fact that their actions are voluntary. Rather, God causes the actions' voluntary character, since he acts in each thing according to what is proper to it.

Obj. 2. Persons have ends as each is constituted. But it is not in our

---

[59]ST I, Q. 83, A. 1.

power to be any kind of thing. Rather, this comes from nature. Therefore, it is natural for us to pursue our ends. Therefore, we do not by free choice pursue the end.

Reply Obj. 2. Human beings have two kinds of properties: one kind from nature and the other kind from something added. But the properties of human beings are from nature either regarding the intellectual part of the soul or regarding the body and powers connected to the body. Therefore, since human beings have the natural property of intellection, they by nature desire their last end, happiness. And this appetite is natural and not subject to free will.

And regarding the body and the powers connected to it, human beings can have natural properties insofar as they have arrangements from imprints of material causes. But such causes cannot make an imprint on the intellectual part of the soul, since that part is not the actuality of a material substance. Therefore, persons have ends as they are constituted by material properties inasmuch as such arrangements incline human beings to choose or reject particular things. But those inclinations are subject to the judgment of reason, which lower appetites obey. And so such inclinations are not prejudicial to freedom of choice.

And there are added properties such as characteristic dispositions and emotions, which incline individuals to one thing rather than another. But those inclinations are likewise subject to the judgment of reason. And the properties are also subject to reason insofar as it lies in our power to acquire them, whether by causing them or disposing ourselves toward them, or to remove them. And so there is nothing regarding these properties inconsistent with freedom of choice.

6. Is free choice a power?[60]

I answer that powers and characteristic dispositions are the sources of our acts. Therefore, the source of acts of free choice needs to be a power or a characteristic disposition or a power with a characteristic disposition, and two considerations show that the source is neither a characteristic disposition nor a power with a characteristic disposition.

First, if the source of free choice is a characteristic disposition, the disposition will be natural, since it is natural for human beings to have free choice. But we have no natural disposition for things subject to free choice, since nature inclines us toward the objects of natural dispositions, and the things toward which nature inclines us are not subject to free choice. And so it is contrary to the nature of free choice that the source of acts of free

[60]ST I, Q. 83, A. 2.

choice be a natural characteristic disposition. And it is contrary to the naturalness of free choice that the source of acts of free choice be a characteristic disposition that is not from nature. And so we conclude that the source of acts of free choice is in no way a characteristic disposition.

Second, characteristic dispositions are the means whereby we dispose ourselves well or ill regarding actions or being acted upon. But free choice is indifferently disposed toward choosing well or ill. And so the source of acts of free choice cannot be a characteristic disposition.

Therefore, we conclude that the source of acts of free choice is a power.

7. Is free choice an appetitive power?[61]

I answer that we have free choice because we can undertake one thing and reject another, and this is to elect. Cognitive power and appetitive power work together to produce election. Regarding cognitive power, there needs to be deliberation, whereby we judge what is to be preferred to something else. And regarding appetitive power, there needs in desiring to be acceptance of what we judge by deliberation. And election is appetitive because election chooses means to our end, and this object as such has the nature of a useful good. But good is the object of appetite. And so election is chiefly the act of an appetitive power. And so free choice is an appetitive power.

Production

The human soul cannot be part of God's substance. The rational soul is a subsistent form and as such can neither come to be out of anything preexisting nor be produced by the power of semen. Therefore, God creates the human soul, and only he can do so. He creates the human soul when he infuses it into the human body to form the human substance, that is, the human being.

1. Is the soul part of God's substance?[62]

I answer that it is impossible that the soul be part of God's substance. For the human soul sometimes potentially understands, acquires knowledge from things, and has different powers. But all such things are foreign to the nature of God, who is pure actuality, receives nothing from anything else, and has no different parts.

---

[61]ST I, Q. 83, A. 3. [62]ST I, Q. 90, A. 1.

2. Is the soul created?[63]

I answer that only substances are properly and truly beings, and accidents are beings because things are such-and-such by reason of them. And so nonsubsistent forms come to be because complete subsistent things come to be.

But the rational soul is a subsistent form, to which existing and coming into existence belong in the proper sense, and the rational soul cannot come to be out of preexisting matter, whether corporeal or spiritual. Therefore, only creation can produce a rational soul.

3. Does God directly produce the rational soul?[64]

I answer that secondary efficient causes always presuppose something that exists from the primary efficient cause, and they cause by effecting changes. And so only the primary efficient cause, God, can cause without the existence of something being presupposed. And so only God can create. But no transformation of any matter can produce a rational soul. And so only God acting directly can produce a rational soul.

4. Was the human soul produced before the body?[65]

I answer that God instituted the first things in their complete natural condition, as the species of each thing required. But the soul, as part of human nature, has its natural completion only insofar as it is united to the body. And so it would not have been proper for the soul to be created without a body.

5. Does semen produce the intellectual soul?[66]

I answer that the active powers in matter cannot expand their activity to produce immaterial effects. But the source of intellection in human beings, since it has an activity in which the body does not share, transcends matter. And so the power in semen cannot produce the source of intellection.

Second, the power in semen causes by the power of the soul of the begetter, as the soul actualizes and makes use of the body. But the body does not share in the activity of the intellect. And so the power of intellection as such cannot extend to the semen. Therefore, the intellect comes from something outside the body.

---

[63] ST I, Q. 90, A. 2.
[64] ST I, Q. 90, A. 3.
[65] ST I, Q. 90, A. 4.
[66] ST I, Q. 118, A. 2.

Third, the intellectual soul has an activity that does not depend on the body. Therefore, the intellectual soul is subsistent and immaterial. Therefore, begetting cannot produce it, and only God can.

Objection. The nutritive, sensory, and intellectual souls in human beings are essentially one and the same soul. But as in other animals, semen produces the sensory soul in human beings. And so the animal and the human being are produced successively, the animal with the sensory soul first. Therefore, semen also produces the intellectual soul.

Reply Obj. A soul preexists in the embryo: first the nutritive soul, then the sensory soul, and finally the intellectual soul. The previous form passes away when the more perfect form comes, since the coming-to-be of one thing is always the passing away of another. But the subsequent form possesses whatever the prior form had, and still more. And so both human beings and other animals arrive at their ultimate substantial form by the coming-to-be and passing away of several forms. Therefore, God creates the intellectual soul at the end of the process of human generation, a soul that is also sensory and nutritive, at which time the preexisting forms pass away.

6. Were human souls created at the same time at the beginning of the world?[67]

I answer that the human soul is not the human being, nor is the union of body and soul an accidental union. Moreover, human beings understand by receiving images from the senses and having recourse to sense images. And so the human soul needs to be united to the body.

Second, if it is natural for the human soul to be united to the body, it is contrary to nature for the human soul to be without a body, and the soul apart from the body lacks the perfection of its nature. And it was unfitting that God should begin his work with things incomplete and at variance with nature. For example, God did not make human beings without hands or feet, and hands and feet are natural parts of human beings. Therefore, much less did he make the souls without bodies. And so we should acknowledge without reservation that God creates souls when they are infused into bodies.

---

[67]ST I, Q. 118, A. 3.

4

The Ultimate Human End: Happiness

Happiness is the ultimate human end. See Glossary, s.v. Happiness. *It is the cause of the will's movement and of the choice of means to the end. The object of the will is universal good, and so only God, the uncreated good, can satisfy the will. If the human will knows only that God exists, it does not attain knowledge of what God is in himself, and so it is not completely satisfied. Only the vision of God's essence can make human beings happy.*

There cannot be happiness without accompanying pleasure. A rightly directed will is both antecedently and concomitantly necessary for happiness (i.e., the will needs to be directed toward God both in this life and in the vision of God). For imperfect happiness in this life, we need a body. For perfect happiness in the next life, which consists of the vision of God, we do not, although the scope of perfect happiness increases when the blessed regain their bodies. And we also need bodily perfections, external goods, and the company of friends for happiness in this life. Human beings can acquire virtue in this life by their natural powers and thereby attain imperfect happiness in this life. But the vision of God transcends their natural powers, and so they cannot attain perfect happiness by those powers. God's wisdom ordains that perfect happiness be the reward of meritorious good deeds.

1. Does human life have an ultimate end?[1]

I answer that whenever things are intrinsically related to one another, the things subordinate to the first thing are necessarily taken away if the latter is taken away. There cannot be an infinite regress regarding causes of motion because there would then be no first cause of motion, and the other causes cannot cause motion if the first cause is taken away.

There are two orders of ends: the intentional order and the order of execution, and there needs to be something first in both orders. In the intentional order, the first thing is the cause that moves the will, and so nothing would move the will if that cause were taken away. And the cause of execution is the cause initiating activity, and so no one would begin to do anything if that cause were taken away. The intentional cause is the ultimate end, and the cause of execution is the first means to achieve that

---

[1]ST I–II, Q. 1, A. 4.

end. If there were no ultimate end, nothing would be sought, no activity would reach fruition, and an efficient cause's striving would not come to a state of rest. And no one would begin to do anything if there were no first cause of means to the end, and the process of deliberation would go on endlessly.

But nothing prevents things that are incidentally, not intrinsically, related from being unlimited in number, since there is no fixed number of incidental causes. And so there may incidentally be an unlimited number of ends and means.

2. Does the happiness of human beings consist in a created good?[2]

I answer that happiness is a complete good, one that completely satisfies the will. Otherwise, there would be no ultimate end if something else remained to be sought. But the object of the will, the human appetite, is universal good. And so nothing but universal good can satisfy the human will. But every creature has limited goodness. Therefore, universal good does not consist in a created good. And so only God can satisfy the human will, and human happiness consists in God alone.

3. Does human happiness consist in beholding God's essence?[3]

I answer that our ultimate and complete happiness consists only in beholding God's essence. To prove this, we need to consider two points. First, human beings are not completely happy as long as something remains for them to desire. Second, we note the perfection of any power by the nature of the power's object. But the object of the intellect is what something is, that is, the thing's essence. And so the more the intellect knows the thing's essence, the more perfect the intellect is. Therefore, if the intellect should know the nature of an effect and not be able to know the nature of the effect's cause, the intellect can know that the cause exists but not attain the cause absolutely. And then human beings retain a natural desire to know what the cause is. This desire belongs to wonderment and inquiry. For example, a person aware of an eclipse of the sun considers the necessity of the event having a cause and wonders about the cause and investigates it. And this inquiry is not satisfied until the person comes to know the nature of the cause.

Therefore, if the human intellect, knowing the nature of created effects, should know nothing about God except that he exists, the intellect's perfection does not yet attain the first cause absolutely and retains a natural desire to seek the cause. And so the human intellect is not yet completely

---

[2]ST I–II, Q. 2, A. 8. [3]ST I–II, Q. 3, A. 8.

happy. For complete happiness, the intellect needs to attain the essence of the first cause, and then the intellect will possess its perfection by union with God as its object. And human happiness consists only in this object.

Objection. A higher perfection belongs to a higher nature. But to behold God's essence is a perfection that belongs to his intellect. Therefore, the ultimate perfection of the human intellect does not reach so far and falls short of beholding God's essence.

Reply Obj. We can understand an end in two ways. We understand an end in one way regarding the thing desired, and then the ends of higher and lower natures are the same. We understand an end in a second way regarding attainment of the thing desired, and then the ends of higher and lower natures differ according to the natures' different dispositions toward the thing desired. Therefore, the happiness of God, whose intellect beholds his essence comprehensively, is superior to the happiness of human beings and angels, who behold his essence but not comprehensively.

4. Is pleasure necessary for happiness?[4]

I answer that pleasure is necessary for happiness as something attendant. For pleasure results from the fact that an appetite is satisfied in the good it has attained. And so there cannot be happiness without attendant pleasure, since happiness consists in nothing but the possession of the highest good.

5. Is it necessary to comprehend God in order to be happy?[5]

I answer that three things are necessary for happiness: the vision of God, which is perfect knowledge of our intelligible end; comprehension, which imports the presence of our end; pleasure or enjoyment, which imports the satisfaction of the lover in the beloved.

Objection. For the mind to attain knowledge of God is great happiness. But to comprehend God is impossible. Therefore, there is happiness apart from comprehending God.

Reply Obj. We speak about comprehension in two ways. In one way, comprehension denotes the inclusion of the comprehended object in the comprehending subject, and then everything that finite things comprehend is finite. And so, in this meaning of comprehension, no created intellect can comprehend God. In the second way, comprehension denotes only the possession of something now actually possessed. For example, we say that a person has another in his or her grasp when the person lays hold

[4]ST I–II, Q. 4, A. 1. [5]ST I–II, Q. 4, A. 3.

of the other. And it is in this way that comprehending God is necessary for happiness.

6. Is a rightly directed will necessary for happiness?[6]

I answer that the will is rightly directed antecedently by being duly ordered to our ultimate end. But nothing attains its end unless it is duly ordered to its end. And so no one can attain happiness unless the person antecedently has a rightly directed will. And so a rightly directed will is antecedently necessary for happiness.

Our ultimate happiness consists in the vision of God's essence, which is the very essence of goodness, and so a rightly directed will is concomitantly necessary for happiness. And so the will of those beholding God's essence necessarily loves everything else in subordination to God, just as the will of those not beholding God's essence necessarily loves under the aspect of good everything the will loves. And this very fact causes the will to be rightly directed.

And so a rightly directed will is both antecedently and concomitantly necessary for happiness.

7. Is the body necessary for human happiness?[7]

I answer that there are two kinds of happiness: imperfect happiness, which we have in this life, and perfect happiness, which consists in the vision of God. We evidently need a body for happiness in this life. For happiness in this life consists of intellectual activity, whether activity of the theoretical or practical intellect. And there cannot be intellectual activity in this life apart from sense images, which are present only in bodily organs. And so the happiness capable of being possessed in this life depends in some respect on the body.

With respect to perfect happiness, reason shows that there can be such happiness for the soul apart from an existing body. For intellectual activities need a body only for sense images. But we evidently cannot behold God's essence by means of sense images. And so perfect human happiness, since it consists in the vision of God's essence, does not depend on the body. And so the soul can be happy apart from the body.

Perfections belong to things in one way as constitutive of a thing's essence. For example, the soul is necessary for human perfection as constitutive of the human essence. Perfections belong to things in a second way as contributing to a thing's well-being. For example, bodily comeliness and mental agility belong to suitable human perfection. But activity

---

[6]ST I–II, Q. 4, A. 4. [7]ST I–II, Q. 4, A. 5.

depends on the nature of the thing acting, and so the more perfect the soul regarding its nature, the more perfectly will the soul have capacity for its characteristic activity, in which happiness consists. Therefore, the body, although it does not belong to the perfection of human happiness in the first way, belongs to the perfection of human happiness in the second way.

Objection. Happiness satisfies desire. But the separated soul still desires to be united to the body, and so the soul's desire is not satisfied. Therefore, the soul cannot be happy when separated from the body.

Reply Obj. The separated soul's desire is completely satisfied regarding the object of its desire, namely, in possessing what suffices to satisfy its desire. But the separated soul's desire is not completely satisfied regarding the subject that desires, in that the one desiring does not possess the desired good in every way that one would wish to possess it. And so, when persons regain their bodies, their happiness increases in scope but not in intensity.

8. Is any bodily perfection necessary for happiness?[8]

I answer that a good disposition of the body is necessarily required for happiness in this life. For such happiness consists in completely virtuous activity, and indisposition of the body can hinder human beings in every kind of virtuous activity.

And it is natural for the soul to be united to the body, and so it cannot be the case that the soul's perfection should exclude its natural perfection. And so perfect disposition of the body is necessary for full happiness both as a condition and as a consequence. Perfect disposition of the body is a necessary condition in order that the body not burden the soul. And perfect disposition of the body is a necessary consequence of perfect happiness, since the happiness of the soul overflows into the body in order that the body may also obtain its perfection.

9. Are any external goods necessary for happiness?[9]

I answer that external goods are necessary for such imperfect happiness as we can possess in this life, since external goods are means that contribute to happiness, which consists in virtuous activity. For example, human beings in this life need bodily necessities for intellectually virtuous and practically virtuous activity, and they need even more things as means to perform practically virtuous deeds.

But external goods are in no way necessary for perfect happiness, which consists in the vision of God. All external goods are necessary either to

---

[8]ST I–II, Q. 4, A. 6. [9]ST I–II, Q. 4, A. 7.

sustain our animal bodies or for the activities we perform by reason of our animal bodies, activities that befit human life. And the perfect happiness consisting in the vision of God will be either in the soul apart from the body or in the soul united to a spiritual body no longer animal. And so external goods are in no way necessary for perfect happiness, since they are ordered to animal life.

And the happiness of contemplation in this life, since, being God-like, it comes closer to perfect happiness than the happiness of activity does, has less need of such material goods.

10. Is the company of friends necessary for happiness?[10]

I answer that to be happy in the present life, persons do not need friends for their usefulness, since happy persons are self-sufficient. Nor do they need friends for pleasure, since happy persons take complete pleasure in their own virtuous activity. But happy persons in the present life need friends for good acts, namely, that they may do good for friends, take pleasure in seeing friends do good, and be helped by friends to do good. For human beings need the aid of friends to act well, both in deeds of the practical life and in activities of the contemplative life.

Although the company of friends is not absolutely necessary for perfect happiness in our heavenly home, since human beings have in God the entire fullness of their perfection, the company of friends enhances happiness. The mere fact that spiritual creatures see one another and rejoice in their companionship helps them extrinsically.

11. Can human beings attain happiness?[11]

I answer that happiness denotes attainment of the perfect good. But human beings are capable of receiving the perfect good, both because their intellect can apprehend the universal and perfect good, and because their will can desire that good. And so human beings can attain happiness. And human beings are capable of the vision of God, in which perfect happiness consists.

12. Can human beings be happy in this life?[12]

I answer that happiness is a perfect and sufficient good. Therefore, happiness excludes every evil and fulfills every desire. But not every evil can be excluded from this life. For example, the present life is subject to many unavoidable evils, both to ignorance on the part of the intellect and to dis-

---

[10]ST I–II, Q. 4, A. 8. [11]ST I–II, Q. 5, A. 1. [12]ST I–II, Q. 5, A. 3.

ordered desire on the part of the will, and to many sufferings on the part of the body. Similarly, human beings by nature desire that the goods they possess perdure. But the present life, contrary to our desire, passes away, and goods of the present life are transitory. Therefore, our desire for good cannot be satisfied in this life.

Second, happiness specifically consists in the vision of God's essence. But human beings cannot attain that vision in this life. Therefore, they cannot have perfect happiness in this life.

13. Can human beings by their natural powers attain happiness?[13]

I answer that human beings, as they acquire virtue, can by their natural powers attain the imperfect happiness they can possess in this life. But perfect human happiness consists in the vision of God, which essentially exceeds the nature of human beings and every creature. For every creature knows by nature according to the modality of its substance, and every knowledge in the modality of created substance falls short of beholding God's essence, which infinitely surpasses every created substance. And so neither a human being nor any creature can by its natural power attain the ultimate happiness.

Objection. Nature does not fail to provide necessary things. But nothing is so necessary for human beings as the means whereby they attain their ultimate end. Therefore, human nature does not lack such means. Therefore, human beings can attain happiness by their natural powers.

Reply Obj. Nature does not fail to provide necessary things for human beings even though it did not give human beings any source whereby they could attain happiness. For nature did endow human beings with free choice, the means whereby they could direct themselves to God, who would make them happy.

14. Are any good deeds necessary for human beings to attain happiness?[14]

I answer that a rightly directed will is simply a will properly ordered to our ultimate end. Therefore, a rightly directed will is necessary for us to attain happiness. But this does not prove that activity of human beings need precede their happiness. For God could simultaneously cause their will to incline rightly toward their end and cause their will to attain their end.

But the order of his wisdom requires that he not do so. To possess the perfect good without undergoing change belongs to the thing that by nature possesses it. But to possess happiness by nature belongs to God

[13]ST I–II, Q. 5, A. 5. [14]ST I–II, Q. 5, A. 7.

alone. And so it belongs to God alone that no prior activity bring him to a state of happiness.

Happiness surpasses every created nature. Therefore, no creature as such suitably attains happiness without undergoing change by activity, and creatures strive for happiness by activity. God's wisdom ordered angels, whom nature ranks as superior to human beings, to attain happiness by undergoing the change of one meritorious act. But human beings attain happiness by undergoing the changes of many meritorious acts. And so human happiness is the reward of virtuous activities.

Objection. Rom. 4:6 says that God bestows righteousness on human beings without regard to their deeds. Therefore, no deeds on their part are necessary in order for them to attain happiness.

Reply Obj. The text is speaking about the righteousness of hope, which we have by the grace that makes us righteous, and such grace is not bestowed on us because of our previous deeds. For such grace is the starting point of the activity whereby we strive for happiness, not the end point of activity, as happiness is.

5

Human Acts

The Voluntary and the Involuntary

Things that proceed directly from the will are voluntary (e.g., one studies because one wills to study). Things proceed indirectly from the will when they happen because the will does not will to do something (e.g., one does not study because one does not will to study) or wills not to do something (e.g., one does not study because one wills not to study). The things proceeding indirectly from the will are voluntary if the person has the capacity and the duty to act.

Force can prevent external bodily actions commanded by the will, but the will's own acts cannot be coerced. Force externally causes things, and forced things, if contrary to the will, are involuntary. Deeds done out of fear are voluntary in the concrete case, that is, as concretely willed, but involuntary if considered apart from the concrete case, that is, in that the will would not will the deed were there no fear. Concupiscence causes voluntary things if the will wills the objects of lust. See Glossary, s.v. Concupiscence.

Ignorance is related to the will's activity in three ways: (1) as accompanying the will's activity; (2) as a consequence of the will's activity; and (3) as preceding the will's activity. Ignorance accompanies the will's activity when one does not know what one is doing but would do it if one did know (e.g., a hunter, thinking to kill a deer, kills an enemy whom he wishes to kill). Such ignorance does not cause something involuntary, since the deed is not contrary to the will, nor does it cause something voluntary, since one cannot will what one does not know. Ignorance is a consequence of the will's activity if the ignorance is voluntary, either because one wills not to know, or because one is negligent in considering what one can and should consider. Ignorance is antecedent to the will's activity if the ignorance is not voluntary and yet causes one to will what one otherwise would not will (e.g., if a hunter, not knowing that a passerby is in the line of fire and taking adequate precautions, shoots and kills the passerby). Such ignorance causes deeds to be absolutely involuntary.

1. Can things be voluntary without any act?[1]

I answer that things that proceed from the will are voluntary. But things proceed from other things in two ways. Things proceed directly when

[1]ST I–II, Q. 6, A. 3.

other things cause them. For example, heat causes things to become hot. Things proceed indirectly when they happen because other things do not act. For example, we attribute the sinking of a ship to its pilot if the pilot stopped piloting his ship. But we do not always attribute the consequences of persons' inaction to them because they do not act. We do so only when they have the ability and the duty to act. For example, we would not attribute the sinking of a ship to a pilot if the pilot were unable to pilot the ship, or if the pilot were not commissioned to pilot the ship.

The will can and sometimes ought to prevent nonwilling and nonacting. And so we impute such nonwilling and nonacting to the will, as if the nonwilling and nonacting proceeded from the will. And so things can be voluntary apart from any act, sometimes without an external act, as when the will wills not to act, and sometimes even without an internal act, as when the will does not will.

2. Can force coerce the will?[2]

I answer that the will can be coerced regarding acts commanded by the will but executed by other powers (e.g., walking and speaking, which are commanded by the will and executed by the power of locomotion), since force can prevent external bodily members from executing commands of the will. But the will cannot be coerced regarding its own acts.

The reason for the latter is that acts of the will are simply inclinations that come from an internal knowing source, just as appetites from nature are inclinations that come from internal noncognitive sources. But coerced or forced things come from external sources. And so it is contrary to the will's act that it be coerced or forced. For example, force can carry stones upward, but the stones' forced movement cannot be the product of their natural inclination. Similarly, force can carry human beings along, but it is contrary to the nature of force that the forced acts be products of the will of human beings.

Objection 1. Anything can be coerced by something more powerful. But something, namely, God, is more powerful than the human will. Therefore, at least God can coerce the human will.

Reply Obj. 1. God is more powerful than the human will and can move it. But if this were to be done by force, an act of the will would no longer accompany it, nor would the will itself be inclined. Rather, the thing done by force would be something contrary to the will.

Obj. 2. Everything affected by a cause acting upon it is coerced by the

---

[2]ST I–II, Q. 6, A. 4.

cause. But the will is acted upon, and the cause acting upon the will sometimes moves it. Therefore, the will is sometimes coerced.

Reply Obj. 2. Movements are only forced if they occur in opposition to the internal inclinations of the things acted upon. Otherwise, all accidental changes and comings-to-be of elementary material substances would be contrary to nature and forced. But accidental changes and comings-to-be of elementary material substances are from nature, since the matter or subjects of changes and comings-to-be have from nature the capacity for such dispositions. And likewise, if desirable things move the will by reason of the will's own inclinations, the movements of the will are voluntary, not forced.

3. Does force cause something involuntary?[3]

I answer that things from nature and voluntary things proceed from an internal cause, and forced things proceed from an external cause. Therefore, as force causes things contrary to nature in irrational beings, so force causes things contrary to the will in rational beings. But things contrary to the will are involuntary. And so force causes involuntary things.

4. Does fear cause something absolutely involuntary?[4]

I answer that deeds done out of fear are voluntary, absolutely speaking, although involuntary in one respect. For things exist absolutely insofar as they are actual, and they exist in one respect insofar as they are only conceptual. But deeds done out of fear are actual in the way in which they are done, in the way in which they exist here and now and under other individual conditions. And so deeds done out of fear are voluntary insofar as they exist here and now, namely, as they in the concrete case prevent the greater feared evil. For example, a ship's crew out of fear of danger voluntarily jettisons the ship's cargo during a storm. And so the deed is absolutely voluntary. And so also the deed has the nature of something voluntary, since the source of the deed is internal to the source. But it is only conceptual that we understand deeds done out of fear as deeds contrary to the will, as deeds existing apart from the concrete case. And so such deeds are involuntary in one respect, that is, as we consider them apart from the concrete case.

5. Does concupiscence cause something involuntary?[5]

I answer that something is voluntary because the will inclines toward it. But concupiscence inclines the will to will the objects of lust. And so concupiscence causes something voluntary.

---

[3]ST I–II, Q. 6, A. 5. [4]ST I–II, Q. 6, A. 6. [5]ST I–II, Q. 6, A. 7.

6. Does ignorance cause something involuntary?[6]

I answer that ignorance can cause something involuntary, since ignorance deprives persons of the prerequisite knowledge for something voluntary. But some ignorance does not deprive persons of such knowledge. And so we need to note that ignorance is related to the will's activity in three ways: (1) as accompanying the will's activity; (2) as a consequence of the will's activity; (3) as preceding the will's activity.

Ignorance accompanies the will's activity when persons do not know what they are doing but would still do it if they did know. For example, a person who, thinking to kill a deer, kills an enemy whom he wishes to kill. And such ignorance does not cause something involuntary, since it does not cause anything contrary to the will. But such ignorance causes something not voluntary, since persons cannot actually will what is unknown.

Ignorance is a consequence of the will's activity if the ignorance is voluntary. This happens in two ways. Ignorance is voluntary in one way if an act of the will inclines to ignorance (e.g., if a person wills not to know in order to be excused or not drawn away from sinning). We call such ignorance affected. Ignorance is voluntary in a second way if it is of things that we can and should know. There is ignorance in this sense if persons do not consider what they can and should consider, or if their ignorance results from emotion or habitual disposition, or if they do not take care to acquire the knowledge that they ought to possess. And ignorance of the general precepts of the law is ignorance in the latter way, since such ignorance is the result of negligence. Ignorance in any of these ways is voluntary and so cannot cause something absolutely involuntary. But such ignorance causes something involuntary in one respect, since the ignorance precedes the will's inclination to do something, and the will would not have the inclination if the person had knowledge.

Ignorance is antecedent to the will's activity if the ignorance is not voluntary and yet causes human beings to will what they otherwise would not will. Such would be the case should human beings not know some circumstance of an activity, a circumstance they were not obliged to know, and on that account do something that they would not do if they were to know the circumstance. For example, such is the case if someone, not knowing that a passerby is traveling along a road and after taking precautions, shoots an arrow that kills the passerby. Such ignorance causes things to be absolutely involuntary.

---

[6]ST I–II, Q. 6, A. 8.

The Will

The will needs something to activate it and something to specify the act. The end of the will is good in general, and the will activates other powers of the soul to their acts regarding particular goods. The intellect presents its object to the will and activates the will by way of formal causality, that is, by specifying the object of the will's action. Sense appetites render objects desirable and so activate the will regarding the objects. The will, by willing the end, activates itself to will means to the end, that is, activates itself to act. No external cause other than God can cause the will to will. Human beings by nature will the will's end, good in general, and things belonging to powers of the soul, subsistence, life, and the like, which are particular goods regarding the natural human constitution.

Since persons in this life are able not to think about any object, no object in this life moves the will necessarily to act. Regarding specification of the object of the will's act, the universal good, happiness, necessarily activates the will, but particular goods, since they are not good in every respect, do not. Unless emotions completely restrain reason, the will does not necessarily tend to the things to which emotions incline. God activates the will in such a way that the will's movement remains free in matters of free choice.

1. Does the intellect move the will?[7]

I answer that something actual is necessary to bring potential things to actuality, and this causes change. But the powers of the soul have potentiality for different actualities in two ways, one with respect to acting or not acting, and the second with respect to doing this or doing that. For example, the power of sight at times actually sees something and at other times does not, and the power of sight at times sees something white and at other times sees something black. Therefore, the powers of the soul need something to move them in two respects, namely, with respect to performing acts and with respect to specifying acts. And the first of these regards the powers, which are sometimes active and sometimes passive, and the other regards the objects that specify the powers' acts.

An efficient cause moves the powers themselves. But every efficient cause acts for the sake of an end. Therefore, the end is the source of the powers' movements. And so skills linked to ends activate skills linked to means. For example, the skill of piloting governs the skill of shipbuilding. But good in general, which has the nature of end, is the object of the will. And so the will in this respect moves other powers of the soul to their acts,

---

[7]ST I–II, Q. 9, A. 1.

since we employ other powers of the soul when we will to do so. For the end and perfection of all other powers of the soul are included in the will's object as particular goods, and skills or powers linked to a general end always activate skills or powers linked to particular ends included in the general end. For example, the commander of an army, whose end is the entire army's deployment, by his command deploys one of his captains, whose end is the deployment of a single company.

The object, by specifying the powers' acts, moves the powers by way of formal causality. But the first formal cause is being and truth in general, which constitutes the object of the intellect. And so the intellect by this kind of influence, by presenting its object to the will, moves the will.

2. Do sense appetites move the will?[8]

I answer that things apprehended as good and suitable move the will as the will's object, and the suitability of things is predicated on the condition of the subject to whom the object is proposed. For we predicate *suitability* relationally, and so *suitability* depends on both termini of the relation. And so the sense of taste, when differently disposed, perceives things as agreeable or disagreeable. And the emotions of sense appetites cause human beings to be disposed in certain ways. And so, as emotions affect human beings, things seem to them suitable that do not seem so apart from their current emotional state. For example, things seem good to angry persons that do not seem good to composed persons. And it is thus, as regards the object, that sense appetites move the will.

3. Does the will move itself?[9]

I answer that it belongs to the will to move other powers of the soul by reason of the end that is the will's object. And as the intellect, by knowing first principles, brings itself from potentiality to actuality regarding knowledge of conclusions, so the will, by willing the end, moves itself to will means to the end.

Objection. The intellect moves the will. Therefore, if the will moves itself, then two causes at the same time move the same thing, and this conclusion seems inappropriate. Therefore, the will does not move itself.

Reply Obj. The will does not move itself in the same respect that the intellect moves the will. Rather, the intellect moves the will by reason of the will's object, while the will, regarding performance of acts, moves itself by reason of its end.

---

[8]ST I–II, Q. 9, A. 2. [9]ST I–II, Q. 9, A. 3.

4. Does only God as external cause move the will?[10]

I answer that movements of the will, like the movements of nature, are from within. But only something that is in some way the cause of a thing's nature can cause the thing's natural movement. For example, human beings may throw stones up in the air, but the movement is not natural to the stones, and only the cause of the stones' nature causes their natural movement. And so no external cause that is not the cause of human beings' power to will can cause voluntary movements of the will.

Two arguments prove that only God can cause the power to will. First, the will is a power of the rational soul. But only God by creation causes such a soul. Therefore, only God can cause the power to will. Second, the will is ordered to universal good. But only God is universal good. Therefore, only God can cause the power to will. And everything else is good because it participates in God's goodness and is a particular kind of good, and particular causes do not impart universal inclinations. And so also no particular efficient cause can cause prime matter, which potentially has every form.

Objection. God causes only good things. Therefore, if only God were to move the will of human beings, their will would never be moved to evil, although it is the will whereby human beings sin or live righteously.

Reply Obj. As the universal cause of motion, God moves the will of human beings to the universal object of the will, that is, the good, and human beings can will nothing apart from this universal movement. But human beings by their power of reason determine themselves to will this or that, and particular things are real or apparent goods. Nonetheless, God sometimes specially moves certain individuals specifically to will certain good things, as in the case of those he moves by his grace.

5. Does nature move the will to will anything?[11]

I answer that we sometimes call the intrinsic causes in changeable things their nature, and these causes consist of matter and form. In another way, we call any substance, or even any being, a substance, and we in this way call characteristics proper to things by reason of their substance natural to the things. These characteristics intrinsically belong to the things. And we trace nonessential characteristics of things to the essential characteristics of the things as the source. And so, in this way of understanding nature, the source of the essential characteristics of things is from nature. This is clearly evident in the case of the intellect, since we by nature know the first principles of our intellectual knowledge. Just so, it is

---

[10]ST I–II, Q. 9, A. 8. [11]ST I–II, Q. 10, A. 1.

also necessary that the source of the will's movements be something we by nature will.

Characteristics proper to things by reason of their substance are natural to the things, and so the characteristics proper to things necessarily come from nature. And as the first principles that the intellect by nature knows are the source of the intellect's movements, so the things that the will by nature wills are the source of the will's movements.

The source of the will's movements is good in general, which is the will's natural object and its final end. And this good includes absolutely everything by nature belonging to the persons willing. For we desire not only the things that belong to the power of the will, but also the things that belong to each power of the soul and the things that belong to the whole human being. And so human beings by nature will the will's object, things belonging to different powers of the soul, and subsistence, life, and the like, which regard our natural constitution. And the object of the will includes all these things as particular goods.

6. Do objects of the will necessarily move the will?[12]

I answer that the will is moved in two ways. In one way, the will is moved with respect to performing its acts. In the second way, the will is moved with respect to specifying its acts, and objects do this. But persons are able not to think about any object and so not to will it. Therefore, no object moves the will necessarily in the first way.

But with respect to the second way, if an object universally good in every respect should present itself to the will, the will necessarily strives for it if the will happens to will anything. For the will could not will the contrary. And if an object not good in every respect should present itself to the will, the will will not necessarily be inclined to it.

Since lack of any good has an aspect of nongood, only the good that is complete and lacking nothing is the kind of good that the will cannot not will. That good is happiness. And we can understand any other, particular good, inasmuch as it lacks some good, as nongood. So considered, it can be rejected or approved by the will, which can be inclined to the same thing in different respects.

7. Do lower appetites necessarily move the will?[13]

I answer that human beings disposed in certain ways by their emotions judge things to be agreeable and good that they would not judge to be such apart from their present emotions. Emotions may affect human be-

---

[12]ST I–II, Q. 10, A. 2. [13]ST I–II, Q. 10, A. 3.

ings in two ways. Emotions affect human beings in one way such that reason is completely restrained, so that human beings do not have the use of reason (e.g., in the case of those driven insane by anger or sexual lust). And there is the same incapacity to reason in such persons as in the case of irrational animals, since such persons have no movement of reason and so no movement of the will.

And emotions at times do not completely engross reason, and the judgment of reason remains to some degree free. Therefore, to the degree that reason remains free and not subject to emotion, to that degree the will does not necessarily tend to the things to which the emotions incline. And so either human beings have no movement of the will, and emotion alone rules, or the movement of their will, if there be such movement, does not necessarily result from emotion.

8. Does God move the will in a necessary way?[14]

I answer that it belongs to God's providence to preserve the nature of things, not to destroy them. Therefore, God moves everything according to its condition, so that he causes necessary causes to produce necessary effects and contingent causes to produce contingent effects. But the human will is an efficient cause indeterminately disposed to effect many things, not determined to effect one thing. Therefore, God moves the will in such a way that the will is not determined to effect one thing. He moves the will in such a way that the will's movement remains contingent and only necessary regarding things to which nature moves the will.

Objection. Irresistible efficient causes necessarily move things. But God, since he has unlimited power, cannot be resisted. Therefore, God moves the will in a necessary way.

Reply Obj. God's will extends both to the deeds done by the things he moves, and to the way in which deeds are done in accord with the things' nature. And so it would be more contrary to God's causal motion if he were to move the will in a necessary way (which way does not belong to the will's nature) than if he were to move the will in a free way (since free movement belongs to the will's nature).

Intention

The tendency of a thing's movement toward something results from the action of the cause moving the thing. The will moves other powers of the soul, and so

---

[14]ST I–II, Q. 10, A. 4.

intention is an act of the will rather than an act of the intellect. Intention always concerns an end, whether the ultimate end or an intermediate end. Human beings can simultaneously intend several related things, one as proximate end and another as ultimate end (e.g., to take medicine to restore health, and health to be happy). Human beings can also simultaneously intend several unrelated things if one thing is useful for another thing. There are two movements of the will when a person is moved to will ends and means independently. There is only one movement of the will when the will wills means for the sake of an end.

1. Is intention an act of the intellect or an act of the will?[15]

I answer that intention signifies tending toward something, and both the action of the cause moving a thing and the movement of the movable thing tend toward something. But the tendency of the thing's movement toward something results from the action of the cause moving the thing. And so intention belongs first and foremost to the cause that moves a thing to an end. And so builders and those in authority move others under their command to what the builders and those in authority intend. But the will moves all other powers of the soul to ends. And so intention in the strict sense is evidently an act of the will.

2. Does intention concern only the final end of human beings?[16]

I answer that intention is related to an end as the terminus of the will's movement. But the will's movement can have a terminus in two ways. The will's movement has a terminus in one way as the absolutely final terminus, in which the movement comes to rest, and this is the terminus of the entire movement. The will's movement has a terminus in a second way as an intermediate terminus, which completes one phase of the movement and begins another phase. For example, when A moves C through B, C is the final terminus, and B is an intermediate terminus. And intention can concern both. And so intention need not always concern the final end of human beings, although intention always concerns an end.

3. Can one intend two things at the same time?[17]

I answer that human beings can simultaneously intend many things if the things are related to one another, since intention concerns both proximate and ultimate ends. And persons simultaneously intend both proximate and ultimate ends. For example, persons simultaneously intend to take medicine and to restore health.

---

[15]ST I–II, Q. 12, A. 1. [16]ST I–II, Q. 12, A. 2. [17]ST I–II, Q. 12, A. 3.

And human beings can intend several things if they are independent of one another. This is indicated by the fact that human beings choose one thing over another because one thing is better than another. And one of the reasons why one thing is better than another is because one thing is useful for more things than another thing is, and so human beings can choose one thing over another for that reason. And so human beings evidently intend several things at the same time.

4. Do we intend an end and will means to that end by the same act?[18]

I answer that the will is moved in one way to ends and means independently and in themselves. And then there are absolutely two movements of the will, one to the end and one to the means.

The will is moved in a second way to ends and means by willing the means because of the end. And then one and the same movement of the will tends toward the end and the means. For example, willing to take medicine for the sake of health involves only one movement of the will. And this is so because the end is the reason why the will wills the means. The same act fastens on the object and the reason for the object. Just so, there is only one act of the intellect in assenting to conclusions because of principles, although the intellect considers principles and conclusions by different acts if it considers them independently.

Choice

Choice is a combination of desire (will) and deliberation (reason). Reason precedes willing and orders the will's acts, since reason presents objects to the will as good. And so choice belongs to reason formally, that is, by way of formal causality. But choice belongs to the will materially and substantially, that is, as the matter subject to the order of reason. Ends as such (e.g., the health of patients as the end of doctors) are not subject to choice (e.g., one has no choice about the nature and end of practicing medicine). But one end may be the means to another end and in this way subject to choice (e.g., to become a doctor in order to practice medicine). Choice always concerns human action, at least intervening action to cause or use things. Choice concerns possible things. It concerns particular goods, which reason can consider under their good or deficient aspect as suitable or unsuitable means to happiness, and so human beings

[18]ST I–II, Q. 12, A. 4.

choose particular goods freely. But human beings necessarily will the perfect good, happiness, and cannot will to be unhappy.

1. Is choice an act of the will or an act of the power of reason?[19]

I answer that choice has an aspect that belongs to the power of reason and an aspect that belongs to the will. But one thing is the form, as it were, in relation to another if the two things form a unit. And as animals are a combination of body and soul, so choice is a combination of desire and deliberation.

Acts of the soul belonging essentially to one power or disposition get their form or species from a higher power or disposition insofar as the higher power or disposition orders the lower. For example, if a person should perform an act of bravery out of love of God, the act indeed belongs to courage regarding the act's subject matter, but to love regarding the act's form.

And reason in one way precedes willing and orders the will's acts, namely, as the will strives for its object by an order of reason, since cognitive powers present their objects to appetitive powers. Therefore, the acts whereby the will strives for things presented to it as good belong materially to the will and formally to the power of reason, since reason orders the will to ends. But the substance of acts of the will is disposed as matter subject to the order imposed by the higher power of reason. And so choice is substantially an act of the will, not an act of the power of reason, since movements of the soul toward chosen goods effect choice. And so choice is an act of the will.

2. Does choice concern only means and never the end?[20]

I answer that choice results from decisions or judgments, which are conclusions, as it were, of practical syllogisms. And so the things that stand as conclusions of practical syllogisms are subject to choice. But in practical matters, the end is the principle, not the conclusion. And so the end is not subject to choice.

In theoretical matters, nothing prevents the principle of one demonstration being the conclusion of another demonstration or science. Just so, something functioning in one activity as an end may also be ordered to something else as a means. And something functioning as an end is in this way subject to choice. For example, health is the end of doctors' activity, and so this end is not subject to their choice. Rather, doctors' exercise of

---

[19]ST I–II, Q. 13, A. 1. [20]ST I–II, Q. 13, A. 3.

choice presupposes that health is the final cause of their choosing means. But bodily health is ordered to the soul's good, and so bodily health or sickness is subject to choice by those responsible for the soul's health. The final end of human beings, however, is in no way subject to their choice.

Objection. Virtue causes persons to choose rightly, and every deed done for the sake of virtue belongs to other powers. But that for the sake of which deeds are done is an end. Therefore, choice concerns ends.

Reply Obj. Virtuous ends are ordered to happiness as the final end of human beings. And it is thus that we can choose those ends.

3. Does choice concern only our actions?[21]

I answer that ends are either human actions or things. And there need to be intervening human actions if the ends are things. This is true either because human beings cause the things that are the ends (e.g., as doctors cause health, which is their end) or because human beings use or enjoy the things that are the ends (e.g., as money or its possession is the end sought by the avaricious). And the same is true about the means. For the means need to be either human actions or things with intervening human actions, actions whereby human beings cause or use the means. And it is in this way that choice always concerns human action.

4. Does choice concern only possible things?[22]

I answer that human choices are always related to human actions. But the things we do are possible for us to do. And so we need to say that choice concerns only possible things. Similarly, we choose something because it conduces to an end. But one cannot attain an end by means of something that is impossible. Means, which are the object of choice, are related to ends as conclusions are related to principles. But possible principles do not yield necessary conclusions. And so ends are possible only if the means thereto are possible. But no one is moved to the impossible. And so no one would strive for an end unless the means thereto seem possible. And so impossible things are not subject to choice.

Objection. Choice is an act of the will. But there is willing of impossible things. Therefore, there is choice of impossible things.

Reply Obj. Willing is in between understanding and external action, since the intellect presents an object to the will, and the will causes external action. Therefore, since the will's movement proceeds from the soul to things, we consider the source of the will's acts in relation to the intellect,

---

[21]ST I–II, Q. 13, A. 4. [22]ST I–II, Q. 13, A. 5.

which understands things as generally good, and we consider the end or completion of the will's acts in relation to external actions, which are the means whereby persons strive to attain things. And so we consider the completion of the will's acts insofar as there are good things for persons to do. And these things are possible. Incomplete willing concerns things that are impossible, and some call such willing velleity, namely, that persons would will such things if the things were possible. But choice denotes acts of the soul already determined to what persons are to do. And so choice in no way concerns anything but possible things.

5. Do human beings choose necessarily or freely?[23]

I answer that human beings can will and not will, can act and not act, and they can will this or that, do this or that. For the will can strive for whatever reason can understand as good, and reason can understand as good both willing and acting, and nonwilling and nonacting. And regarding particular goods, reason can consider their good aspect and their deficient aspect and accordingly understand them as things to be chosen or shunned.

But the perfect good, happiness, is the only good that reason cannot understand under any aspect of evil or deficiency. And so human beings necessarily will their happiness and cannot will to be unhappy. But choice, which concerns means, concerns other, particular goods. And so human beings choose freely, not necessarily.

Objection. Human beings are not moved to one thing rather than another if the two things are completely equal. For example, if hungry persons have within their grasp two separate, equally distant portions of equally appetizing food, they are not moved more to one than to the other. Far less can persons choose things understood to be of less worth than other things. Therefore, if one of several things presented to a person's will seems to be of greater worth than the others, the person cannot choose any of the others. But every choice concerns what seems better in some way. Therefore, human beings always choose necessarily.

Reply Obj. If two things equal in one respect are presented to a person, nothing prevents the person from considering a superior characteristic regarding one of them, or the person's will from tending to that one rather than the other.

---

[23]ST I–II, Q. 13, A. 6.

Deliberation

There is uncertainty in practical matters, and so reason needs to inquire before it judges about what things are to be done, what things to be chosen. We deliberate about doubtful things, contingent things useful for our actions. We do not deliberate about things beyond doubt, whether activities requiring set skills or activities of no consequence. Deliberation is analytic, beginning with the end we intend to obtain until we reach a decision about what we should do to obtain it. It presupposes the end, knowledge of particulars, and truths of theoretical and practical sciences as sources. It ceases when a means to the end is chosen.

1. Is deliberation an inquiry?[24]

I answer that choice results from judgments of reason about things to be done. And there is much uncertainty in practical matters, since human actions deal with contingent particulars, and contingent particulars can vary. But reason does not produce judgments about doubtful and uncertain things without a preceding inquiry. And so reason needs to inquire before judging about what is to be chosen, and we call such an inquiry deliberation.

2. Does deliberation concern only our actions?[25]

I answer that we need to consider many conditions and circumstances about contingent particulars in order to know contingent things with certainty. And so, deliberative inquiry, properly speaking, pertains to contingent particulars. True knowledge about such things does not rank as high as knowledge desirable in itself, such as knowledge of universal and necessary things. But we seek knowledge about contingent particulars insofar as such knowledge is useful for action, since actions concern contingent particulars. And so deliberation, properly speaking, concerns our actions.

Objection. If human beings were to deliberate only about their own deeds, no one would deliberate about things to be done by others. But this conclusion is false. Therefore, deliberation does not concern only our deeds.

Reply Obj. We seek deliberation about the deeds of others insofar as others are one with us. We are united to others by bonds of affection, as, for example, one is as solicitous about a friend's concerns as about one's own. Or we are united to others in an instrumental way, since the chief cause and an instrumental cause are as if one cause. And so masters deliberate about what their slaves are to do.

---

[24]ST I–II, Q. 14, A. 1. [25]ST I–II, Q. 14, A. 3.

3. Does deliberation concern all our actions?[26]

I answer that we inquire about doubtful things, and things related to human activity may be beyond doubt in two ways. Things are beyond doubt in one way because they come to fixed ends in fixed ways, as in the case of skills that have fixed ways of proceeding. For example, scribes do not deliberate about how they should draw letters of the alphabet, since their craft determines how they are to do so. Things are beyond doubt in a second way because it matters little whether they are done in this or that way. Things that help or hinder little with respect to attaining ends are trivial, and reason understands trivial things as if they were nothing.

4. Is the process of deliberation analytic?[27]

I answer that every inquiry needs to begin from some source. If the source be both prior in knowledge and prior in reality, the process of inquiry is synthetic, since causes are more elementary than effects. But if the source is prior in knowledge and subsequent in reality, the process of inquiry is analytic, as when we judge about evident effects in terms of their causes. And the source in deliberative inquiry is the end, which is prior in intention but subsequent in reality. And so deliberative inquiry needs to be analytic, namely, to start with what we intend to obtain in the future, and to continue until we reach a decision about what we are to do right away.

5. Is the process of deliberation endless?[28]

I answer that deliberative inquiry is actually limited in respect to its source, and there are two sources of deliberative inquiry. One source, the end, is by the very nature of things proper to deliberative inquiry. Deliberation does not concern the end, but we presuppose the end as the source of deliberation. The second source is from a different kind of thing, and such sources presupposed by deliberative inquiry comprise everything perceived by the senses (e.g., that this particular thing is bread or iron) and everything known in a universal way by theoretical or practical science (e.g., that God forbids adultery, or that human beings cannot survive without suitable nourishment). And those deliberating do not inquire about these sources.

Deliberative inquiry is also actually limited in respect to its term, and the term is something in our immediate power to accomplish. As ends by their nature cause deliberative inquiry, so means by their nature conclude

---

[26]ST I–II, Q. 14, A. 4. [27]ST I–II, Q. 14, A. 5. [28]ST I–II, Q. 14, A. 6.

deliberative inquiry. And so what presents itself as the first thing to be done, by its nature brings deliberative inquiry to a final conclusion, at which point deliberative inquiry ceases.

Nothing, however, prevents deliberation from being potentially endless insofar as an unlimited number of things present themselves as things for deliberation to inquire about.

Consent

Consent denotes the act of the will whereby the will inclines toward something and takes pleasure in it, and so consent is an appetitive act. The inclination of the will toward the ultimate human end, happiness, is pure volition, but inclinations of the will toward particular things determined by deliberation as means to the end constitute consent in the proper sense.

1. Is consent an act of appetitive power or an act of cognitive power?[29]

I answer that consenting signifies an inclination of the senses toward something, and it belongs to the external senses to know things physically present. And the intellect knows universal natures, which it can know without difference both when individual things are physically present and when individual things are physically absent. Because acts of the will are inclinations toward the things, those inclinations, as they cleave to the things, by analogy get a name from sense perception, as if they acquire knowledge of the things to which they cleave, as they take pleasure in the things. And consenting is accordingly an act of appetitive power.

2. Does consent concern ends or means?[30]

I answer that consent denotes the inclination of a movement of the will toward something preexisting in the power of the person so inclining, and there is a sequence of actions. We need first to conceive an end, then to desire the end, then to deliberate about the means, then to desire the means. But the will by nature strives for the final end. And so the inclination of the will's movement toward the understood final end has the nature of pure volition and not the nature of consent.

But things consequent to the final end, as means, are subject to deliberation. And so consent can concern them, since movements of the will are attached to the things decided by deliberation. But desire of means pre-

---

[29]ST I–II, Q. 15, A. 1. [30]ST I–II, Q. 15, A. 3.

supposes the decisions of deliberation. And so the inclinations of movements of the will toward the decisions of deliberation constitute consent in the proper sense. But deliberation concerns only means. And so consent in the proper sense concerns only means.

Objection. To desire means is to choose. Therefore, if consent were to concern only means, consent would seem not to differ from choice in any respect. But this is not true. Therefore, consent does not concern only means.

Reply Obj. Choice adds to consent a relationship regarding the preference of one thing over another, and so there still remains a choice after consent. For we may by deliberation discover that several means conduce to an end, and we consent to each when we approve of each, and we by choosing prefer one of the approved means over the others. But if there should be only one means of which we approve, there is only a conceptual and not a real difference between consent and choice. Then there is consent insofar as we approve the means in order to do something, and there is choice insofar as we prefer the approved means over those of which we disapprove.

Acts Commanded by the Will

Commanding is essentially an act of reason, since ordering in a communicative way belongs to reason. But the will is the primary power that causes the movement of other powers of the soul. And so the will is the primary power that causes the very fact that reason by its commands moves other powers of the soul.

Reason can judge that it is good to will things and can command that the will will the things.

Reason is reflexively conscious of itself, and so it can order and command things related to its own acts. It can always command itself to act, that is, to think. But regarding the objects of its acts, it cannot command the intellect to understand things. Nature orders assent to some understood things (first principles), and assent in such cases is not subject to our command. But other understood things do not compel the intellect to assent (e.g., that John should marry Joan), and so assent or dissent in such cases is subject to the command of reason.

Reason governs imagination, and so acts of sense appetites are in this respect subject to the command of reason. But the condition and disposition of the body is not subject to the command of reason. And so acts of sense appetites are not totally subject to the command of reason. Also, sense perception and imagination may suddenly arouse movements of sense appetites that are beyond the command of reason.

Acts of vegetative powers (e.g., digestion), which are noncognitive natural powers, are not subject to the command of reason.

Bodily movements by sense powers (e.g., locomotion) are subject to the command of reason, but bodily movements by noncognitive natural powers (e.g., sneezing) are not.

1. Is commanding an act of reason or an act of the will?[31]

I answer that an act of reason may precede an act of the will, or vice versa, since we can cause acts of the will and acts of reason to act upon the other, namely, as reason reasons about willing, and the will wills to reason. And since subsequent acts retain the power of prior acts, there may at times be some acts of the will that retain some of the power of acts of reason, and conversely, there may be some acts of reason that retain some of the power of acts of the will.

Commanding is essentially an act of reason, for those commanding, by indicating or giving commands, order those commanded to do things. And so to order things in a communicative way belongs to reason. Reason can indicate or give commands in one way in the indicative mood, as when one person says to another, "This is what you should do." And reason sometimes gives a command in the imperative mood, as when one person says to another, "Do this." But the primary power that causes the movement of other powers of the soul is the will. Therefore, the will's power causes the very fact that reason by its commands moves other powers of the soul, since a secondary cause only causes by reason of the power of the primary cause. And so we conclude that commanding is an act of reason, although commanding presupposes an act of the will. And the commands of reason by the power of the will move other powers to perform their acts.

2. Do we command acts of the will?[32]

I answer that commands are simply acts of reason that causally order things to be done. And as reason can judge that it is good to will things, so reason can order things to be done by commanding that human beings should will things. And so acts of the will can be commanded.

Objection 1. The soul commands itself to will, but the soul does not will. But willing is an act of the will. Therefore, we do not command acts of the will.

Reply Obj. 1. The soul wills when it completely commands itself to will. But the soul sometimes does not completely command, since different considerations impel reason to command or not to command. And so reason wavers between the two outcomes and does not completely command.

---

[31]ST I–II, Q. 17, A. 1. [32]ST I–II, Q. 17, A. 5. [33]ST I–II, Q. 17, A. 6.

Obj. 2. If some acts of the will are commanded, the same reasoning leads to the conclusion that all of them are. But if every act of the will is commanded, there necessarily results an infinite regression. For an act of the will precedes the act of reason that commands, and if that act of the will is also commanded, another act of reason in turn precedes this command. And so on. But an infinite regress is improper. Therefore, we do not command acts of the will.

Reply Obj. 2. Because commands are acts of reason, the acts subject to reason are commanded. But the first act of the will is not from an order of reason but from a natural desire or a higher cause. And so there is no need to regress endlessly.

3. Do we command acts of reason?[33]

I answer that reason is reflexively conscious of itself. And so it can order things related to its own acts and command its acts as well as the acts of other powers of the soul.

With respect to performing the acts, reason can always command activity, as when we tell someone to pay attention and think. With respect to objects of the acts, reason cannot command the act whereby the intellect understands the truth about something. Such an act is not within our power to command, since it occurs by the power of illumination, whether the illumination be natural or supernatural. And so, with respect to such an object, acts of reason do not lie within our power and cannot be commanded.

But there is a different kind of act when reason assents to what it understands. If the things reason understands are such that the intellect by nature assents to them (namely, first principles), it does not lie within our power to assent or dissent. Nature orders assent, and so the assent is not subject to our command. But some understood things do not convince the intellect to such an extent that the intellect cannot for some reason assent or dissent, or at least withhold assent or dissent. And assent or dissent in such cases lies within our power and is subject to our command.

4. Do we command acts of sense appetite?[34]

I answer that sense appetites differ from the intellectual appetite, the will, in that sense appetites are the powers of bodily organs, and every act of powers utilizing bodily organs depends not only on the soul's power but also on the disposition of the bodily organs. For example, as seeing depends on the power of sight and the condition of the eyes, so also acts of

---

[34]ST I–II, Q. 17, A. 7.

sense appetites depend on the power of the appetites and the disposition of the body.

What happens regarding the soul's powers results from apprehension. But the understanding of reason governs the perception of imagination, which concerns the particular, since universal active powers govern particular active powers. And so the acts of sense appetites are in this respect subject to the command of reason. But the condition and disposition of the body is not subject to the command of reason. And so the movements of sense appetites are in this respect impeded from being totally subject to the command of reason.

Perceptions by the power of imagination or the senses may at times suddenly arouse movements of sense appetites, and then such movements are beyond the command of reason, although reason could have prevented them if it had foreseen them. And so reason governs the concupiscible and irascible appetites by political or kingly rule, which is rule over free persons not totally subject to commands, not by despotic rule.

5. Do we command acts of the vegetative soul?[35]

I answer that some acts issue from natural appetites, and other acts from animal and intellectual appetites, since every kind of efficient cause seeks its end in a particular way. Natural appetites do not result from any cognition, as animal appetites and the intellectual appetite do. But reason commands by way of cognitive power. And so reason can command acts that issue from animal appetites and the intellectual appetite, but not acts that issue from natural appetites. But the powers of nutrition and reproduction are natural powers. And so acts of the vegetative soul are not subject to the command of reason.

6. Do we command the acts of our external bodily members?[36]

I answer that our bodily members are organs of the powers of the soul, and so bodily members are disposed to obey reason in the way in which the powers of the soul are disposed to obey reason. But our sense powers are subject to the command of reason, and our powers from nature are not. And so every movement of bodily members by our sense powers is subject to the command of reason, and bodily members' movements resulting from the powers of nature are not.

Objection. Sex organs are at times aroused unsuitably and apart from any desire, and they at other times fail to be aroused when there is desire. Therefore, the movements of our bodily members do not obey reason.

---

[35]ST I–II, Q. 17, A. 8. [36]ST I–II, Q. 17, A. 9.

Reply Obj. Mental perceptions arouse our sense organs, namely, as the intellect and imagination represent things that result in emotions of the soul, and the emotions result in movements of these bodily members. But natural changes, namely, those of heat and cold, are necessary for sex organs to be aroused, and natural changes are not subject to the command of reason. And so these bodily members are not aroused at the command of reason. Like the heart, sex organs are a primary source of life, and primary sources of life are potentially the whole living thing. And so these bodily members have their specific movements from nature, since first things need to be from nature.

6

Moral Goodness and Malice

Human Acts in General

Human actions are good insofar as they share in existing, and evil inasmuch as they lack the completeness of existing proper to human actions. The chief good in human action consists in the suitability of the objects of the actions, since objects specify actions, and the chief evil is an unsuitable aspect regarding the objects. Second, human actions will be evil if they lack any requisite circumstance (e.g., proper place, proper time). Third, the goodness of human actions depends on the end or purpose of the actions. See Glossary, s.v. Cause, Intention.

The objects of some human actions may not comprise anything belonging to the order of reason (e.g., going for a walk), and such human actions are in themselves morally indifferent. Human actions, individually considered, need to have some circumstance, at least an intended end that causes the actions to be good or evil. Human actions that take place without reflection are not, properly speaking, human acts. Whenever a circumstance concerns a particular order of reason, the circumstance necessarily specifies the moral act as good or evil.

1. Are some human acts evil?[1]

I answer that we predicate *good* and *evil* of actions as we predicate *good* and *evil* of things, since each thing produces action in the way in which the thing exists. And each thing has as much good as it has existing, since *good* and *being* are convertible terms.

But only God possesses the entire fullness of existing in an indivisible and noncomposite way, and all other things possess the fullness of existing proper to them in different ways. And so some things may possess existing in one respect and yet lack something regarding the fullness of existing proper to them. For example, the fullness of human existing requires a composite of body and soul that possesses all the powers of the soul and the means of knowledge and motion. And so human beings lacking any of these things lack part of the fullness of their proper existing. Therefore, human beings have as much goodness as they have existing, and they lack

[1]ST I–II, Q. 18, A. 1.

goodness insofar as they lack part of the fullness of existing. For example, it is good for a blind person to be alive, and it is an evil for such a person to lack the power of sight. But the fullness of a thing's existing belongs to the nature of good. Therefore, things lacking part of their proper fullness of existing are good in one respect, as beings, but not absolutely good.

Therefore, every human action is good inasmuch as it shares in existing, and it is evil inasmuch as it lacks the fullness of existing proper to human action. Such is the case when human action lacks either the measure determined by reason or the proper place or the like.

2. Are human actions good or evil by reason of their objects?[2]

I answer that human actions, like other things, are good or evil by reason of the fullness of their existing or the lack thereof. But the chief thing evidently belonging to the fullness of things' existing is what gives them their species. As forms give things of nature their species, so objects give actions their species. For example, final termini specify motions. And as we note the chief goodness of things of nature by reason of their forms, so we note the chief goodness of moral acts by reason of their suitable objects. And so also some call objects good by reason of their kind (e.g., using one's own property).

And the chief evil in things of nature consists in the failure of the things they produce to attain their specific form (e.g., when human beings beget something nonhuman). Just so, the chief evil in the case of moral actions consists in something regarding the actions' objects (e.g., taking property that belongs to another). Such objects are evil by reason of their kind.

Objection. The goodness of effects depends on their causes, not the converse. But actions cause the objects of active powers. Therefore, human actions are not good or evil by reason of their objects.

Reply Obj. The objects of human action are sometimes not the objects of active powers. For example, appetitive powers are passive in one respect, since desirable objects move our appetites, although the powers cause human actions.

Nor do the objects of active powers always have the nature of effects. They are such only after they have been transformed. For example, digested food is an effect of the nutritive power, but undigested food is the matter on which the nutritive power acts. And because objects are somehow effects of active powers, the object is the end of a power's action and gives the action its form and species.

---

[2]ST I–II, Q. 18, A. 2.

And although the goodness of effects does not cause the goodness of actions, actions are good because they are able to produce good effects. And so the very relation of actions to their effects is the reason why the actions are good.

3. Do circumstances determine whether human actions are good or evil?[3]

I answer that the entire fullness of perfections of things of nature does not derive from their substantial form, which gives them their species. Added accidents contribute a great deal. For example, shape, color, and the like contribute a great deal to the fullness of human perfection. And evil results if any such accident lacks a proper form.

Just so, the entire fullness of the goodness of human actions does not consist in the actions' species. Rather, added accidents contribute something to the goodness of human actions and are requisite circumstances of the actions. And so human actions will be evil if they lack anything necessary as a requisite circumstance.

4. Do ends determine whether human actions are good or evil?[4]

I answer that as the existing of contingent things depends on their efficient cause and their form, so the goodness of such things depends on their end. And so human actions have the aspect of goodness from the ends on which they depend, in addition to the unqualified goodness existing in the actions.

Human actions have four kinds of goodness. One kind is the goodness they have as action and being. The second kind is the goodness they have by reason of their species. The third kind is the goodness they have by reason of their circumstances. And the fourth kind is the goodness they have by reason of their ends, the actions' relationship to the cause of their goodness, as it were.

5. Are any human acts by their species morally indifferent?[5]

I answer that objects specify acts, and objects related to the source of human acts, reason, specify human (i.e., moral) acts. And so there will be specifically good human acts if the objects of the acts comprise things in accord with the order of reason (e.g., giving alms to the needy). And there will be specifically evil human acts if the objects of the acts comprise things contrary to the order of reason (e.g., stealing, which is the taking of property belonging to another). But the objects of human acts may not

---

[3]ST I–II, Q. 18, A. 3. [4]ST I–II, Q. 18, A. 4. [5]ST I–II, Q. 18, A. 8.

comprise anything belonging to the order of reason (e.g., picking up straw from the ground, going to the country). And such human acts are by their species morally indifferent.

6. Are any human acts, individually considered, morally indifferent?[6]

I answer that human acts, individually considered, are either morally good or morally evil. This is so because moral acts are good both by reason of their objects and by reason of their circumstances. Every individual human act needs to have some circumstance, at least regarding an intended end, that causes the act to be good or evil. For, since it belongs to reason to order, acts that issue from reason by deliberation, if they are not ordered to proper ends, are by that very fact contrary to reason and have the character of evil. And if the acts are ordered to proper ends, they are in accord with the order of reason and have the character of good. But human acts are necessarily either ordered or not ordered to proper ends. And so every act by human beings that issues from reason by deliberation, every act individually considered, is necessarily morally good or evil.

If human acts do not issue from reason by deliberation but from some fancy (e.g., when men stroke their beard, or persons move their hands or feet), such acts are not, properly speaking, moral or human acts, since acts have that character from reason. And so such acts will be morally indifferent, being outside the class of moral acts, as it were.

7. Do circumstances constitute moral acts in species of good or evil?[7]

I answer that as forms of nature constitute the species of things of nature, so forms as conceived by reason constitute the species of moral acts. A nature is determined to attain one thing, and its process of doing so cannot go on and on. Therefore, it necessarily reaches a final form, from which we understand its specific difference, besides which there can be no other specific difference. This is why we cannot in the case of things of nature understand accidents as specific differences.

But the reasoning process is not determined to attain one thing, and reason, when it attains something, can always go further. And so what reason in one act understands as an added circumstance, reason can then order and understand as the specifying object's chief characteristic. For example, the character of property belonging to another specifies the act of taking such property, since that is why we classify the act in the species

---

[6]ST I–II, Q. 18, A. 9. [7]ST I–II, Q. 18, A. 10.

of theft. And if we were additionally to consider the character of where and when an act takes place, we shall consider place or time as a circumstance. But because reason can also order regarding place, time, and the like, reason can understand the characteristic of place regarding the act's object as contrary to the order of reason. For example, reason ordains that one should not do wrong in a sacred place, and so stealing property from a sacred place adds a particular contrariety to the order of reason. And so place, which we hitherto considered to be a circumstance, we now consider as the object's chief characteristic contrary to reason. And so whenever a circumstance regards a particular order of reason, whether the circumstance be in accord with, or contrary to, the order of reason, the circumstance necessarily specifies the moral act, whether as good or evil.

Interior Acts of the Will

Good and evil acts of the will are specifically different acts, and objects specifically differentiate human acts. And so human acts are good or evil by reason of the acts' objects. The will's goodness depends exclusively on the one thing that intrinsically causes the goodness of its acts, namely, its objects. Since reason presents objects to the will, the will's goodness depends on reason, just as the will's goodness depends on the will's object. The fact that human reason rules the human will and measures its goodness derives from the eternal law, that is, God's reason. See Glossary, s.v. Law (eternal).

A will that wills contrary to erroneous reason is evil in one respect, since reason happens to understand the object as evil, and the will inclines to the object as evil. For example, such would be the case if a person believes that it is evil to drink any alcohol, and the person willfully drinks a glass of wine. If reason errs voluntarily, whether directly or due to negligence, such an erroneous reason does not excuse the will from being evil, since the error springs from ignorance of God's law, which the person can know and is obliged to know. Such would be the case if a person's erroneous reason judges that adultery is permissible. See Glossary, s.v. Conscience, Law (natural). *But the will is excused if the error springs from ignorance of a circumstantial fact. Such would be the case if one erroneously thinks that a coat one takes is one's own.*

1. Does the will's goodness depend on the will's object?[8]

I answer that good and evil intrinsically differentiate the will's acts. And so good and evil acts of the will are specifically different acts. But objects

---

[8]ST I–II, Q. 19, A. 1.

specifically differentiate human acts. And so human acts are good or evil by reason of the acts' objects.

Objection. Good alone is the object of the will. Therefore, if the will were to be good by reason of the will's object, every act of the will would be good and no act of the will evil.

Reply Obj. An apparent, not a real, good is sometimes the will's object, and an apparent good does not have the character of good as absolutely suitable. And so acts of the will are sometimes evil.

2. Does the will's goodness depend exclusively on the will's object?[9]

I answer that the primary thing in any genus is in some respect simpler and consists of fewer things. For example, the primary material substances are simple things. And so the primary thing in any genus is in some respect simple and consists of only one thing. But the goodness or malice of human acts originates from the will's acts. And so we note the will's goodness or malice by that one thing, although we can note the goodness or malice of other human acts by various things.

But the one thing that is the source in any genus is such intrinsically, not incidentally, since we trace everything incidentally such to something intrinsically such. And so the will's goodness depends exclusively on the one thing that intrinsically causes the goodness in the will's acts, namely, its object, and not on circumstances, which are accidents of the will's acts.

3. Does the will's goodness depend on reason?[10]

I answer that the will's goodness depends in the strict sense on the will's object. But reason presents the object to the will. For understood objects are objects proportional to the will, and sensibly perceived and imagined objects are objects proportional to sense appetites. This is because reason understands, and the will strives for, universal good, and cognitive sense powers perceive, and appetitive sense powers strive for, only particular goods. And so the will's goodness depends on reason in the same way that the will's goodness depends on the will's object.

4. Does the will's goodness depend on the eternal law?[11]

I answer that effects produced by several subordinated causes depend more on the primary cause than on the secondary causes, since secondary causes can act only in the power of the primary cause. But the fact that

[9]ST I–II, Q. 19, A. 2. [10]ST I–II, Q. 19, A. 3. [11]ST I–II, Q. 19, A. 4.

human reason rules the human will and measures the will's goodness derives from the eternal law, that is, God's reason. And so the will's goodness depends much more on God's eternal law than on human reason, and we need to have recourse to eternal reason when human reason is insufficient.

5. Is the will evil if it wills contrary to erroneous reason?[12]

I answer that a will that wills contrary to erroneous reason or conscience in morally indifferent matters is somehow evil because of the will's object, on which the will's goodness or malice depends. This is because reason happens to understand the object as evil, not because of the nature of the object, and the will's object is what reason presents to the will. Therefore, the will takes on the character of evil by tending toward something that reason proposes as evil. And good things can likewise take on the character of evil, or evil things the character of good, because reason so understands them.

For example, if erroneous reason presents abstinence from fornication, which is good, as evil, the will tends toward it as something evil. And so the will will be evil because it wills something that happens to be evil because reason so understands it, not something intrinsically evil. Similarly, belief in Christ is intrinsically good and necessary for salvation, but the will tends toward that good only insofar as reason presents it. And so the will tends toward belief in Christ as evil, if reason so presents it, because it happens to be evil as reason understands it, not because it is intrinsically evil.

6. Is the will good if it wills in accord with erroneous reason?[13]

I answer that this question is equivalent to asking whether erroneous conscience excuses. The answer depends on whether ignorance causes involuntary things, and acts have moral good or evil insofar as they are voluntary. Therefore, if reason or conscience should err voluntarily, whether directly or due to negligence (in that persons do not will to know what they are obliged to know), such an error of reason or conscience does not excuse the will so willing in accord with erroneous reason from being evil. But if the error comes from ignorance of a particular circumstance without any negligence on the person's part, such an error of reason or conscience excuses the person, and so the person's will is not evil when so willing in accord with erroneous reason.

For example, if erroneous reasons should tell a man that he should have intercourse with another's wife, the will in accord with such an erroneous reason is evil, since the error springs from ignorance of God's law, which

---

[12]ST I–II, Q. 19, A. 5. [13]ST I–II, Q. 19, A. 6.

he is obliged to know. But if reason should err in thinking that the woman lying with him is his wife, and he happens to have intercourse with her when she seeks from him the right of a wife to intercourse with her husband, his will is excused and so not evil. This is because the error springs from ignorance of the circumstance, which excuses the person, and the ignorance causes something involuntary.

External Human Acts

The goodness or malice of human acts in relation to what human beings intend to attain by the acts depends entirely on the will. But the goodness or malice in the acts' requisite matter and circumstances depends on reason, and intending good ends does not suffice to make external acts good. See Glossary, s.v. Cause (final), Intention.

1. Does the goodness or malice of external acts depend exclusively on the will's goodness?[14]

I answer that external acts have two kinds of moral good or evil. One kind is by reason of the acts' requisite matter and circumstances, and the other kind by reason of the acts' relation to ends. The whole goodness or malice in the relation of external acts to ends depends on the will. But the goodness or malice in the acts' requisite matter and circumstances depends on reason, and the will's goodness depends on such goodness insofar as the will tends toward it.

A single defect suffices to make things evil, but integral goodness is required to make things good in every respect. Therefore, if the will is good by reason of its object and end, the external act is good. But the will's goodness in intending good ends does not suffice to make external acts good. External acts are evil if the will is evil either because it intends evil ends, or because it wills evil acts.

Emotions

Emotions, which are movements of sense appetites, are morally good or evil insofar as they are subject to the command of reason and the will, and they are voluntary either because the will commands them, or because the will fails to forbid them. See Glossary, s.v. Emotions.

---

[14]ST I–II, Q. 20, A. 2.

1. Do emotions have moral good and evil?[15]

I answer that emotions in themselves, namely, as movements of irrational appetites, have no moral good or evil, which depends on reason. But emotions insofar as they are subject to the command of reason and to the will have moral good or evil. For sense appetites are more closely connected to reason and the will than external bodily members are. But the movements and acts of external bodily members are morally good or evil insofar as the movements and acts are voluntary. And so emotions, insofar as they are voluntary, are much more morally good or evil than the movements and acts of external bodily members are. And emotions are voluntary either because the will commands them, or because the will does not forbid them.

---

[15]ST I–II, Q. 24, A. 1.

7

Love

Kinds

One has a love of desire for a good that one wills for oneself or another and a love of friendship for the other for whom one wills a good. The love of friendship, love of another, is love without qualification, and the love of desire, love of a good for another, is love with qualification.

1. Do we appropriately distinguish two kinds of love, namely, the love of friendship and the love of desire?[1]

I answer that to love is to will good for something. Therefore, movements of love strive for two things, namely, the good that one wills for something (whether for oneself or another) and the thing for which one wills the good. Therefore, one has a love of desire for the good one wills for another, and one has a love of friendship for the one for whom one wills the good.

This division has an order of priority. For one loves without qualification and as such what one loves with a love of friendship, and one does not love without qualification and as such but for the other what one loves with a love of desire.

For things that possess existing are beings without qualification, and things that exist in something else are beings with qualification. Just so, things that themselves possess goodness are good without qualification, the good convertible with being, and the good belonging to something else is good with qualification. And so the love whereby one loves something that it have good is love without qualification, and the love whereby one loves something that something else have good is love with qualification.

Objection. There are three kinds of friendship: the useful, the pleasurable, and the worthy. But there is desire in useful and pleasurable friendships. Therefore, we should not contradistinguish desire from friendship.

Reply Obj. In useful and pleasurable friendships, one wills good things for friends, and the character of friendship is preserved in such friendships in this respect. But because that good is additionally related to one's own

[1]ST I–II, Q. 26, A. 4.

pleasure or utility, useful and pleasurable friendships are subsumed under love of desire and so lack the true character of friendship in this respect.

Causes

Likeness in possessing the human form causes a love of friendship. The affection of one person extends to another as the other is one with oneself, and persons accordingly will good for another just as they do for themselves. Likeness in possessing potentially what another actually possesses causes a love of desire. Regarding love of desire, one loves oneself more than one loves another.

1. Does likeness cause love?[2]

I answer that there are two ways of likeness. In one way, all like things actually possesses the same thing. For example, two things that possess whiteness are like things. In the second way, one thing possesses potentially and by an inclination what something else possesses actually. For example, a heavy material substance situated out of its proper place is like such a substance situated in its proper place. Or else a potential thing is like an actual thing insofar as potentialities are like actualities.

Therefore, the first way of likeness causes a love of friendship or benevolence. For two things alike in possessing the same form are by that fact somehow one in that form. For example, two human beings are the same in being specifically human, and two white persons are the same in being white. And so the affection of one person extends to another as the other is one with the person, and persons will good for others just as they do for themselves. And the second way of likeness causes a love of desire or a friendship of utility or pleasure. For everything with potentiality, inasmuch as it is such, by its nature seeks to actualize its potentiality, and things endowed with powers of sensing and knowing take pleasure in doing so.

Persons loving with a love of desire, in willing the good they desire, love themselves in the strict sense. But all persons, since they are substantially one with themselves but one with others in likeness of form, love themselves more than others. And so persons, if others prevent them from gaining a desired good, hate the others because the others prevent them from gaining their good, not because the others are like them. And so potters quarrel because they lessen one another's profits.

---

[2]ST I–II, Q. 27, A. 3.

Objection. Persons love in others what they themselves would not wish to be. For example, persons who would not wish to be actors love actors. But this would not happen if likeness were to be the specific cause of love, for human beings would in that case love in others what they themselves possessed or wished to possess. Therefore, likeness does not cause love.

Reply Obj. There is a proportional likeness even in persons loving in another what they do not love in themselves, since the persons are related to what they love in themselves as the other is related to what the persons love in the other. For example, if a good singer loves a good writer, there is a proportional likeness in such a love insofar as each possesses what is proportional to the person with respect to the person's skill.

Effects

Love is the efficient cause of the external union of the lover and the beloved, since love moves the lover to desire and seek the company of the beloved as fitting for, and belonging to, the lover. Love is the formal cause of the union of affection, which results when persons conceive others as part of their own well-being (love of desire) and friends as other selves (love of friendship).

Mutual indwelling is an effect of love regarding understanding, since the beloved abides in the understanding of the lover, and the lover strives to discern particulars of the beloved's innermost being.

Mutual love is an effect of love regarding desire, since the beloved is in the lover's affection by reason of some satisfaction. The lover is satisfied by pleasure in the beloved or the qualities of the beloved when the beloved is present, or by desiring the beloved when the beloved is absent, or by striving for good things for the beloved with a love of friendship because of deep satisfaction in the beloved. Conversely, the lover is in the beloved by a love of desire, which seeks to possess the beloved completely, and by a love of friendship, which reckons the friend's good or bad fortune and the friend's will as the lover's own.

Thus the lover, reckoning the friend identical with the lover, is in the beloved, and the beloved, reckoning the friend identical with the beloved, is in the lover. The mutual indwelling in a love of friendship is reciprocal, since friends mutually love one another and will and do good things for one another.

1. Is union an effect of love?[3]

I answer that a lover is united to the beloved in two ways. One kind of union is in an external way (e.g., when the beloved is in the company of

[3]ST I–II, Q. 28, A. 1.

the lover). The second kind of union is by way of affection. We need to consider this way by the lover's prior understanding, since movements of the will follow understanding. Love of desire and love of friendship result from an understanding of the beloved's unity with the lover. Persons, when they love something by desiring it, conceive the thing as part of their well-being, and persons, when they love someone with a love of friendship, will good for the other just as they will good for themselves. And so persons willing good for others as for themselves conceive friends as other selves.

Therefore, love is the efficient cause of the first kind of union, an external union, since love moves lovers to desire and seek the company of the beloved as fitting for them and belonging to them. And love is the formal cause of the second kind of union, a union of affection, since love itself is such a union or bond.

2. Is mutual indwelling an effect of love?[4]

I answer that mutual indwelling is an effect of love with respect to the power of understanding. For the beloved is in the lover as the beloved abides in the understanding of the lover, and the lover, not resting content with a superficial grasp of the beloved, strives to search out particulars belonging to the beloved's innermost being and to enter the beloved's innermost being.

And mutual love is an effect of love with respect to the power of desiring. For the beloved is in a lover as the beloved is in the lover's affection by reason of some satisfaction. Thus a lover in the company of the beloved takes pleasure in the beloved or the good things of the beloved. Or a lover not in the company of the beloved strives with desire for the person beloved with a love of desire. Or a lover strives with a love of friendship for the good things the lover wills for the beloved, not because of any extrinsic reason (i.e., desiring something for the sake of another thing or willing another's good for the sake of something else) but because of a deeply rooted satisfaction in the beloved. And so we also speak of intimate love and the depths of love.

And conversely, a lover is in the beloved in one way by a love of desire, and in another way by a love of friendship. A love of desire is not satisfied with gaining or enjoying the beloved in any external or superficial way but seeks to possess the beloved completely, reaching the inner things of the beloved. And regarding a love of friendship, a lover is in the beloved insofar as the lover reckons the friend's good or bad fortune as the lover's own,

---

[4]ST I–II, Q. 28, A. 2.

and reckons the friend's will as the lover's own, so that the lover seems to experience and to be affected by the friend's good or bad fortune. And so it is characteristic of friends to will the same things and to grieve and rejoice in the same things.

And so a lover, reckoning things belonging to a friend as the lover's own, would seem to be in the beloved, as if the lover has become identical with the friend. And conversely, a beloved is in the lover, since the beloved wills and acts for the sake of the friend as for the beloved's own sake, as if reckoning the friend identical with the beloved. There is mutual indwelling in a love of friendship in a third way, a reciprocal way, since friends mutually love one another, and will and do good things for one another.

8

Habits

In General

Habits are dispositions in some way related to action. They are suitable or unsuitable in relation to human nature, which is the source of human action, or in relation to the human end, which is either action itself or an effect attained by action. Powers are primarily and intrinsically related to acts, and so habits belonging to powers (e.g., justice to the will) chiefly signify a relation to the powers' acts (e.g., the habit of justice to the will's just acts). The prerequisites of habits are: (1) that the subjects in which habits inhere differ from the objects of habits as potentialities from actualities; (2) that things can be determined in several ways and to different things; and (3) that several things be apportioned to act in concert to dispose a subject to one of the objects for which the subject has potentiality. See Glossary, s.v. Actuality, Habit, Potentiality, Power.

1. Do habits signify a relation to acts?[1]

I answer that it belongs to every habit by its nature to have a relation to acts in some way, since it belongs to the nature of habit to signify a disposition in relation to a thing's nature as habits are suitable or unsuitable. But a thing's nature, which is the end of the thing's coming to be, is further ordered to another end, which is either action or an effect that one attains through action. And so habit signifies a relation both to the nature of something and as a consequence to an action, as the action is the nature's end or conduces to the nature's end. And so habit is a disposition whereby something is well or ill disposed, either intrinsically (i.e., by the thing's nature) or in relation to something else (i.e., in relation to the thing's end).

And there are some habits that first and foremost also signify a relation to acts regarding the subjects in which they inhere, since habits primarily and intrinsically signify a relationship to a thing's nature. Therefore, if the nature of the things in which habits inhere consists in the very relation to acts, then the habits chiefly signify a relation to the acts. But it is evidently the nature and essence of powers to be sources of acts. And so every habit belonging to a power as the habit's subject chiefly signifies a relation to acts.

---

[1]ST I–II, Q. 49, A. 3.

Objection. Health, leanness, and beauty are sometimes habits. But we do not predicate these things in relation to acts. Therefore, it is not essential that habits be sources of acts.

Reply Obj. Health is a habit or habitual disposition in relation to a thing's nature. But natures as sources of action consequently signify a relation to acts. And so human beings or their bodily members are healthy when they can perform the actions of healthy human beings. And the same is true in the case of other habits of human beings.

2. Are habits necessary?[2]

I answer that habits signify dispositions in relation to a thing's nature and to a thing's activity or end, and such dispositions dispose the thing well or ill to such activity or such an end. There are three prerequisites for things to need to be disposed toward something else. The first prerequisite is that the disposed subject be other than the object toward which it is disposed and be disposed toward the object as potentiality to actuality. And so there is no need for habits or dispositions in the case of God, whose substance is his activity and who exists for himself. The second prerequisite is that things can be determined in several ways and to different things. And so there is no need for habits or dispositions in things with potentiality for only one thing, as in the case of heavenly bodies. The third prerequisite is that several things act in concert to dispose a subject toward one of the objects for which the subject has potentiality, and that these things be apportioned in different ways so as to dispose the subject well or ill toward its form or action. And so the simple qualities of material elements, which befit the elements' nature in a fixed way, are not dispositions or habits. But health, beauty, and the like, which signify an apportionment of several things able to be apportioned in different ways, are. And so habits are dispositions, and dispositions are arrangements of things with spatial or potential or specific parts.

Therefore, habits are necessary, since there are many beings whose natures and actions need several things to act in concert, and these things can be apportioned in different ways.

Subjects in Which Habits Inhere

Bodily actions springing from nature (e.g., circulation of the blood) are determined to one thing, and so no habit disposes the body for such actions. Bodily

---

[2]ST I–II, Q. 49, A. 4.

actions springing from the soul by means of the body (e.g., acts of courage) belong chiefly to the soul and secondarily to the body as the body is disposed to be readily apt for the soul's action. Regarding the disposition of the body as a subject for its form (the soul), the body has habitual dispositions such as health, beauty, and the like, but these dispositions are imperfect habits, since they can be easily altered.

Habits inhere in the soul by reason of the soul's powers. Sense powers, insofar as they are subject to the command of reason and to the will, can have habits whereby the powers are well or ill disposed toward contrary things. The potential intellect can have habitual understanding, habitual scientific knowledge, and habitual theoretical wisdom. And the will especially needs habits that rightly dispose it regarding its exercise of choice. See Glossary, s.v. Intellect, Intellectual Virtues, Moral Virtues, Senses.

1. Does the body have any habits?[3]

I answer that habits are dispositions in things with potentiality for forms or actions. But habits signify dispositions toward action. Therefore, no habit exists chiefly in the body as its subject. For every bodily action springs either from a natural characteristic of the body or from the soul that moves the body. Therefore, regarding actions that spring from nature, no habit disposes the body, since the powers of nature are limited to one thing, and habitual dispositions are needed only if subjects have potentiality for many things. And actions that spring from the soul by means of the body belong chiefly to the soul and secondarily to the body. Habits are proportional to actions, and so like actions produce like habits. And so dispositions for such actions exist chiefly in the soul. But dispositions can exist in the body secondarily as the body is disposed and made apt to be readily at the service of the soul's action.

If, however, we are speaking about the disposition of a subject toward its form, then a habitual disposition can exist in the body, which as subject we relate to the soul as form. And it is in this way that health, beauty, and the like are habitual dispositions. But these dispositions do not completely possess the character of habit, since the dispositions' causes by their nature can be easily altered.

2. How is the soul the subject of habits?[4]

I answer that as related to human nature, habits cannot inhere in the soul, since the soul itself is the form that completes human nature. And so a habit or disposition can in this respect be in the body by reason of the

---

[3]ST I–II, Q. 50, A. 1. [4]ST I–II, Q. 50, A. 2.

body's relation to the soul rather than in the soul by reason of the soul's relation to the body. (But regarding a habit related to a higher [divine] nature in which human beings may share, nothing prevents the habit, namely, grace, from being in the soul by the soul's essence.)

Habits related to action, however, inhere especially in the soul, since the soul is disposed toward many actions, not limited to one action, and a disposition for many things is required for habits. But the soul causes actions by its powers. And so habits inhere in the soul by reason of those powers.

3. Can the soul's sense powers have habits?[5]

I answer that as sense powers act at the instigation of nature, they are ordered to one thing, just as nature is. And so, like the powers of nature, sense powers lack habits insofar as the powers act at the instigation of nature.

But as sense powers act at the command of reason, they can then be ordered to various things. And so sense powers can have habits whereby the powers are well or ill disposed toward certain things.

Objection. Sensory parts are common to ourselves and irrational animals. But irrational animals have no habits, since they have no will, and we posit will in the definition of [moral] habit. Therefore, sense powers have no [moral] habits.

Reply Obj. The sense powers of irrational animals, if the animals are left to themselves, act at the instigation of nature, not at the command of reason. And so irrational animals have no habits ordered to actions, although the animals have dispositions like health and beauty in relation to their nature.

But the reason of human beings disposes irrational animals by conditioning them to do things in this or that way. And so we can in a way attribute habits to irrational animals. But this conditioning of animal behavior lacks the character of [moral] habit with respect to animals using the will, since they do not have the power to will or not will, which seems to belong to the nature of [moral] habits. And so, properly speaking, irrational animals cannot have any habits ordered to actions.

4. Does the intellect have habits?[6]

I answer that the intellect retains potentiality in some regard even when brought to actually knowing, although not in the same way that it has potentiality before learning or discovering. Therefore, the potential intellect is the subject in which inhere the habits of scientific knowledge whereby the intellect is capable of contemplating even when it is not actually doing so.

---

[5]ST I–II, Q. 50, A. 3. [6]ST I–II, Q. 50, A. 4.

Second, as powers belong to the things to which their actions belong, so habits belong to the thing to which their actions belong. But acts of understanding and contemplating are the intellect's own acts. Therefore, the habits whereby the intellect contemplates likewise inhere in the intellect.

5. Does the will have habits?[7]

I answer that every power that can be disposed to act in different ways needs habits whereby it would be rightly disposed toward its acts. But the will, as a power of reason, can be disposed to act in different ways. And so there are habits in the will, habits whereby the will would be rightly disposed toward its acts. And the very nature of habits makes evident that they are chiefly related to the will, since they are the means that persons use whenever they will to act.

Causes

As dispositions of subjects to their forms or natures, habits may be natural in two ways: (1) by reason of human nature itself (e.g., the disposition to laugh); and (2) by reason of the bodily nature or constitution of individuals (e.g., John's healthy or sickly constitution). In the former case, all human beings have the dispositions. In the latter case, different individuals may possess different degrees of the dispositions, which can spring entirely from nature (e.g., health entirely from an individual's bodily constitution), or partially from nature and partially from an external source (e.g., health from both the individual's bodily constitution and the restorative powers of medicine).

As dispositions of subjects toward action, habits belonging to the soul's powers can be natural by reason of human nature itself or by reason of the bodily constitution of individuals. Human beings, however, possess these natural habits partially from an external source. For example, the intellect has natural habits inchoatively by reason of human nature itself and partially from an external source (e.g., the habit of understanding first principles by intelligible forms derived from sense images). And the intellect has natural habits of reason inchoatively by reason of the bodily constitution of individuals (e.g., better sense powers and better brains render some individuals more readily fit to understand than other individuals). See Glossary, s.v. Intellectual Virtues, Principle. *The will has natural habits inchoatively only as to the source of the habits, not as to the substance of the habits, that is, the first principles governing human action are sources of moral virtues but not the moral virtues them-*

[7]ST I–II, Q. 50, A. 5.

selves. See Glossary, s.v. Moral Virtues. *And the will has natural habits by reason of the bodily constitution of individuals (e.g., the bodily constitution of some individuals inclines them more to chastity or patience than the bodily constitution of other individuals does).*

The intellect and the will are partially passive powers, that is, they are only active when they are acted upon. Self-evident propositions convince the intellect to give firm assent to conclusions. And so single acts of reason can produce habits of scientific knowledge (e.g., the habit of deducing theorems from postulated axioms). See Glossary, s.v. Science (Aristotelian). *But single acts of reason cannot so completely dominate the will that the will will strive uniformly in accord with human nature, that is, acquire morally virtuous habits.*

Regarding particular reason, whereby the cogitative power in conjunction with memory and imagination judges that particular things are helpful or harmful, the same acts need to be repeated over and over in order that the things be firmly impressed on memory. For example, one needs repeatedly to watch and wait for the proper traffic signals before crossing streets in order for such action to become habitual.

Powerful single acts can produce bodily dispositions (e.g., one dose of strong medicine can restore health).

1. Do any habits spring from nature?[8]

I answer that things can be natural by reason of a thing's specific nature (e.g., human beings are by reason of their nature capable of laughter) and by reason of the individual thing's nature (e.g., Socrates is sickly or healthy by reason of his individual nature, his own constitution). Also, things can be natural in two ways regarding each nature: in one way in that entire things spring from nature; in the second way in that things spring from nature in one respect and from an external source in another respect. For example, persons' entire health springs from nature if they restore themselves to health, and their health springs partially from nature and partially from an external source if medicine helps them to restore their health.

As dispositions of subjects in relation to their forms or natures, habits may be natural in each way. For example, some dispositions from nature are requisite for the human species, and there are no human beings without those dispositions. But because such dispositions enjoy some latitude, different human beings may possess different degrees of the dispositions according to the nature of individuals. Such dispositions can spring either

[8]ST I–II, Q. 51, A. 1.

entirely from nature, or partially from nature and partially from an external source (e.g., if medical skills help to restore persons to health).

And habitual dispositions toward action, habits whose subjects are the soul's powers, can be natural by reason of our specific nature insofar as habits belong to the soul, which, as the form of the body, is the specific source. And habitual dispositions toward action can be natural by reason of the nature of individuals regarding their bodies. But in neither way do human beings (unlike angels, in whom nature implants intelligible forms) possess natural habits entirely from nature.

Therefore, human beings have some habits that spring partially from nature and partially from an external source. The intellect can have natural habits inchoatively, both by reason of our specific nature (e.g., understanding first principles by means of intelligible forms derived from sense images) and by reason of the nature of individuals (e.g., as particular bodily organs render some persons more fit to understand well, since we need cognitive sense powers for intellectual activities).

Regarding the soul, the will has natural habits inchoatively only as to the source of the habits and not as to the substance of the habits. For example, the first principles of universal law are called the seedbeds of virtue because the inclination of habits toward their object seems to be the beginning of the habits and belongs to the nature of powers, not to the habits.

Regarding the body, there are appetitive habits inchoatively by reason of the nature of individual human beings. For example, the bodily constitution of some persons disposes them toward chastity or meekness or the like.

2. Do acts produce any habits?[9]

I answer that there are in some efficient causes only the active source of their activity. For example, there is in fire only the active source of generating heat. The acts of such efficient causes cannot produce habits in the causes. This is why things of nature cannot become habituated or unhabituated to anything.

Other efficient causes have active and passive sources of their acts. For example, the will produces its acts insofar as the intellect, by presenting objects, moves the will, and the power of the intellect, as it reasons about conclusions, has self-evident propositions as the active source of its acts. And so efficient causes by such acts can produce habits regarding the acts' source that, itself moved, causes movement. For the acts of efficient

---

[9]ST I–II, Q. 51, A. 2.

causes dispose whatever is acted upon and moved by something else. And so repeated acts produce characteristics in passive and moved powers, and such characteristics are habits. For example, morally virtuous habits are produced regarding appetitive sense powers as reason so moves the powers, and habits of scientific knowledge are produced in the intellect as first principles so move the intellect.

3. Can one act produce a habit?[10]

I answer that acts produce habits as active sources move passive powers to act. But in order that characteristics be produced in passive things, active things need to dominate what is passive. And so we perceive that fire does not immediately enkindle combustible material, since fire cannot immediately dominate the material. Rather, fire little by little gets rid of the material's contrary dispositions. And so fire imparts its likeness on the material when it completely dominates the material.

And the active source that is reason cannot in one act completely dominate the will, since the latter is disposed in different ways and toward different things, and acts of reason judge that things should be sought in particular ways and circumstances. And so reason in one act does not so completely dominate the will that the latter for the most part strives for one and the same thing in accord with nature. Rather, uniform striving in accord with nature belongs to [morally] virtuous habits. And so many acts, not one, produce [morally] virtuous habits.

There is a passive source in intellectual powers that is the potential intellect itself, regarding which the active source can by one act completely dominate the intellect's power. For example, a self-evident proposition convinces the intellect to give firm assent to a conclusion. And so single acts of reason can produce habits of scientific knowledge. But a probable proposition cannot do this. And so many acts of reason are needed to produce habits of probable knowledge.

And there is another passive source in intellectual powers that is particular reason (i.e., the cogitative power with the powers of memory and imagination), and the same acts of the lower cognitive powers need to be repeated over and over in order that things be firmly impressed on memory.

And single acts can produce bodily dispositions if active sources have great power. For example, strong medicine sometimes immediately brings about health.

---

[10]ST I–II, Q. 51, A. 3.

9

Virtue

Essence

Thomas uses the definition of Peter Lombard as the point of departure for his treatment of virtue.[1] *Good characteristic dispositions are the formal cause of virtue. Something belonging to the mind, something rational, constitutes the subject matter, the material cause of virtue. Virtue is directed toward good action, and so good action is the end, the final cause, of virtue. God is the efficient cause of infused virtues (e.g., charity), but human beings acquire some virtues (e.g., courage) by their own activity. Successive sections deal with intellectual virtues, which are directed toward good activity of the intellect, moral virtues, which are directed toward good action of the will and sense appetites, and the relation between the two kinds of virtue. See Glossary, s.v.* Cause, Intellectual Virtues, Moral Virtues, Virtue.

1. How do we appropriately define virtue?[2]

I answer that according to the definition usually attributed to virtue, virtue is a good characteristic of the mind, the characteristic by which we live rightly, of which no one makes wrong use, and which God works in us apart from any work of ours. This definition completely embraces the whole nature of virtue, since we compose the complete nature of anything from all of its causes, and the aforementioned definition includes all the causes of virtue.

In calling virtue a good characteristic, we understand virtue's formal cause by its genus and specific difference, since *characteristic* is virtue's genus, and *good* is its specific difference. (The definition would be more exact if it were to substitute *habit*, which is the proximate genus of virtue, for *characteristic*.)

Virtue has the matter with which it deals and the matter in which it rests, namely, its subject. The matter with which virtue deals is the object of a virtue. But since objects limit virtue to specific kinds of virtue, and we are now giving the definition of virtue in general, we could not posit such

[1]Peter Lombard, *Sentences* II, dist. 27, A. 2.

[2]ST I–II, Q. 55, A. 4.

matter in the definition. And so we substitute virtue's subject for its material cause by saying that virtue is a good characteristic *of the mind*.

And action is the end of virtue, since virtues are habits related to action. Some habits (i.e., vices) are always directed to evil, some habits are at times directed to good and at times directed to evil, and some habits (i.e., virtues) are always directed to good. And so we say that virtues are habits *by which we live rightly*, in order to distinguish virtues from vices. And we say that virtues are habits *of which no one makes wrong use*, in order to distinguish virtues from the habits that are sometimes directed to evil.

And the efficient cause of infused virtue, which is the virtue defined here, is God. And that is why the definition adds: *which God works in us apart from any work of ours*. But if we omit this clause, the rest of the definition will be common to all virtues, both those acquired and those infused.

Intellectual Virtues

There are three kinds of theoretical intellectual virtues. One kind is the habit of theoretical first principles, which disposes the intellect to understand self-evident propositions (e.g., the principle of contradiction). The second kind consists of habits of scientific knowledge (e.g., biology, physics), which dispose the intellect to demonstrate ultimate truths about this or that kind of thing. The third kind is the habit of theoretical wisdom (theology, philosophy), which disposes the intellect to reason about the first cause of all things, namely, God. Theoretical wisdom, because of its object, is the greatest intellectual virtue. See Glossary, s.v. Principle, Science (Aristotelian), Theoretical Wisdom.

There are two kinds of practical intellectual virtues: skills and practical wisdom. Skills (e.g., shipbuilding) are practical intellectual virtues about rightly making external things. Practical wisdom is the practical intellectual virtue about rightly doing things (i.e., rightly ordered internal desire in producing and using external things). For practical wisdom, human beings need to be rightly disposed regarding their end. Since moral virtues produce the right disposition towards the human end, human beings need moral virtues, which produce right desire, for practical wisdom. Human beings need practical wisdom to be suitably disposed in choosing means to the human end. See Glossary, s.v. Practical Wisdom (Prudence), Skills.

1. Are theoretical wisdom, scientific knowledge, and understanding the three habits of the theoretical intellect?[3]

I answer that virtues of the intellect enable it fully to contemplate truth, and we can contemplate truth in two ways: as self-evident and as known

[3]ST I–II, Q. 57, A. 2.

through something else. The intellect immediately perceives the truth of self-evident principles. And the habit that enables the intellect fully to contemplate such truths is understanding, that is, the habit of first principles.

And the intellect by rational inquiry, not immediately, perceives truths that it knows through something else. Such truths can be the ultimate conclusions of rational inquiry in two ways: as ultimate in one kind of knowledge and as ultimate in regard to all human knowledge. Scientific knowledge enables the intellect fully to contemplate truths that are ultimate in this or that kind of knowable thing. And so, since there are different kinds of knowable things, there are different habits of scientific knowledge. But there is only one theoretical wisdom, which contemplates the highest cause. And so theoretical wisdom appropriately judges and integrates everything, since we can completely and comprehensively judge only by tracing things to their first cause.

2. Are skills intellectual virtues?[4]

I answer that skills are simply right reasoning about works to be produced, and the goodness of works consists in the intrinsic goodness of the products. For example, craftsmen as such deserve praise for the quality of the works they produce, not for the disposition of the will with which they produce the works.

Thus skills, strictly speaking, are habits related to action, but they have something in common with theoretical habits, since it also belongs to the latter how contemplated things are disposed, not how the human will is disposed toward contemplated things. For example, it does not matter how appetitive powers of the soul dispose geometricians, whether they are happy or angry, provided they demonstrate truths, just as it does not matter how the will of craftsmen is disposed. And so skills are essentially virtues in the same way that theoretical habits are, namely, inasmuch as both produce works that are good only regarding the ability to produce the works well and not regarding the works' use, which is the special good that complementary virtues seek.

3. Does the virtue of practical wisdom differ from the virtue of skills?[5]

I answer that some habits have the character of virtue only because they cause the ability to produce good works, and other habits have the character of virtue because they cause both the ability to produce good works and good use of the works. Skills cause only the ability to produce good

---

[4]ST I–II, Q. 57, A. 3. [5]ST I–II, Q. 57, A. 4.

works, since skills are not concerned about what craftsmen desire. But practical wisdom causes both the ability to produce good works and good use of the works, since practical reason, as presupposing rightly ordered desire, is concerned about what persons desire.

The reason for this difference is because skills are right reasoning about things to be made, and practical wisdom is right reasoning about things to be done. But making and doing are different, since making (e.g., building) is an action that passes into external matter, and doing (e.g., seeing, willing) abides in the cause that acts. And so practical wisdom is ordered to such human acts, which consist of the exercise of powers and habits, in the same way that skills are ordered to external productions, since both practical wisdom and skills consist of right reasoning about the things to which each is ordered.

Ends in regard to human acts are disposed like principles in theoretical matters. And so, for practical wisdom (i.e., right reasoning about things to be done), human beings need to be rightly disposed regarding ends, and right desire results in such a disposition. And so, for practical wisdom, human beings need moral virtues, which produce right desire. But the good of artifacts is the good proper to the works, not the good proper to the human will. And so skills do not presuppose right desire.

Therefore, the virtue of practical wisdom is evidently a virtue that differs from the virtue of skills.

Objection. Good deliberation belongs to practical wisdom. But some skills (e.g., military skill, navigational skill, medical skill) involve deliberation. Therefore, practical wisdom is indistinguishable from skill.

Reply Obj. Practical wisdom deliberates rightly about things belonging to the entire life of human beings and the final goal of human life. But some skills involve deliberation about things that belong to the skills' own ends. And so we call some persons wise commanders or wise ship captains because they deliberate rightly about warfare or seafaring, but we do not call them absolutely wise. Rather, we call absolutely wise only those who deliberate rightly about things of benefit to the entire life of human beings.

4. Do human beings need the virtue of practical wisdom?[6]

I answer that living rightly consists of acting rightly. And in order for persons to act rightly, they need not only do certain things but also do them in certain ways, namely, act by right choice, not simply out of im-

---

[6]ST I–II, Q. 57, A. 5.

pulse or emotion. And since means are the object of choice, rectitude in choosing has two requirements, namely, the requisite end and the means suitably ordered to that end. And the virtues that perfect the soul's will, whose object is the human good and end, suitably dispose human beings to their requisite end. But for there to be things suitably ordered to the requisite end, a habit of reason needs directly to dispose human beings, since deliberating and choosing, which concern means, are acts of reason. And so reason needs to have an intellectual virtue that perfects reason to be suitably disposed toward means. And this virtue is practical wisdom. And so the virtue of practical wisdom is necessary for living rightly.

Objection. We deliberate rightly by practical wisdom. But human beings can act both by their own good counsel and by another's. Therefore, in order to live rightly, human beings do not themselves need to possess practical wisdom, but it suffices for them to follow the counsel of wise persons.

Reply Obj. When human beings do good things because moved by another's counsel and not because of their own reason, their actions are not yet altogether perfect as regards their reason directing them and as regards their will moving them to act. And so, although they do good things, they nonetheless do not do them rightly in an absolute sense, and acting rightly in an absolute sense is living rightly.

5. Is theoretical wisdom the greatest intellectual virtue?[7]

I answer that the object of theoretical wisdom surpasses the objects of all the other intellectual virtues, since theoretical wisdom contemplates the highest cause, God. And because we judge about effects by their causes, and about lower causes by their higher cause, theoretical wisdom is able to judge, has the function of disposing, and is architectonic in relation to every other intellectual virtue.

Moral Virtues

Emotions as movements of sense appetites ordered by reason can coexist with moral virtues. Emotions are the objects of some moral virtues (e.g., courage, moderation), and acts of the will the object of other moral virtues (e.g., justice), which exist without emotion.

---

[7]ST I–II, Q. 66, A. 5.

Moral virtues are inchoatively natural to human beings by reason of their specific rational nature, inasmuch as reason by nature knows certain first moral principles (e.g., one should take reasonable means to preserve one's life), and inasmuch as the will has a natural desire for good according to reason. And moral virtues are natural to human beings by reason of their individual bodily constitution, inasmuch as bodily constitutions dispose individuals to particular moral virtues (e.g., patience). Repeated human acts governed by reason can produce moral virtues for the good measured by reason. Moral virtues aim at the mean between too much and too little. The mean of some moral virtues (e.g., courage, moderation) is a mean of reason, a mean that reason imposes on internal emotions in different ways according to the constitution of each individual. But justice concerns external things, and so the mean of justice is a mean in external things, a mean that renders to each person what is due to that person, neither more nor less.

There are four cardinal virtues, which are related in various ways to the formative source of moral virtues, the good of reason. Practical wisdom consists of the very contemplation of reason. Justice consists of reason controlling human actions. Moderation consists of reason controlling emotions that incite human beings to act contrary to reason. Courage consists of reason controlling emotions that incite human beings not to act when they should. Practical wisdom inheres in reason, justice in the will, moderation in the concupiscible appetite, and moderation in the irascible appetite.

Incomplete virtues, which are tendencies only to particular kinds of good deeds, are not connected, but complete virtues, which are tendencies to do good deeds rightly, are connected. For example, courage cannot exist as a complete virtue without the restraint of moderation or the right order of justice or the judgment of practical wisdom. No moral virtue is possible without practical wisdom, nor can human beings possess practical wisdom without possessing moral virtues, which dispose human beings to the proper ends of things to be done.

Moral virtues, insofar as they result in the good related to the supernatural end of human beings, need to be infused by God and cannot exist without the supernatural virtue of charity. Charity causes practical reason to be rightly disposed toward the supernatural end.

Justice is the most excellent moral virtue, since it is more closely related to reason than the other moral virtues are, since it inheres in the rational appetite (the will), and since its object concerns human (i.e., rational) actions in relation to oneself and others. Courage, which subjects desire to reason in things proper to life, ranks the highest of moral virtues concerning emotions. And moderation, which subjects desire to reason in things ordered to life, namely, food for the life of the individual and sex for the life of the species, ranks the next highest. These three virtues, with practical wisdom, are the most worthy virtues.

1. Can emotions accompany moral virtues?[8]

I answer that if we, like the Stoics, should call emotions inordinate affections, emotions cannot exist in a virtuous person in such a way that there would be consent to the emotions after deliberation. But if we should call emotions any movements of sense appetites, then emotions as ordered by reason can exist in virtuous persons. And so virtues are states of repose from emotions as and when emotions are inappropriate.

2. Are emotions the object of every moral virtue?[9]

I answer that moral virtues perfect the will by ordering the will to the good of reason. But the good of reason consists of what reason controls and orders. And so everything that reason can order and control can be the object of moral virtues. But reason orders both the emotions of sense appetites and the actions of the will, and emotions do not inhere in the will. And so emotions are not the object of every moral virtue. Rather, emotions are the object of some moral virtues, and actions of the will the object of other moral virtues.

3. Can there be any moral virtue apart from emotion?[10]

I answer that if we should define emotions as movements of sense appetites, then moral virtues with emotions as their object, as their special matter, evidently cannot exist without emotions. This is so because such moral virtues, were they to exist without emotions, would then cause sense appetites to be completely inactive, and it is not part of virtues that things subject to reason be devoid of their acts. Rather, it is part of virtues that things subject to reason, by performing their acts, execute the commands of reason. And so, as virtues dispose bodily members for the members' requisite acts, so virtues dispose sense appetites for the appetites' own rightly ordered movements.

And moral virtues with actions of the will as their object (e.g., justice) can exist without emotions, since these virtues direct the will to its own acts, and its own acts do not consist of emotions. But joy, at least the joy inhering in the will, nonetheless results from just acts, and the joy inhering in the will is not an emotion. When perfect justice multiplies this joy, the joy will redound to sense appetites, since lower powers accompany the movements of higher powers. And so, by reason of such an overflow, the more virtues shall be perfect, the more emotion they cause.

---

[8]ST I–II, Q. 59, A. 2. [9]ST I–II, Q. 59, A. 4. [10]ST I–II, Q. 59, A. 5.

4. Do we have virtues by nature?[11]

I answer that things are natural to human beings in two ways: by reason of their specific nature and by reason of their individual nature. Each thing belongs to a species by reason of its form, and the thing is individuated by its matter. But the form of human beings is the rational soul, and their matter is the body. Therefore, what befits human beings by reason of their rational soul is natural to them by reason of their species, and what is natural to them by reason of the particular composition of their body is natural to them by reason of their individual nature. For what is specifically natural to human beings regarding their body is in one respect related to the soul, since such a body is related to such a soul.

Virtues are in both ways somehow inchoatively natural to human beings. Virtues are natural to human beings by their specific nature inasmuch as their reason by nature has knowledge of some principles, both about things that we can know and about things to be done, and these principles are the seeds of intellectual and moral virtues. Virtues are also natural to human beings by their specific nature inasmuch as the will has a natural desire for the good in accord with reason. And virtue is natural to human beings by their individual nature inasmuch as the body's disposition better or worse disposes individuals toward certain virtues. For sense powers are actualities of parts of the body, and the parts' disposition helps or hinders the powers in their acts. And so the parts' disposition helps or hinders the powers of reason, which the sense powers serve.

But we do not completely possess these virtues from nature. For natures are determined to one and the same course of action, and one and the same course of action does not bring these virtues to perfection. Rather, virtues are perfected in different ways, according to the different things with which the virtues deal and according to different circumstances.

5. Do repeated acts produce virtues in us?[12]

I answer that the virtues of human beings specifically perfect human beings in goodness. But the nature of good consists of manner, kind, and rank, or of number, weight, and measure. Therefore, we need to assess the human beings by a norm, and that norm is twofold, namely, human reason and God's law. But God's law is a higher norm. And so his law governs more things than human reason does. And so God's law governs whatever reason does, but the converse is not true.

---

[11]ST I–II, Q. 63, A. 1.

[12]ST I–II, Q. 63, A. 2.

Human acts, insofar as they spring from reason, under whose power and rule the good measured by the norm of human reason consists, can produce virtues ordered to that good. But human acts, whose source is reason, cannot produce virtues that dispose human beings for the good measured by God's law and not by human reason. Rather, only God's action can produce such virtues. Regarding such virtues, God works them in us apart from our action.

Objection. Sin is incompatible with virtue. But human beings can avoid sin only through God's grace. Therefore, only God's gift, not our repetition of acts, can produce virtues in us.

Reply Obj. Divinely infused virtues, especially if considered in their perfection, are incompatible with any mortal sin. But humanly acquired virtues may be compatible with sinful, even mortally sinful, acts. For the exercise of habits that we possess is subject to our will, and one sinful act does not destroy the habits of acquired virtues, since habits, not acts, are directly contrary to habits. And so, although human beings cannot without grace avoid mortal sin so as never to sin mortally, they are nonetheless not prevented from acquiring virtuous habits, whereby they may abstain for the most part from evil deeds and especially deeds very contrary to reason.

There are also some mortal sins that human beings can in no way avoid without grace, namely, sins directly contrary to the theological virtues, which we possess by the gift of grace.

6. Is the mean of moral virtues a real mean or one of reason?[13]

I answer that we can understand the mean of reason in one way as the mean existing in acts of reason, as if the acts of reason have been brought to a mean. But moral virtues perfect acts of the will, not acts of reason. And so the mean of moral virtues is not a mean of reason in this sense. The mean of reason in another sense is the mean that reason imposes on some matter, and then the mean of moral virtues is a mean of reason, since moral virtue consists in the mean by conforming to right reason.

But the mean of reason may also sometimes be a real mean (e.g., in justice), and then the mean of moral virtue needs to be a real mean. And the mean of reason is sometimes not a real mean, and then we understand the mean in relation to ourselves, and such is the mean in the case of every moral virtue other than justice. Justice is different because justice concerns actions, which consist in external things, and we need absolutely and as such to establish what is right about external things. And so the

---

[13]ST I–II, Q. 64, A. 2.

mean of reason in the case of justice is the same as the mean of things, namely, in that justice renders to each person what is due to that person, neither more nor less. But other moral virtues concern internal emotions, about which we cannot in one and the same way establish what is right, since human beings are disposed toward emotions in various ways. And so we need to establish the right order of reason in emotions in relation to ourselves, whom emotions affect.

7. Are there four cardinal virtues?[14]

I answer that we can understand the number of things by their formal sources or by the subjects in which they inhere, and we, by understanding virtues in both ways, find that there are four cardinal virtues.

The formal source of moral virtues is the good of reason. We may consider the good of reason in one way as it consists in the very contemplation of reason, and then there will be one chief virtue, practical wisdom. And we may consider the good of reason in a second way as we impose the orders of reason on things, and this way concerns either actions, and then there is the virtue of justice, or of emotions, and then there need to be two virtues. For we need to impose orders of reason on emotions because emotions resist reason. Some emotions incite us to act contrary to reason, and so we need to control our emotions. Such control of emotions is the virtue of moderation. And some emotions (e.g., fear of danger) keep us from doing what reason dictates, and so human beings need to be strengthened regarding what is proper to reason so as not to yield to their emotions. Such strength of character is the virtue of courage.

If we consider the subjects in which moral virtues inhere, we find the same number of cardinal virtues. One subject, the one practical wisdom perfects, essentially belongs to reason, and three subjects share in reason. One of the latter subjects is the will, the one in which the virtue of justice inheres, the second is the concupiscible appetite, the one in which the virtue of moderation inheres, and the third is the irascible appetite, the one in which the virtue of courage inheres.

8. Are moral virtues interconnected?[15]

I answer that incomplete virtues (e.g., moderation and courage) are tendencies in us only toward particular kinds of good deeds, whether we have such inclinations by nature or habituation. Moral virtues so understood are not connected. For example, some individuals who are not ready to act

---

[14]ST I–II, Q. 61, A. 2. [15]ST I–II, Q. 65, A. 1.

chastely are nonetheless by their natural constitution or habitual behavior ready to act generously.

Complete moral virtues are habits that incline us to do good deeds rightly, and moral virtues so understood are connected. If we distinguish the cardinal virtues by the general characteristics proper to each (judgment to practical wisdom, right order to justice, restraint to moderation, strength of soul to courage), it is evident why the virtues are connected. For example, strength of soul is not to be praised as a virtue if it is without moderation or right order or judgment. And the same is true about the other cardinal virtues.

And if we distinguish cardinal virtues by their matter, the virtues are connected because persons can possess no moral virtues apart from practical wisdom. For it belongs to moral virtues, as habits of choosing, to make right choices. And right choice requires not only an inclination to a requisite end, which morally virtuous habits directly bring about, but also that persons directly choose means to such an end, which practical reason does by deliberating about, judging, and commanding the means.

Likewise, neither can persons possess practical wisdom without possessing moral virtues. For practical wisdom is right reasoning about things to be done, and such reasoning proceeds from the ends of things to be done, as principles, and moral virtues rightly dispose persons to those ends. And so we cannot possess practical wisdom without moral virtues. And so moral virtues are connected.

9. Can there be moral virtues without the theological virtue of charity?[16]

I answer that human beings can by their acts acquire moral virtues insofar as those virtues result in the good related to ends that do not surpass the natural capacity of human beings. And moral virtues so acquired can exist without charity, as they did in the case of many pagans.

But moral virtues, insofar as they result in the good related to our final supernatural end, perfectly and truly possess the character of virtue and cannot be acquired by human acts. Rather, God infuses such virtues, and they cannot exist without charity. For such moral virtues cannot exist without practical wisdom, and practical wisdom cannot exist without moral virtues, since moral virtues cause us to be rightly disposed toward certain ends, and practical reason reasons from those ends. And for practical wisdom to reason rightly, it is far more necessary that human beings be rightly disposed regarding their supernatural end, which is accom-

---

[16]ST I–II, Q. 65, A. 2.

plished by charity, than that they be rightly disposed regarding other ends, which is accomplished by moral virtues. Similarly, in theoretical matters, right reasoning most of all requires the first indemonstrable principle (i.e., that contradictory propositions cannot be simultaneously true). And so infused practical wisdom cannot exist without charity, and infused moral virtues, which cannot exist without practical wisdom, likewise cannot exist without charity.

Only infused virtues are perfect and virtues in an absolute sense, since they rightly dispose human beings for their final end absolutely. But other virtues, acquired virtues, are virtues in one respect, not absolutely, since they rightly dispose human beings regarding their final end in particular kinds of things to be done but not regarding their final end absolutely.

10. Is justice superior to other moral virtues?[17]

I answer that virtues are specifically greater or lesser absolutely or in some respect. A virtue is absolutely greater insofar as it reflects a greater good of reason, and justice, as more closely connected to reason, surpasses all other moral virtues. For the subject in which justice resides is the will, and the will is the rational appetite. And the object or matter of justice concerns actions, and actions dispose human beings in regard to themselves and in relation to others. And so justice is the most excellent of virtues.

Other moral virtues concern emotions. Regarding those virtues, the greater the things concerning which movements of desire are subject to reason, the more each virtue reflects the good of reason. But the greatest thing belonging to human beings is life, on which all other things depend. And so courage, which subjects movements of desire to reason in things proper to life and death, is the chief moral virtue that deals with emotions, although courage is subordinate to justice. And so the virtues most esteemed by others are necessarily the greatest, since virtue is the power to do good. And so others most of all esteem those who are courageous and those who are just, since the virtue of the former is useful in war, and the virtue of the latter is useful both in war and in peace.

After courage ranks moderation, which subjects desire to reason regarding things directly ordered to life, both regarding the life of the individual and the life of the species, namely, food and sex, respectively.

And so these three virtues, together with practical wisdom, are the most worthy virtues. But particular virtues are greater in some respect as they assist or adorn one of the chief virtues.

---

[17]ST I–II, Q. 66, A. 4.

Relation of Moral Virtue to Intellectual Virtue

Human beings need to have the requisite intention of the human end, and moral virtues, which incline the will to that end, accomplish this. But human beings also need to understand the means to the end, and practical wisdom accomplishes this by deliberating, judging, and commanding. And so there can be no moral virtue without practical reason, nor moral virtue without understanding the first principles of practical reason (e.g., one should take reasonable means to maintain one's life).

Human beings can have theoretical intellectual virtues and practical intellectual skills without having moral virtue. But practical wisdom is impossible without moral virtue. For valid arguments about particular things require both universal principles and particular principles, and to be rightly disposed regarding particular things, one needs habits that cause one to judge rightly about things to be done. And so human beings need moral virtues for right reasoning about things to be done, that is, for practical wisdom.

Absolutely speaking, intellectual virtues, which perfect reason, are more excellent than moral virtues, which perfect the will. But in relation to acts, moral virtues, whose function is to activate other powers, is more excellent.

1. Can there be moral virtue without intellectual virtue?[18]

I answer that there can be moral virtue without the intellectual virtues of theoretical wisdom, scientific knowledge, and skills but not without understanding and practical wisdom. There can be no moral virtue without practical wisdom, since moral virtues are habits related to choice, that is, habits that cause right choice. And two things are necessary in order that choice be right. First, there needs to be the requisite intention of the human end, and moral virtues, which incline the will toward the good befitting reason, the good that is the requisite end, accomplish this. Second, human beings need to understand rightly the means to the requisite end, and human beings can only do so if their reason rightly deliberates, judges, and commands. Such activities of reason belong to practical reason and the virtues associated with it.[19] And so there can be no moral virtue without practical wisdom.

And so neither can there be moral virtue without understanding. For it is by understanding that we know the first principles that we know by nature, both in theoretical and practical matters. And so, just as right rea-

---

[18]ST I–II, Q. 58, A. 4.

[19]Three virtues are associated with practical wisdom as its potential parts: deliberating rightly; judging about deeds according to the general law; and judging about exceptions to the general law. See ST I–II, Q. 57, A. 6.

soning in theoretical matters, since it springs from the first principles known by nature, presupposes understanding of the principles, so also does practical wisdom, which consists of right reasoning about things to be done.

Objection. Moral virtues cause human beings to incline to act rightly. But some human beings have such inclinations from nature even without judgments of reason. Therefore, there can be moral virtue without intellectual virtue.

Reply Obj. An inclination from nature toward a virtuous good is a virtuous beginning but not completely virtuous. For the stronger such inclinations are, the more dangerous they may be unless they are united to right reason, which makes right choices of means suitable for the requisite end. Similarly, the faster a blind horse runs, the more forcibly it collides with something, and the worse its injury. And so, although moral virtues do not consist of right reason, they both are in accord with right reason and need to be done with right reason.

2. Can there be intellectual virtue without moral virtue?[20]

I answer that there cannot be practical wisdom apart from moral virtue, although there can be other intellectual virtues apart from moral virtue. For practical wisdom consists of right reasoning about things to be done, both in general and in particular, and actions involve particular things. And right reasoning requires the principles from which valid arguments spring. And valid arguments about particular things require both universal principles and particular principles. Regarding universal principles about things to be done, the natural understanding of principles (whereby they know that they should not do anything evil), or even some practical scientific knowledge, rightly disposes human beings. But this does not suffice to reason about particular things. For emotions in particular cases may sometimes overwhelm those universal principles or scientific knowledge.

In order that human beings be rightly disposed regarding particular principles about things to be done, that is, regarding ends, human beings need to be perfected by habits that cause right judgment about ends to be somehow natural to them. And moral virtues accomplish this. For virtuous persons judge rightly about virtuous ends, since persons perceive ends in the way in which persons are disposed. And so human beings need to possess moral virtues in order to reason rightly about things to be done, and such right reasoning is practical wisdom.

---

[20]ST I–II, Q. 58, A. 5.

3. Are moral virtues more excellent than intellectual virtues?[21]

I answer that we can call things greater or lesser in two ways: in one way, absolutely; in the other way, in some respect. But nothing prevents something from being absolutely better and not being better in some respect. For example, it is better to philosophize than to be rich, but not in the case of one experiencing need.

When we consider something according to its specific nature, we consider it absolutely. But virtues are specified by their objects. And so, absolutely speaking, virtues with more excellent objects are more excellent. But the object of reason is more excellent than the object of the will, since reason understands things as universal, and the will inclines toward real things, which exist as individual. And so, absolutely speaking, intellectual virtues, which perfect reason, are more excellent than moral virtues, which perfect the will.

But in relation to acts, moral virtues, which perfect the will, and whose function is to move other powers to act, are more excellent.

And virtues are virtues because they are the sources of acts, since virtues perfect powers. Therefore, it also follows that the character of virtue belongs more to moral virtues than to intellectual virtues, although intellectual virtues are, absolutely speaking, more excellent habits.

---

[21]ST I–II, Q. 66, A. 3.

10

Law

Essence

Thomas lists four essential elements of law. First, law is an order of reason, since the source of human acts is reason, which rules and measures them by ordering human beings to their end and commanding means to the end. Second, law is ordered to the common good, and every law regarding particular acts has the character of law only because of that order. Third, lawmaking belongs to the whole people or a public personage that has the care of the community. Fourth, laws need to be promulgated if they are to impose obligation on those subject to the laws.

1. Does law belong to reason?[1]

I answer that law is a rule and measure of acts that induces persons to act or refrain from acting, and the rule and measure of human acts is reason, which is the primary source of human acts. For it belongs to reason to order us to our end, which is the primary source of our prospective action, and the source in any kind of thing is the rule and measure of that kind of thing. And so we conclude that law belongs to reason.

Objection. Law induces those subject to the law to act rightly. But inducing to act rightly belongs in the strict sense to the will. Therefore, law belongs to the will rather than to reason.

Reply Obj. Reason has from the will the power to induce activity, since reason commands means because one wills ends. But an act of reason needs to rule the will regarding the means commanded in order that the willing have the nature of law. And the will of the ruler in this way has the force of law. Otherwise, the willing of the ruler would be injustice rather than law.

2. Is law always ordered to the common good?[2]

I answer that law belongs to the source of human acts, since law is their rule and measure. As reason is the source of human acts, so something in

[1]ST I–II, Q. 90, A. 1. [2]ST I–II, Q. 90, A. 2.

reason is the source of all other kinds of acts. And so law needs chiefly and especially to belong to the source.

The first source in practical matters, with which practical reason is concerned, is the ultimate end. But the ultimate human end is happiness or blessedness. And so law especially needs to regard the order to blessedness. And law in the strict sense needs to concern the order to happiness in general, since every part is related to a whole as something imperfect to something perfect. And so just laws constitute and preserve happiness and its particulars by citizens sharing in a political community, since the political community is the perfect community.

Regarding any kind of thing, the one most such is the source of the others, and the others are such by their relation to that one. For example, fire, which is hottest, causes heat in composite material substances, which are hot because they share in fire. But law is primarily such because of its order to the common good. And so every precept regarding particular acts has the nature of law only because of its order to the common good. And so every law is ordered to the common good.

3. Is any person's reason competent to make law?[3]

I answer that law in the strict sense primarily and chiefly concerns ordering things to the common good. But ordering things to the common good belongs either to the whole people or to persons acting in the name of the whole people. And so lawmaking belongs either to the whole people or to a public personage that has the care of the whole people. For as in all other matters, ordering things to ends belongs to those to whom the ends belong.

Objection. Lawmakers aim to induce human beings to virtue. But any human being can lead others to virtue. Therefore, the reason of any human being is competent to make law.

Reply Obj. Private persons cannot effectively induce others to virtue, since private persons can only offer advice and have no coercive power if their advice is rejected, and law should have coercive power in order to induce others effectively to virtue. But the people or a public personage has such coercive power and the right to inflict punishment. And so it belongs only to the people or a public personage to make law.

4. Is promulgation an essential component of law?[4]

I answer that laws are imposed on others as rules or measures. But rules and measures are imposed by being applied to those ruled and measured.

---

[3]ST I–II, Q. 90, A. 3. [4]ST I–II, Q. 90, A. 4.

And so laws, in order to oblige persons, need to be applied to those who are to be ruled by the laws. But the promulgation leading persons to knowledge achieves such application. And so promulgation is necessary for laws to be in force.

And so law is defined by the four characteristics I have mentioned: law is an order of reason for the common good by one who has the care of the community, and is promulgated.

Objection. The natural law most has the nature of law. But the natural law does not need to be promulgated. Therefore, promulgation is not an essential component of law.

Reply Obj. The natural law is promulgated by God when he implants it in the minds of human beings so that they know it by nature.

Kinds

God's reason governs the whole community of the universe. This is the eternal law. Rational creatures share in his providence by the use of reason to provide for themselves, and so they share in the eternal law whereby they have a natural inclination toward their requisite end and proper activity. This participation in the eternal law is the natural law. Human reason needs to go beyond the general principles of the natural law to particular regulations, and such regulations devised by reason are human laws. Revealed divine law, the Old Law before Christ and the New Law after Christ, were necessary to direct human life. Sudden movements of sense appetites to act outside the control of, or contrary to, reason, which we call concupiscence, are "law" only inasmuch as they are just punishment of Adam's sin. See Glossary, s.v. Concupiscence, Law.

1. Is there an eternal law?[5]

I answer that law is simply a dictate of practical reason by a ruler who governs a perfect community. But supposing that God's providence rules the world, his reason evidently governs the entire community of the universe. And so the plan of governance of the world existing in God as ruler of the universe has the nature of law. And since God's reason conceives eternally, not temporally, such law is eternal.

2. Is there a natural law in us?[6]

I answer that law, since it is a rule or measure, can belong to things in two ways: in one way to those who rule and measure; in a second way to

---

[5]ST I–II, Q. 91, A. 1. [6]ST I–II, Q. 91, A. 2.

those ruled and measured, since things are ruled and measured insofar as they partake of the rule or measure. But the eternal law rules and measures everything subject to God's providence. And so everything shares in some way in the eternal law, namely, insofar as all things have inclinations to their own acts and ends from its imprint on them. But rational creatures are subject to God's providence in a more excellent way than other things, since rational creatures also share in God's providence in providing for themselves and others. And so they share in the eternal plan whereby they have their natural inclination to their requisite activity and end. And we call such participation in the eternal law by rational creatures the natural law.

Objection. The freer one is, the less one is subject to law. But human beings are freer than other animals because human beings have free choice. Therefore, since other animals are not subject to a natural law, neither are human beings.

Reply Obj. Even irrational animals, like rational creatures, share in the eternal law in their own way. But because rational creatures share in the eternal law by using their intellect and reason, their participation in the eternal law is law in the strict sense, since law belongs to reason. And irrational creatures do not share in the eternal law by the use of reason. And so we can call the latter participation law only by analogy.

3. Are there human laws?[7]

I answer that law is a dictate of practical reason. But there are similar processes of theoretical and practical reason, since both proceed from principles to conclusions. Therefore, we advance in theoretical reason from indemonstrable first principles, naturally known, to the conclusions of different sciences, conclusions discovered by exercising reason, not implanted in us by nature. Just so, human reason needs to advance from the precepts of the natural law, as general and indemonstrable first principles, to matters to be more particularly regulated. And such regulations devised by human reason are human laws, provided that the other conditions belonging to the nature of law are observed.

Objection. The natural law shares in the eternal law. But the eternal law renders all things most orderly. Therefore, the natural law suffices for ordering human affairs. Therefore, there is no need for human laws.

Reply Obj. Human reason cannot partake of the complete dictates of God's reason but partakes of them in human reason's own way and incompletely. And so regarding theoretical reason, we by our natural participation

---

[7]ST I–II, Q. 91, A. 3.

in God's wisdom know general principles but do not specifically know every truth, as God's wisdom does. Just so regarding practical reason, human beings by nature partake of the eternal law as to general principles but not as to particular specifications of particular matters, although such specifications belong to the eternal law. And so human reason needs to proceed further to determine the particular prescriptions of human law.

4. Did human beings need a divine law?[8]

I answer that there are four reasons why direction of human life needs to have divine law in addition to the natural law and human laws.

First, law directs our acts in relation to our ultimate end. And if human beings were ordered only to an end that did not surpass the proportion of their natural ability, they would not, regarding reason, need to have any direction superior to the natural law and human laws derived from the natural law. But human beings are ordered to eternal blessedness, which surpasses their proportional natural human capacity. Therefore, God needed to lay down a law superior to the natural law and human laws in order to direct human beings to this end.

Second, because of the uncertainty of human judgment, especially regarding contingent and particular matters, different persons may judge differently about various human actions, and so even different and contrary laws result. Therefore, in order that human beings can know beyond doubt what they should or should not do, a divinely revealed law, regarding which error is impossible, was needed to direct human beings in their actions.

Third, human beings can make law regarding things they can judge, and they can judge only sensibly perceptible external acts, not hidden internal movements. But human beings need to live righteously regarding both kinds of acts in order to attain complete virtue. And so human laws could not prohibit or adequately order internal acts, and divine law needed to supplement human laws.

Fourth, human laws cannot punish or prohibit all evil deeds, since, in seeking to eliminate all evils, one would thereby also take away many goods and not benefit the common good necessary for human companionship. Therefore, there needed to be a divine law forbidding all sins in order that every evil be forbidden and punished.

5. Is there only one divine law?[9]

I answer that division causes number, and we distinguish things in two ways: in one way as things altogether specifically different (e.g., horses

---

[8]ST I–II, Q. 91, A. 4. [9]ST I–II, Q. 91, A. 5.

and oxen); in a second way as complete and incomplete in the same species (e. g., adults and children). And it is in the latter way that we distinguish divine law into the Old and the New Law. And so the condition of the Old Law is comparable to that of a child subject to a tutor, and the condition of the New Law comparable to an adult no longer subject to a tutor.

We note the perfection and imperfection of the two Laws in three regards. First, it belongs to any law to be directed to the common good as its end. The common good may be a sensibly perceptible and earthly good, and the Old Law was directly ordered to such a common good. And so the people were invited at the very institution of the Old Law to occupy the earthly kingdom of the Canaanites (Ex. 3:8–17). Or the common good may be an intelligible and heavenly good, and the New Law orders human beings to such a common good. And so Christ at the very outset of his preaching invited human beings to the kingdom of heaven (Mt. 4:17).

Second, it belongs to the divine law to direct human acts regarding the order of righteousness, and the New Law surpasses the Old Law in regard to righteousness by ordering internal spiritual acts.

Third, it belongs to the divine law to induce human beings to observe the commandments. The Old Law accomplished this by fear of punishments, but the New Law accomplishes this by love, which the grace of Christ pours into our hearts.

6. Is there a law of concupiscence?[10]

I answer that law belongs essentially to those who rule and measure, and belongs by participation to those ruled and measured. And so every inducement or order in things subject to law is law by participation. But there are two ways in which lawmakers can induce their subjects to things. In one way, lawmakers directly induce their subjects to things, and sometimes different subjects to different actions. In this regard, we can distinguish different kinds of laws (e.g., military law and commercial law). In a second way, lawmakers indirectly induce their subjects to things, namely, when lawmakers deprive subjects of an office and thereby transfer them to another position in society and to another kind of law. For example, a soldier discharged from the army will be transferred to the law governing farmers or merchants.

Therefore, God, the lawmaker, subjects different creatures to different inducements, so that what is in one way law for one kind of creature is in another way contrary to the law for another kind of creature. For example,

---

[10]ST I–II, Q. 91, A. 6.

ferocity is in one way the law for dogs and in another way contrary to the law for sheep. Therefore, it is the law for human beings, which is allotted by God's order according to their condition, that they act according to reason. And this law was so effective in our first condition that nothing outside reason or contrary to reason could come upon Adam surreptitiously. But when Adam withdrew from God, he fell subject to the impulses of his sense appetites. And this happens in particular to each human being the more the individual has withdrawn from reason, so that the individual in a way resembles beasts, who are borne along by the impulses of their sense appetites.

Therefore, in other animals, the very inclinations of sense appetites, inclinations called concupiscence, directly have the nature of law in an absolute sense, although in the analogous way we can speak of law in such things. And in human beings, such inclinations of sense appetites do not have the nature of law. Rather, they are deviations from the law of reason. But since divine justice stripped human beings of original justice and the full force of reason, the impulses of sense appetites that drive human beings have the nature of law inasmuch as such impulses are a punishment and the result of divine law depriving them of their dignity.

Effects

The proper effect of law is to make those subject to the law good. Only laws striving for the common good ruled by divine justice are unqualifiedly good.

1. Does law make human beings good?[11]

I answer that law is simply a ruler's dictate of reason whereby he governs his subjects, and the virtue of every subject is to be duly subject to the ruler. Just so, the virtue of the irascible and concupiscible powers consists of being duly obedient to reason. And the virtue of every subject consists of being duly subject to the ruler in this way, and every law is ordered to being obeyed by those subject to it. And so it belongs to law to induce subjects to their requisite virtue. Therefore, since virtue makes its possessors good, the proper effect of law is to make its subjects good, either absolutely or in some respect. If the aim of the lawmaker strives for real good, the common good regulated by divine justice, law makes human beings absolutely good. But if the aim of lawmakers is set upon what is not absolutely good but what is useful or desirable for themselves or contrary

[11] ST I–II, Q. 92, A. 1.

to divine justice, then law makes human beings relatively good, namely, in relation to such a regime. So also does good belong to things in themselves evil. For example, we speak of good robbers, since they act suitably to accomplish their end.

Objection 1. Law is ordered to the common good. But some ill disposed regarding their own good are well disposed regarding what belongs to the common good. Therefore, it does not belong to law to make human beings good.

Reply Obj. 1. Since every human being is part of a political community, no human being can be good unless rightly related to the common good. Nor can a whole be rightly constituted except by parts rightly related to it. And so the common good of a political community can be rightly disposed only if its citizens, at least those to whom its ruling belongs, are virtuous. But it suffices as regards the good of the community that other citizens be virtuous enough to obey the commands of the law. And so the virtue of a ruler and that of a good man are the same, but the virtue of an ordinary citizen and that of a good man are not.

Obj. 2. Some laws are tyrannical. But a tyrant strives for his own good, not the good of his subjects. Therefore, it does not belong to law to make human beings good.

Reply Obj. 2. A tyrannical law, since it is not in accord with reason, is not a law, absolutely speaking. Rather, it is a perversion of law. And yet such a law strives to make citizens good inasmuch as it partakes of the nature of law. For it partakes of the nature of law only insofar as it is a dictate for his subjects and strives to make them duly obedient, that is, to make them good in relation to such a regime, not absolutely good.

The Eternal Law

The plan of divine wisdom causes the movement of everything to its requisite end and so has the character of law. Every rational creature knows the plan of divine wisdom in its effects, at least regarding the general principles of the natural law. All human laws, as plans of government subordinate to the supreme ruler and partaking of right reason, are derived from the eternal law. Human laws govern only human beings subject to the laws, but the movements and activities of everything are subject to the eternal law. Human beings partake of the eternal law in a conscious way, since they know the eternal law in some regard and have an inclination from nature toward things consonant with the eternal law. The virtuous are completely subject to the eternal law, and the wicked suffer the punishment that the eternal law dictates for those who fail to observe it.

1. Is the eternal law a supreme plan in God?[12]

I answer that as there preexists in every craftsman a plan for the things he produces by his skill, so there needs to exist in every ruler an orderly plan for the things his subjects should do. And as the plan for the artifacts of a craft is the craft or ideal type of the artifacts, so the plan of a ruler for his subjects' actions has the nature of law, provided that the other conditions regarding the nature of law are observed. But God in his wisdom creates all things and is related to them like a craftsman to the products of his craft. God also governs all the actions and movements in particular kinds of creatures. And thus, as the plan of divine wisdom has the nature of a craft or type or idea because all things are created through it, so the plan of divine wisdom causing the movement of all things to their requisite ends has the nature of law. And so eternal law is simply the plan of divine wisdom that directs all the actions and movements of created things.

2. Do all know the eternal law?[13]

I answer that we can know things in two ways: in themselves and in their effects, which have likenesses of the things. For example, those not looking at the sun know it in the effects of its rays. Therefore, no one except the blessed, who see God by his essence, can know the eternal law as it is in itself. But every rational creature knows it in some of its radiating effects, whether greater or lesser effects. Every knowledge of truth is a radiation and participation of eternal law, which is incommunicable truth. For everyone knows truth to some extent, at least regarding the general principles of the natural law. But some share more or less in knowing truth regarding other things. And so they also know more or less of the eternal law.

3. Is every law derived from the eternal law?[14]

I answer that law signifies a plan directing acts to ends. But in the case of all interrelated causes, the power of a secondary cause needs to be derived from the power of a primary cause, since a secondary cause causes only insofar as the primary cause moves the secondary cause. And so we perceive the same regarding all who govern, that the chief ruler communicates his plan of government to secondary administrators. For example, a king by issuing commands communicates his plan for the affairs of a political community to subordinate administrators. And also in the case of things requiring the skill of craftsmen, a master builder communicates his plan for the activities requiring those skills to subordinate craftsmen, who

---

[12]ST I–II, Q. 93, A. 1. [13]ST I–II, Q. 93, A. 2. [14]ST I–II, Q. 93, A. 3.

carry out the manual work involved. Therefore, since the eternal law is the plan of government in the supreme ruler, all plans of government in subordinate rulers need to be derived from the eternal law. But such plans of subordinate government consist of all the other laws besides the eternal law. And so all laws are derived from the eternal law insofar as they partake of right reason.

Objection. Nothing evil can come from the eternal law. But some laws are evil. Therefore, not every law comes from the eternal law.

Reply Obj. Human law has the nature of law insofar as it is in accord with right reason, and then it is derived from eternal law. And human law is evil insofar as it withdraws from reason, and then it has the nature of brute force rather than of law. But insofar as some likeness of law is preserved in an evil law because one empowered to make law ordered it, it is also in this respect derived from the eternal law.

4. Are necessary and eternal things subject to the eternal law?[15]

I answer that the eternal law is the plan of divine governance. Therefore, everything subject to divine governance is also subject to the eternal law, and things not subject to eternal governance are not subject to the eternal law. And we can consider the distinction between the two kinds of things in regard to matters that concern us. For example, things that human beings can do are subject to human governance, but things that belong to the nature of human beings (e.g., having souls or hands or feet) are not subject to human governance. Therefore, everything belonging to created things, whether contingent or necessary, belongs to the eternal law, but things belonging to the divine nature or essence are in reality the eternal law itself and not subject to the eternal law.

5. Are contingent natural things subject to the eternal law?[16]

I answer that human law and the eternal law, the law of God, differ. For human law governs only rational creatures subject to human beings. This is because law directs actions proper to those subject to governance. And so, strictly speaking, no one imposes a law on one's own actions. But all the things done regarding the use of irrational things subject to human beings are done by the actions of the human beings causing the things done. For irrational creatures so used are acted upon by other things and do not act upon themselves. And so human beings cannot impose law on irrational things, however much the latter things are subject to human beings. But human beings can impose law on rational beings subject to

[15]ST I–II, Q. 93, A. 4. [16]ST I–II, Q. 93, A. 5.

them, insofar as human beings by precepts or declarations communicate to their subjects rules to govern the subjects' actions.

And as human beings by their declarations imprint an inner source of action on other human beings subject to them, so also God imprints on all the things of nature the sources of their activities. And so God in this respect commands the whole of nature. And all movements and actions of the whole of nature in this respect are also subject to the eternal law. And so irrational creatures, as directed by divine providence, not by understanding God's commands, are subject to the eternal law in another way than rational creatures are.

Objection. The eternal law is most efficacious. But deficiencies occur in contingent natural things. Therefore, such things are not subject to the eternal law.

Reply Obj. Deficiencies occurring in natural things, although outside the order of particular causes, are not outside the order of universal causes, and especially of the first cause, God, whose providence nothing can escape. And because the eternal law is the plan of divine providence, deficiencies of natural things are subject to the eternal law.

6. Are all human affairs subject to the eternal law?[17]

I answer that things are subject to the eternal law in two ways: as they partake of the eternal law in a conscious way, and as they partake of the eternal law as causes act on them. Irrational creatures are subject to the eternal law in the second way. But because rational natures, along with what they have in common with all creatures, have something proper to them as rational, they are subject to the eternal law in both ways. This is because they know the eternal law in some regard, and each rational creature has an inclination from nature toward things consonant with the eternal law.

Both ways are incomplete and in some way destroyed in the wicked, in whom the natural inclination to virtue is perverted by vicious habits, and the natural knowledge of goodness is darkened by emotions and sinful habits. And both ways are more complete in the virtuous, since knowledge of faith and of wisdom is added to their natural knowledge of goodness, and the inner causal activity of grace and virtue is added to their natural inclination toward goodness.

Therefore, the virtuous are completely subject to the eternal law, since they always act in accord with it. And the wicked are incompletely subject

---

[17]ST I–II, Q. 93, A. 6.

to the eternal law regarding their own actions, since they incompletely recognize and incline to goodness. But what their actions lack is proportionately supplemented by what they undergo, namely, as they suffer what the eternal law dictates for them insofar as they fail to do what befits the eternal law.

The Natural Law

Reason habitually possesses knowledge of the first principles of the natural law. The first principle of the natural law is that one should seek what is good for human beings and avoid what is evil for them. All precepts of the natural law are based on that principle. Reason by nature understands that everything for which human beings have a natural inclination is good for human beings and to be actively sought, and that everything contrary to a natural inclination is evil for them and to be avoided. First, human beings as substances have a natural inclination to preserve their lives, and so they should use means to do so. Second, human beings as animals have a natural inclination to mate and raise children, and so they should do so. Third, human beings as human beings have natural inclinations to seek truth and live cooperatively in society, and so they should do so. Note that these natural inclinations are the inclinations of human, *that is,* rational, *nature, and so the inclinations are only natural insofar as they are in accord with reason.*

All virtuous acts as such belong to the natural law, since human beings have a natural inclination to act according to reason, that is, virtuously. But some particular virtuous acts (e.g., particular acts of modesty) do not belong to the natural law, since human beings do many things virtuously to which nature does not at first incline them.

Truth in practical matters is the same for all human beings only regarding general principles, not regarding particular conclusions from the principles (e.g., one should return goods to their owners, but there are exceptions). Nor do all know particular conclusions (e.g., emotions or bad habits or evil dispositions may pervert the reason of some). The natural law may vary insofar as divine law or human laws add beneficial things to it. Nothing can be subtracted from the first principles of the natural law, and so the natural law is in this respect altogether immutable. The natural law may vary regarding particular conclusions in relatively few cases (e.g., contrary to the general principle that one should return goods to their owners, one should not return firearms to a homicidal maniac). The general principles of the natural law cannot be excised from the human conscience, although emotions may prevent reason from applying the principles to particular actions. See Glossary, s.v. Conscience. *False opinions or evil customs or bad habits, however, can excise secondary principles.*

1. Is the natural law a habit?[18]

I answer that we can speak of habits in one way in the strict sense and essentially, and then the natural law is not a habit. For the natural law is constituted by reason. But what one does, and the means whereby one does it, are not the same. For example, one makes a fitting speech by means of the habit of grammar. Therefore, since habits are the means whereby one does things, no law can be a habit in the strict sense and essentially.

We can speak of habits in a second way as what we possess by reason of habits. For example, we call faith what we have by reason of the habit of faith. And so, as reason sometimes actually considers precepts of the natural law and sometimes only habitually possesses them, natural law in the latter way is a habit. Just so, the indemonstrable first principles in theoretical matters are principles belonging to the habit of first principles, not the habit itself.

2. Does the natural law include several precepts or only one?[19]

I answer that the precepts of the natural law are related to practical reason as the first principles of scientific demonstrations are related to theoretical reason. For both the precepts of the natural law and the first principles of scientific demonstrations are self-evident propositions. And things can be self-evident in two ways: in one way as such; in a second way in relation to ourselves.

Propositions as such are self-evident when their predicates belong to the nature of their subjects, although such propositions may not be self-evident to those who do not know the definition of the subjects. For example, the proposition *Human beings are rational* is by its nature self-evident, since to speak of something human is to speak of something rational, although the proposition is not self-evident to one who does not know what a human being is. And so there are axioms or universally self-evident propositions, and propositions whose terms all persons know (e.g., *Every whole is greater than one of its parts*) are such. But some propositions are self-evident only to the wise, who understand what the terms signify. For example, for those who understand that angels are not material substances, it is self-evident that angels are not circumscriptively in a place, something not evident to the uneducated, who do not understand the nature of angels.

There is a priority regarding things that fall within the understanding of all persons. For what falls first within our understanding is being, the

---

[18]ST I–II, Q. 94, A. 1. [19]ST I–II, Q. 94, A. 2.

understanding of which is included in everything one understands. And so the first indemonstrable principle is that one cannot at the same time affirm and deny the same thing. And this principle is based on the nature of being and nonbeing, and all other principles are based on it.

And as being is the first thing that without qualification falls within understanding, so good is the first thing that falls within the understanding of practical reason. But practical reason is ordered to action, since every efficient cause acts for the sake of an end, which has the nature of good. And so the first principle in practical reason is based on the nature of good, namely, that good is what all things seek. Therefore, the first precept of the natural law is that we should do and seek good, and shun evil. And all the other precepts of the natural law are based on that precept, namely, that all the things that practical reason by nature understands to be human goods or evils belong to precepts of the natural law as things to be done or shunned.

Since good has the nature of end, and evil the nature of the contrary, reason by nature understands to be good all the things for which human beings have a natural inclination, and so to be things to be actively sought, and understands contrary things to be evil and to be shunned. Therefore, the order of our natural inclinations orders the precepts of the natural law.

First, for example, human beings have an inclination for good by the nature they share with all substances, namely, as every substance by nature seeks to preserve itself. And regarding this inclination, means that preserve our human life and prevent the contrary belong to the natural law.

Second, human beings have more particular inclinations by the nature they share with other animals. And so things that nature has taught all animals, such as the sexual union of male and female, the upbringing of children, and the like, belong to the natural law.

Third, human beings have inclinations for good by their rational nature, which is proper to them. For example, human beings by nature have inclinations to know truths about God and to live in society with other human beings. And so things that relate to such inclinations belong to the natural law (e.g., that human beings shun ignorance, that they not offend those with whom they ought to live sociably, and the like).

3. Do all virtuous acts belong to the natural law?[20]

I answer that if we are speaking about virtuous acts as virtuous, then all virtuous acts belong to the natural law, since everything to which human

---

[20]ST I–II, Q. 94, A. 3.

beings are inclined by their nature belongs to the natural law. But everything is by its nature inclined to the activity that its form renders fitting. For example, fire is inclined to heat things. And so, since the rational soul is the specific form of human beings, everyone has an inclination from one's nature to act in accord with reason. And this is to act virtuously. And so in this regard, all virtuous acts belong to the natural law, since one's own reason by nature dictates that one act virtuously.

But if we should be speaking about virtuous acts as such and such, namely, as in their own species, then not all virtuous acts belong to the natural law. For we do many things virtuously to which nature does not at first incline us, but which human beings by the inquiry of reason have discovered to be useful for living righteously.

Objection. Everyone agrees about things that are in accord with nature. But not everyone agrees about virtuous acts, for things that are virtuous for some are vicious for others. Therefore, not all virtuous acts belong to the natural law.

Reply Obj. The argument of this objection is valid regarding virtuous acts as such and such. For then, because of the different conditions of human beings, some acts may be virtuous for some persons, as proportionate and suitable for them, which are nonetheless vicious for other persons, as disproportionate for them.

4. Is the natural law the same for all human beings?[21]

I answer that things to which nature inclines human beings belong to the natural law, and one of the things proper to human beings is that their nature inclines them to act in accord with reason. And it belongs to reason to advance from the general to the particular. Theoretical reason does so in one way, and practical reason in another way. Since theoretical reason is most concerned about necessary things, which cannot be otherwise, its particular conclusions, like its general principles, are true without exception. But practical reason is concerned about contingent things, which include human actions. And so the more reason goes from the general to the particular, the more exceptions there are, although there is some necessity in the general principles. Therefore, truth in theoretical matters, both first principles and conclusions, is the same for all human beings, although some know only the truth of the principles, which are universal propositions, and not the truth of the conclusions. But truth in practical matters, or practical rectitude, is the same for all human beings only regarding the general principles, not regarding the particular conclusions. And not all of

---

[21]ST I–II, Q. 94, A. 4.

those with practical rectitude regarding particulars know the truth in equal measure.

Therefore, the truth or rectitude regarding the general principles of both theoretical and practical reason is the same for all persons and known in equal measure by all of them. And the truth regarding the particular conclusions of theoretical reason is the same for all persons, but some know such truth less than others. For example, it is true for all persons that triangles have three angles equal to two right angles, although not everybody knows this.

But the truth or rectitude regarding particular conclusions of practical reason is neither the same for all persons nor known in equal measure even by those for whom it is the same. For example, it is correct and true for all persons that they should act in accord with reason. And it follows as a particular conclusion from this principle that those holding goods in trust should return the goods to the goods' owners. And this is true for the most part, but it might in particular cases be injurious, and so contrary to reason, to return the goods (e.g., if the owner should be seeking to attack one's country). And the more the particular conclusion goes into particulars, the more exceptions there are (e.g., if one should declare that entrusted goods should be returned to their owners with such and such safeguards or in such and such ways). For the more particular conditions are added to the particular conclusion, the more ways there may be exceptions, so that the conclusion about returning or not returning entrusted goods is erroneous.

Therefore, we should say that the natural law regarding general first principles is the same for all persons both as to the principles' rectitude and as to knowledge of them. And the natural law regarding particulars, which are conclusions, as it were, from the general principles, is for the most part the same for all persons both as to its rectitude and as to knowledge of it. But the natural law can be wanting in rather few cases both as to its rectitude and as to knowledge of it. As to rectitude, the natural law can be wanting because of particular obstacles. And as to knowledge of the natural law, the law can be wanting because emotions or evil habituation or evil natural disposition has perverted the reason of some. For example, the Germans of old did not consider robbery wicked,[22] although robbery is expressly contrary to the natural law.

5. Can the natural law vary?[23]

I answer that we can understand the mutability of the natural law in one way by the addition of things to it. Then nothing prevents the natural law

---

[22]Cf. Julius Caesar, *Gallic Wars* VI, 23.

[23]ST I–II, Q. 94, A. 5.

from changing by things being added to it, since both divine law and human laws add to natural law many things beneficial to human life.

We can understand the mutability of the natural law in a second way by the subtraction of things from it, namely, that things previously subject to the law cease to be so. Then the natural law is altogether immutable as to its first principles. And as to secondary precepts, certain proper proximate conclusions, as it were, from the first principles, the natural law is not so changed that what it prescribes is not for the most part completely correct. But it can be changed regarding particulars and in rather few cases, due to special causes that prevent observance of such precepts.

Objection 1. The killing of innocent human beings, theft, and adultery are contrary to the natural law. But God altered these precepts. For example, God on one occasion commanded Abraham to slay his innocent son, as Gen. 22:2 relates. And God on another occasion commanded the Jews to steal vessels the Egyptians had lent them, as Ex. 12:35–36 relates. And God on another occasion commanded Hosea to take a fornicating wife, as Hos. 1:2 relates. Therefore, the natural law can vary.

Reply Obj. 1. All human beings, both the innocent and the guilty, die when natural death comes. But God's power inflicts natural death because of original sin. And so, at the command of God, death can without any injustice be inflicted on any human being, whether innocent or guilty.

Likewise, adultery is sexual intercourse with another man's wife, whom the law laid down by God has allotted him. And so there is no adultery or fornication in having intercourse with any woman at the command of God.

And the argument is the same regarding theft, which consists of taking another's property. One does not take without the consent of the owner (i.e., steal) anything that one takes at the command of God, who is the owner of the property.

Nor is it only regarding human affairs that everything God commands is owed to him. Rather, regarding things of nature, everything God does is also in one respect natural.

Obj. 2. Common possession of all property and like freedom for all persons belong to the natural law. But human laws have altered these precepts. Therefore, the natural law can vary.

Reply Obj. 2. We speak of things belonging to the natural law in one way because nature inclines us to them. For example, one should not cause injury to another.

We can speak of things belonging to the natural law in a second way because nature did not introduce the contrary. For example, we could say that it belongs to the natural law that human beings are naked, since nature did not endow them with clothes, which human skills created. It is in this way that we say that common possession of all property and like freedom for all persons belong to the natural law, namely, that the reason of human beings, not nature, introduced private property and compulsory servitude. And so the natural law in this respect varies only by way of addition.

6. Can the natural law be excised from the hearts of human beings?[24]

I answer that the general principles of the natural law cannot be excised from the hearts of human beings. But the natural law is wiped out regarding particular actions insofar as desires or other emotions prevent reason from applying the general principles to particular actions.

And the natural law can be excised from the hearts of human beings regarding secondary precepts, either because of wicked opinions or evil customs or corrupt habits. For example, some did not think robbery a sin or even sins against nature to be sinful.

Human Laws

Human beings need instruction and training to arrive at complete virtue. Force and fear are necessary to restrain the wicked, at least so that they leave others in peace. And so human laws are necessary in order that human beings may live in peace and attain virtue. The laws impose obligation insofar as they are just, and things are just insofar as they are in accord with reason, whose primary rule is the natural law. And so every human law has the character of law insofar as it is from the natural law. Some human laws are conclusions from general precepts of the natural law (e.g., laws prohibiting homicide, which are conclusions from the general principle that one should do no evil to others). Other human laws are further specifications of general principles (e.g., laws punishing criminals in specific ways, which are further specifications from the general principle that criminals should be punished).

Human laws can be distinguished by the way in which they are derived from the natural law: the common laws of peoples (the jus gentium*) as conclusions, and the laws of particular commonwealths (e.g., tax laws) as specifications. Second, human laws can be distinguished by the persons affected (e.g., military law for military personnel). Third, human laws can be distinguished by the type of government of the community (e.g., monarchy, aristocracy, democracy). Fourth, human laws can be distinguished by their subject matter (e.g.,*

---

[24]ST I–II, Q. 94, A. 6.

property law). Some human laws are framed exclusively in general terms (e.g., laws prohibiting homicide), some are general but concern particular persons (e.g., laws defining the powers of particular office-holders), and some apply general laws to particular cases (administrative and judicial decisions).

Human laws are established for the collectivity of human beings, most of whom have imperfect virtue. And so human laws prohibit only the most serious vices inflicting harm on others, such as laws prohibiting homicide and theft. Although there are no virtuous actions that human laws could not command, the laws command only things that can be ordered to the common good.

Just human laws oblige in conscience. Human laws are just if they are ordered to the common good, if lawmakers are authorized to make laws, and if the laws impose proportionally equal burdens on citizens. Conversely, human laws are unjust regarding the human good if they are established to benefit the lawmakers rather than the community, if they exceed the authority of the lawmakers, or if they impose proportionally unequal burdens on citizens. Such laws of themselves do not oblige in conscience but may do so if obedience is necessary to avoid scandal or civil unrest. One should never obey unjust human laws contrary to the divine good (e.g., laws commanding worship of idols).

Only those subject to the authority of the lawmakers are subject to the laws (e.g., only those subject to U.S. jurisdiction are subject to U.S. laws). The authority of a higher power (e.g., the U.S. president) overrides the authority of a lower power (e.g., a U.S. military commander). Rulers with supreme authority are exempt from the coercive power of human laws but should of their own free will subject themselves to the laws. One should not obey a law in particular cases if observance would result in a clear and imminent danger to the community or a component of the common good (e.g., a driver may, with due caution, exceed the legal speed limit in order to bring a severely injured person to a hospital).

Human laws may need to be revised to make them more perfect. And human laws may need to be revised to suit the altered conditions of human beings (e.g., new laws may be needed to prevent terrorist attacks). But the binding force of law is diminished whenever laws are revised, since custom powerfully influences legal observance. In the case of self-governing peoples, repeated external acts contrary to written laws obtain the force of law, since the acts indicate the mind and will of the people. (In the case of peoples that do not govern themselves, rulers' tolerance of such acts indicates the rulers' mind and will.) Rulers should dispense subjects from observing human laws when persons or situations warrant it. And rulers may at times dispense subjects from secondary precepts of the natural law (e.g., the obligation of debtors to repay creditors) but cannot dispense subjects from the general precepts of the natural law or from precepts of divine law.

1. Was it beneficial that human beings establish laws?[25]

I answer that human beings by nature have a capacity for virtue, but they need to arrive at the perfection of virtue by some training. Just so, industriousness helps them regarding their necessities (e.g., food and clothing). And nature gives them sources to provide these necessities, namely, reason and hands, not the full complement of the necessities that nature gives other animals, for whom nature has sufficiently provided covering and food.

But human beings are not readily self-sufficient regarding this training, since the perfection of virtue consists chiefly of human beings' restraint from excessive pleasures, toward which they are most prone. This is especially true of youths, for whom training is more efficacious. And so human beings receive such training, whereby they arrive at virtue, from others. And regarding youths prone to virtuous acts by good natural disposition or habituation, paternal training, which consists of admonitions, suffices.

But some people are wicked and prone to vices and cannot be easily persuaded by words. Therefore, force and fear were needed to restrain them from evil. And so, at least desisting from evil deeds, they would leave others in peace and be themselves at length brought to such habituation to do voluntarily what they hitherto did out of fear and so become virtuous. But such training, which compels by fear of punishment, is the training administered by laws. And so it was necessary to establish laws in order that human beings live in peace and have virtue. For human beings perfect in virtue are the best of animals, and human beings cut off from law and justice are the worst of animals, since human beings, unlike other animals, have the tools of reason to satisfy their disordered desires and beastly rages.

2. Is every human law derived from the natural law?[26]

I answer that laws have binding force insofar as they have justice, and things regarding human affairs are just because they are right according to the rule of reason. But the primary rule of reason is the natural law. And so every human law has as much of the nature of law as it is derived from the natural law, and a human law that diverges in any way from the natural law will be a perversion of law and no longer a law.

We can derive things from the natural law in one way as conclusions from its first principles, like the way in which we draw conclusions from first principles in theoretical sciences. We can derive things from the natural law in a second way as specifications of certain general principles, just

---

[25]ST I–II, Q. 95, A. 1. [26]ST I–II, Q. 95, A. 2.

as craftsmen in the course of exercising their skill adapt general forms to specific things. For example, a builder needs to adapt the general form of a house to this or that shape of a house.

Therefore, some things are derived from general principles of the natural law as conclusions. For example, one can derive the prohibition against homicide from the general principle that one should do no evil to anyone. And some things are derived from general principles of the natural law as specifications. For example, the natural law orders that criminals should be punished, but that criminals be punished in this or that way is a specification of the natural law.

Therefore, human laws are derived from the natural law in both ways. Things derived from the natural law in the first way are not only contained in human laws as established by those laws, but they also have part of their binding force from the natural law. But things derived from the natural law in the second way have all of their binding force from human law.

3. Do we appropriately distinguish different kinds of human laws?[27]

I answer that we can intrinsically distinguish things by what belongs to their nature. For example, the nature of animals includes a soul that is rational or irrational. And so we properly and intrinsically distinguish animals by whether they are rational or irrational, and not by whether they are black or white, which are characteristics altogether outside the nature of animals.

And many characteristics belong to the nature of human laws, and we can properly and intrinsically distinguish human laws by any of those things. For example, it first of all belongs to the nature of human laws that they should be derived from the natural law. And we in this respect divide positive laws into the common law of peoples and the laws of particular commonwealths by the two ways in which things may be derived from the natural law. For precepts derived from the natural law as conclusions from its general principles belong to the common law of peoples (e.g., just buying and selling, and the like, without which human beings cannot live sociably with one another). And living sociably with others belongs to the natural law, since human beings are by nature social animals. But precepts derived from the natural law by way of particular specifications belong to the laws of particular commonwealths, whereby each commonwealth specifies things suitable for it.

---

[27]ST I–II, Q. 95, A. 4.

Second, it belongs to the nature of human laws that they be ordered to the common good of a political community. And we can in this respect distinguish human laws by the different kinds of persons who perform particular tasks for the common good (e.g., priests, who pray to God for the people; rulers, who govern the people; soldiers, who fight for the safety of the people). And so special laws are adapted for such persons.

Third, it belongs to the nature of human laws that they be established by those who govern a political community. In this respect, we appropriately distinguish the human laws of monarchies (rule by one person), aristocracies (rule by the best persons), oligarchies (rule by a few rich and powerful persons), and democracies (rule by the people). There is also a form of government that is a mixture of these forms, and this mixed form of government is the best. The laws of such regimes are prescribed by elders and the people. (Tyranny is another, altogether corrupt form of government, and the laws of tyrannical regimes are not laws.)

Fourth, it belongs to the nature of human laws that they direct human actions, and we in this respect distinguish laws by their different subject matter.

4. Should human laws be framed in particular rather than general terms?[28]

I answer that every means needs to be proportioned to the end. But the end of law is the common good, since laws should be framed for the common benefit of citizens, not for any private benefit. And so human laws need to be proportioned to the common good. But the common good consists of many things. And so laws need to concern many things, both persons, matters, and times. For the political community consists of many persons, and its good is procured by many actions. Nor is it instituted to endure only for a short time but to last for all time through successive generations of citizens.

Objection. Things of the legal order consist of everything laws decree about individual matters, and of judicial decisions, which also concern particular matters, since judges hand down decisions on particular cases. Therefore, laws are framed both in general and in particular terms.

Reply Obj. There are three parts of legal justice (i.e., positive law). There are prescriptions framed only in general terms. And regarding such laws, legal justice does not originally differentiate in particulars but does once established. For example, captives are ransomed at a fixed price.

[28]ST I–II, Q. 96, A. 1.

And there are laws that are general in one respect and particular in another. We call such laws privileges, that is, private laws, since they concern particular persons, although the power of these laws extends to many matters.

And some things are legal because general laws are applied to particular cases, not because the applications are laws. For example, judges hand down decisions that we consider legally binding.

5. Does it belong to human law to prohibit all vices?[29]

I answer that laws are established as certain rules and measures of human action. But measures should be homogeneous with what they measure, since different kinds of things are measured by different kinds of measures. And so laws need to be imposed on human beings according to their condition, since laws ought to be possible regarding both nature and a country's customs. And the power or ability to act results from internal habituation or disposition, since the virtuous and those without virtuous habits do not have the same power to act. Just so, children and adults do not have the same power to act, and so the law is not the same for children and adults. For example, many things are permitted to children that laws prohibit to adults, or even that public opinion censures. Similarly, many things are tolerated in persons of imperfect virtue that would not be tolerated in virtuous persons.

And human law is established for the collectivity of human beings, most of whom have imperfect virtue. And so human law does not prohibit every kind of vice, from which the virtuous abstain. Rather, human law prohibits only the more serious kinds of vice, from which most persons can abstain, and especially those vices that inflict harm on others, without the prohibition of which human society could not be preserved. For example, human laws prohibit homicide, theft, and the like.

Objection. Human law is derived from natural law. But all vices are contrary to the natural law. Therefore, human law ought to prohibit all vices.

Reply Obj. The natural law is our participation in the eternal law, but human law falls short of the eternal law. For laws framed for the governance of political communities permit and leave unpunished many things that God's providence punishes. And so human laws cannot prohibit everything that the natural law prohibits.

---

[29]ST I–II, Q. 96, A. 2.

6. Do human laws command every virtuous action?[30]

I answer that we distinguish specific virtues by their objects. But we can relate all the objects of virtues either to the private good of a person or to the common good of the people. For example, one can perform courageous acts either to uphold the rights of one's friends or to preserve the community. But laws are ordered to the common good. And so there are no virtues regarding the actions of which laws could not command. But laws do not command regarding every action of every virtue. Rather, they only command things that can be ordered to the common good, whether immediately, as when things are done directly for that good, or mediately, as when lawmakers order things belonging to good training, which trains citizens to preserve the common good of justice and peace.

7. Does human law impose obligation on human beings in the court of conscience?[31]

I answer that human laws are either just or unjust, and just laws have obligatory force in the court of conscience from the eternal law, from which they are derived. Laws are just from three perspectives: (1) from their end, namely when they are ordered to the common good; (2) from their authority, namely, when the laws enacted do not surpass the power of the lawmakers; (3) from their form, namely, when they impose proportionally equal burdens on citizens for the common good.

And laws are unjust in one way by being contrary to the human good in the foregoing respects. Laws may be unjust regarding their end, as when authorities impose burdensome laws on citizens to satisfy the authorities' covetousness or vainglory rather than to benefit the community. Or laws may be unjust regarding the authority to make them, as when persons enact laws that exceed the power committed to them. Or laws may be unjust regarding their form, as when burdens, even if ordered to the common good, are disproportionately imposed on the people. Such laws are acts of violence rather than laws, since unjust laws do not seem to be laws. And such laws do not oblige in the court of conscience, except perhaps to avoid scandal or civil unrest, to avoid which human beings ought to yield even their rights.

Laws may be unjust in a second way by being contrary to the divine good (e.g., the laws of tyrants inducing their subjects to worship idols or to do anything else contrary to the divine law). And it is never permissible to obey such laws, since we ought to obey God rather than human beings.

---

[30]ST I–II, Q. 96, A. 3. [31]ST I–II, Q. 96, A. 4.

Objection. Lower powers cannot impose laws on the courts of higher powers. But the power of human beings, which establishes human laws, is inferior to God's power. Therefore, human law cannot impose laws on the court of God, that is, the court of conscience.

Reply Obj. All human power is from God, and so those who resist human power in matters belonging to its scope resist God's order. And so such persons become guilty in respect to their conscience.

8. Is everyone subject to the law?[32]

I answer that two things belong to the nature of law: that law be the rule of human actions, and that law have coercive power. Therefore, human beings can be subject to the law in two ways. They can be subject to law in one way as the ones regulated by the rule. In this regard, all those subject to a power are subject to the laws the power establishes. But one may not be subject to a power because one is absolutely free from subjection to the power. And so those belonging to one political community are not subject to the laws of the ruler of another political community, since such persons are not subject to the ruler's dominion. Or one may not be subject to a power insofar as one is ruled by a higher law. For example, a person subject to a proconsul ought to be ruled by the proconsul's commands except in matters from which the emperor exempted the person. In such matters, a person directed by a higher command is not bound by the command of an inferior power. And so those absolutely subject to the law may not be bound by the law regarding matters about which they are ruled by a higher law.

Regarding the coercive power of law, some are subject to the laws as the coerced to the power coercing. And in this respect, only the wicked, not the virtuous and righteous, are subject to the law. For what is coerced and forced is contrary to the will. But the will of the virtuous is in accord, and the will of the wicked in discord, with the law. And so only the wicked, not the virtuous, are subject to the law in this respect.

Objection. Rulers are exempt from the law. But those exempt from the law are not subject to it. Therefore, not everyone is subject to the law.

Reply Obj. Rulers are exempt from the law regarding its coercive force, since, properly speaking, one is not coerced by oneself, and law has coercive force only by the power of the ruler. Therefore, rulers are exempt from the law because no one can pass sentence on them if they act contrary to the law. But regarding the directive power of law, rulers are subject to the law by their own will. Rulers should follow the law they decree for others. And so, regarding God's judgment, rulers are not exempt from

---

[32]ST I–II, Q. 96, A. 5.

the law regarding its directive power, and they should willingly, not by coercion, fulfill the law.

Rulers are also above the law insofar as they can, if it be expedient, alter the law and dispense from it at certain times and places.

9. Are those subject to the law permitted to act contrary to the letter of the law?[33]

I answer that every law is ordered to the commonweal and has the force and nature of law insofar as it is so ordered. But law has no power to bind morally insofar as it falls short of being ordered to the commonweal. And it often happens that observance of the law, although generally beneficial to the commonweal, is most harmful to it in particular cases. Therefore, since lawmakers cannot envision all particular cases, they direct their aim at the common benefit and establish laws regarding things that generally happen. And so one should not observe a law if a case happens to arise in which observance of the law would be harmful to the commonweal. For example, if a law should decree that the gates of a besieged city remain shut, this is for the most part for the benefit of the commonweal. But if a situation should arise in which enemy soldiers are pursuing some citizens defending the city, it would be most harmful to the community if the gates were not to be opened to admit the defenders. And so, contrary to the letter of the law, the city gates should be opened in such a situation in order to preserve the commonweal, which is the lawmaker's intention.

But not everyone is competent to interpret what may be useful or not useful for the community if observance of the letter of the law does not risk a sudden danger that needs to be immediately resolved. Rather, only rulers are competent to make such interpretations, and they have authority in such cases to dispense citizens from laws. On the other hand, if there be a sudden danger that does not allow enough time to be able to have recourse to a superior, the very necessity includes an implicit dispensation, since necessity is not subject to the law.

10. Should human law be revised in any way?[34]

I answer that human law is a dictate of reason directing human actions. And so there can be two reasons why laws may be rightly revised: one regarding reason; the other regarding human beings, whose actions laws regulate. Regarding reason, it seems to be natural to it to advance step-by-step from the imperfect to the perfect. And so, regarding theoretical sciences, the first philosophers transmitted imperfect doctrines that later

---

[33]ST I–II, Q. 96, A. 6. [34]ST I–II, Q. 97, A. 1.

philosophers corrected. So also, regarding practical matters, the first lawmakers, who strove to discover things useful for the human community but were unable of themselves to consider everything, instituted imperfect laws that were deficient in many respects. And later lawmakers revised these laws, establishing laws that could fail to serve the commonweal in fewer cases.

And regarding human beings, whose actions laws regulate, laws can be rightly revised to suit changed conditions of human beings, and different things are expedient for human beings according to their different circumstances. For example, a law permitting a well-tempered, serious, and diligently community-minded people to choose magistrates to administer the commonwealth is rightly framed. But the power to bestow such offices is rightly taken away from a corrupted people who sell their votes and entrust their governance to scoundrels and criminals, and the power to bestow the offices falls to the choice of a few good persons.

Objection. Human law is derived from the natural law. But the natural law remains immutable. Therefore, human law ought to remain immutable.

Reply Obj. The natural law is a participation in the eternal law, and so the natural law remains immutable. And the natural law has this immutability from the immutability and perfection of the divine reason that establishes human nature. But human reason is mutable and imperfect.

Moreover, the natural law consists of universal precepts that always abide, while laws established by human beings consist of particular precepts that regard different situations that arise.

11. Should human laws always be revised for something better?[35]

I answer that human laws are revised insofar as their revision serves the commonweal. But the very revision of laws, as such, involves some detriment to the commonweal. For custom avails very much for the observance of laws, since things done contrary to common custom, even if in themselves slight, are rather serious. And so the binding force of law is diminished when laws are revised, since custom is removed. And so human laws should never be revised unless the commonweal gains in one respect as much as it loses in the other. And such is the case either because a very great and very clear benefit results from the new law, or because there is a very great necessity due to the fact that the existing law is clearly unjust, or to the fact that observance of the existing law is most harmful. And so,

[35]ST I–II, Q. 97, A. 2.

in framing new laws, there should be an evident benefit in departing from laws long perceived as just.

12. Can customs obtain the force of law?[36]

I answer that all laws come from the reason and will of lawmakers: divine and natural laws from the reasonable will of God, and human laws from human wills regulated by reason. But the deeds of human beings as much as their words indicate their reason and will regarding things to be done. For example, everyone seems to desire as good what one carries out in deed. And human words alter and explain laws insofar as the words explain the internal movements and thoughts of human reason. And so acts, especially when repeated so as to constitute custom, can alter and explain laws, and cause things to obtain the force of law, namely, insofar as repeated external acts most effectively manifest internal movements of the will and the thoughts of reason. For things done repeatedly seem to proceed from deliberate judgments of reason. And so custom has the force of law and abolishes law and interprets law.

Objection 1. Moral good cannot come out of many wicked acts. But those who first begin to act contrary to a law act wickedly. Therefore, many such acts do not produce something morally good. But law is something morally good, since law regulates human actions. Therefore, customs cannot abolish laws so that the customs obtain the force of law.

Reply Obj. 1. Human laws are wanting in particular cases. And so one can sometimes act outside the law, namely, in cases in which the laws are wanting, and yet the actions will not be morally evil. And when such instances are repeated because of alterations in human beings, then customs indicate that laws are no longer useful, just as it would be evident that laws are no longer useful if expressly contrary laws were to be promulgated. But if the same reason for which the original law was useful still persists, the law prevails over the custom, not the custom over the law. One exception may be if the law seems useless simply because it is impossible by reason of a country's customs. For it is difficult to destroy a people's customs.

Obj. 2. Framing laws belongs to public persons, whose business is to govern a community, and so private persons cannot make law. But customs flourish through the acts of private persons. Therefore, custom cannot obtain the force of law so as to abolish laws.

Reply Obj. 2. The people among whom a custom is introduced can be in two situations. If a people is free, that is, self-governing, the consent of the whole people, which custom indicates, counts more in favor of a particu-

---

[36]ST I–II, Q. 97, A. 3.

lar legal observance than the authority of its ruler, who only has the power to frame laws insofar as the ruler acts in the name of the people. And so the whole people can establish laws, but individual persons cannot.

And if the people does not have the free disposition to frame laws for itself or to abolish laws imposed by a higher power, the customs prevailing in such a people still obtain the force of law insofar as those who have the power to impose laws on the people tolerate the customs. For rulers thereby seem to approve what the customs introduce.

13. Can the people's rulers dispense subjects from human laws?[37]

I answer that dispensing, properly speaking, signifies allotting common goods to individuals. And so the heads of households are dispensers, since they with due weight and in due measure distribute to each member of the household both duties and things necessary for living. Therefore, regarding a political community, one person dispenses, since that person in a way orders how individuals should fulfill general precepts.

A precept generally for the convenience of the community may sometimes be unsuitable for a particular person or in a particular case, since the precept would prevent something better or bring about some evil. But it would be most dangerous to commit this to the discretion of each individual, except, perhaps, when there is a clear and present danger. And so those empowered to rule a people have the power to dispense from human laws that rest on the rulers' authority, namely, as regards persons or situations in which the law is wanting, to grant permission not to observe precepts of the law.

But if rulers should grant this permission at their mere whim, without the persons or situations warranting it, they will be unfaithful or unwise dispensers. Rulers will be unfaithful dispensers if they do not aim at the common good, and they will be unwise dispensers if they ignore the reason for granting dispensations.

Objection. Human law, if just, needs to be in accord with the natural and divine laws. But no human being can dispense anyone from the divine and natural laws. Therefore, neither can any human being dispense someone from a human law.

Reply Obj. The general precepts of the natural law, which are never wanting, cannot be dispensed, although human beings sometimes dispense from other precepts of the natural law, which are conclusions, as it were, from the general precepts (e.g., dispensing from the obligation to repay loans owed to traitors, or the like).

---

[37]ST I–II, Q. 97, A. 4.

But every human being is subject to the divine law as private persons are subject to public law. And thus, as only rulers or their representatives can dispense from human laws, so only God or his special representatives can dispense from precepts of the divine law.

The Moral Precepts of the Old Law

Thomas distinguishes three kinds of precepts of the Old Law: moral precepts, ceremonial precepts, and judicial precepts. Moral precepts concern good morals, and human acts are morally good if they are in accord with reason. Judgments of practical reason derive from naturally known first principles (e.g., live cooperatively in society), and so moral precepts of the Old Law necessarily belong to the natural law in some way. Some of these moral precepts (e.g., Thou shalt not steal*) are proximate conclusions that reason can easily draw from the general first principles. Other moral precepts (e.g., respect the elderly) are remote conclusions that require greater reflection and instruction by the wise. Still other moral precepts concern divine things (e.g.,* Thou shalt not take the name of the Lord thy God in vain*), about which human beings need divine instruction.*

Human laws lay down precepts regarding acts of justice and prescribe other virtuous acts only insofar as the acts take on an aspect of justice. But divine law lays down precepts about everything required for communion with God and so about the acts of every virtue (e.g., precepts governing chastity).

The Decalogue includes precepts from God himself, whether precepts easily known from the first principles of the natural law or precepts specially revealed by God. The first principles themselves are not included in the Decalogue, since they are self-evident to natural reason. Nor are remote conclusions from the first principles that the wise discover by careful study, and that God communicates by the instruction of the wise.

The commandments of the first tablet of the Decalogue (e.g., Thou shalt not worship false Gods before me*) direct human beings in relation to God, human beings' ultimate good. The commandments of the second tablet (e.g.,* Honor thy parents*) order the justice to be observed in human society. Both sets of commandments include God's intention that they be observed, and so the commandments cannot be dispensed from. But specific applications of the commandments to be observed in human society to particular acts, namely, whether this or that act is murder or theft, can vary, and so some killing is not murder, and some taking of another's property is not theft.*

Human lawmakers have power only over external acts, but God also has power over internal acts of the will. Divine law and human law punish only deeds done knowingly. Divine law but not human law punishes those willing or intending to do evil. Neither divine nor human law punishes those who observe the law without possessing the corresponding virtue (i.e., the habit) to do so.

Acts of charity as such fall under precepts of the divine law if the precepts lay down specific commands of charity (e.g., to love God, to love one's neighbor). But precepts commanding other virtuous acts (e.g., to honor one's parents) can be observed without possession of the virtue of charity.

1. Do all the moral precepts of the Old Law belong to the natural law?[38]

I answer that moral precepts of the Old Law, as distinguished from its ceremonial precepts and its precepts governing the administration of justice, concern things that as such belong to good morals. But we speak of human morals in relation to reason, which is the specific source of human acts. And so morals in accord with reason are good, and those in discord with reason are evil. As every judgment of theoretical reason derives from the natural knowledge of first principles, so every judgment of practical reason derives from certain naturally known first principles, and one can in various ways proceed from these principles to judge about different things.

There are some things regarding human acts so explicit that, by applying the general and first principles, we can with rather little reflection at once approve or disapprove them. And there are some things that, in order to be judged morally, require much reflection on various circumstances, which only the wise are qualified to study carefully. And there are some things that human beings need the help of divine instruction in order to judge (e.g., articles of faith).

But the moral precepts of the Old Law concern things that pertain to good morals, and such precepts are in accord with reason. And every judgment of human reason is derived from natural reason. And so the moral precepts of the Old Law need to belong to the natural law, albeit in different ways.

The natural reason of each person at once judges that some things as such are to be done or not to be done (e.g., *Honor thy father and thy mother*, *Thou shalt not kill*, *Thou shalt not steal*). And such precepts belong to the natural law absolutely.

And there are some things that the wise after more careful reflection judge should be done. And these things belong to the natural law but in such a way that they need instruction, whereby the wiser teach the less

[38]ST I–II, Q. 100, A. 1.

wise (e.g., *Rise up at the presence of a gray head, and honor the person of the elderly*, and such like).

And there are some things that human reason needs divine instruction to judge, and we thereby learn about divine things (e.g., *Thou shalt not make for thyself a graven image or any likeness*, *Thou shalt not take the name of the Lord thy God in vain*).

2. Do the moral precepts of the Old Law concern all virtuous acts?[39]

I answer that legal precepts are ordered to the common good, and so they need to be distinguished by different kinds of political communities. And so also one kind of laws needs to be framed for a political community ruled by a king, and a different kind of laws needs to be framed for a political community where the people or some powerful persons in the community rule. And there is one kind of community to which human law is ordered, and another kind of community to which divine law is ordered.

Human law is ordered to a political community, which consists of human beings in relation to one another. And human beings are related to one another by external actions, whereby they are in communion with one another. And such communion belongs to the nature of justice, which, properly speaking, gives direction to a human community. And so human law lays down precepts only regarding acts of justice, and it prescribes other virtuous acts, if at all, only insofar as those acts take on an aspect of justice.

But the community for which divine law provides consists of human beings in relation to God, whether in the present or the future life. And so divine law lays down precepts regarding everything that rightly orders human beings for communion with God. But human beings are united to God by their reason or mind, in which is the image of God. And so the divine law lays down precepts about everything that rightly orders human beings' reason, and all virtuous acts bring this about. For example, intellectual virtues rightly order acts of reason, as such, and moral virtues rightly order acts of reason regarding internal emotions and external actions. And so the divine law fittingly lays down precepts about the acts of every virtue. But the divine law does so in such a way that some things, without which the order of virtue, that is, the order of reason, cannot be observed, fall under the obligation of precepts, while things belonging to the well-being of complete virtue fall under the admonition of counsels.

---

[39]ST I–II, Q. 100, A. 2.

3. Do we trace all the moral precepts of the Old Law to the Ten Commandments?[40]

I answer that God himself laid down the Decalogue for the people and laid down the other precepts for them through Moses. The precepts whose knowledge human beings possess from God himself belong to the Decalogue. And the precepts they can know from the first general principles with rather little reflection, as well as those that divinely infused faith reveals, are such.

Therefore, two kinds of precepts are not reckoned among the precepts of the Decalogue. One kind consists of the first and general principles, and these principles need no further promulgation than their inscription on natural reason as self-evident, as it were (e.g., human beings should do evil to no one, and such like). And the second kind consists of the precepts that the wise by careful study discover belong to reason, since God communicates these precepts to the people through the instruction of the wise. Still, both of these kinds of precepts are included in the Decalogue, albeit in different ways. For the first and general principles are included as first principles in proximate conclusions, and, conversely, the precepts known through the wise are included as conclusions in first principles.

Objection. We do not trace the moral precepts of the Old Law to its ceremonial precepts. Rather, we do the converse. But one of the commandments, namely, *Remember that thou keep holy the Sabbath*, is ceremonial. Therefore, we do not trace all the moral precepts of the Old Law to all the commandments of the Decalogue.

Reply Obj. The commandment to observe the Sabbath is moral in one respect, namely, that human beings devote some time to divine things. But we do not reckon the Sabbath among the moral precepts of the Decalogue as to the appointed day, since the commandment in this respect is ceremonial.

4. Can human beings be dispensed from the commandments of the Decalogue?[41]

I answer that there ought to be dispensations from precepts whenever there arise particular cases in which observance of the letter of the law would be contrary to the intention of the lawmaker. First and foremost, the intention of any lawmaker is directed to the common good. Second, the intention of a lawmaker is directed to the order of justice and virtue, which order preserves and attains the common good. Therefore, if precepts are laid down that include the preservation of the common good or

---

[40]ST I–II, Q. 100, A. 3. [41]ST I–II, Q. 100, A. 8.

the order of justice and virtue, the precepts include the intention of the lawmaker and so cannot be dispensed from. For example, if a community were to have a precept that no one should subvert the commonwealth or betray the political community to its enemies, or that no one should do unjust or evil things, such precepts could not be dispensed from.

But if other precepts subordinate to the latter were to be laid down that specify particular ways to preserve the common good or the order of justice and virtue, such precepts could be dispensed from. The precepts could be dispensed from insofar as their nonobservance in particular cases would not cause prejudice to the first precepts, which include the intention of the lawmaker. For example, if a political community, to preserve the commonwealth, were to decree that citizens stand guard on each street of a besieged city, some citizens could be dispensed for the sake of a greater benefit.

The commandments of the Decalogue include the aim of the lawmaker, God. For the commandments of the first tablet, which direct human beings in relation to God, include the order of human beings to their common and ultimate good (i.e., God). And the commandments of the second tablet include the order of justice to be observed in human society, namely, that nothing improper be done to anyone, and that one should render to others what is their due. And so the commandments of the Decalogue cannot be dispensed from at all.

Objection. A prohibition against homicide is included in the commandments of the Decalogue. But human beings seem to dispense from this commandment. For example, the precepts of human law permit human beings such as criminals and enemies to be killed. Therefore, the commandments of the Decalogue can be dispensed from.

Reply Obj. The Decalogue prohibits the killing of human beings insofar as such killing is undeserved, for then the commandment includes the nature of justice. And human law cannot make it lawful that human beings be killed undeservedly. But it is not undeserved that criminals and enemies of the commonwealth be killed. And so this is not contrary to the commandment of the Decalogue, nor is such killing murder, which the commandment of the Decalogue prohibits. Likewise, it is not theft or robbery, which a commandment of the Decalogue prohibits, if property is taken from one who ought to relinquish it.

And so there was no theft when the children of Israel at the command of God took away the spoils of the Egyptians (Ex. 12:35–36), since the spoils were due the Israelites by reason of God's judgment. Likewise, Abraham, when he agreed to kill his son (Gen. 22:1–12), did not consent to murder, since it was proper that Isaac be killed at the command of God, who is the Lord of life and death. God inflicts death on all human beings, just and unjust, for the sin of our first parent, and human beings will not be murderers if they should by divine authority execute judgment, as God is not a murderer. Likewise, Hosea, having sexual intercourse with a fornicating wife or adulterous woman (Hos.1:2–11), is not an adulterer or fornicator, since he had intercourse with a woman who was his by the command of God, who is the author of the institution of marriage.

Therefore, the commandments of the Decalogue, regarding the nature of justice that they include, cannot be changed. But specifications applying the commandment to particular acts, namely, specifications whether this or that be murder, theft, or adultery, are variable. The specifications sometimes change only because of divine authority, namely, regarding matters that God alone instituted, such as marriage and the like. The specifications also sometimes change because of human authority, as in matters committed to human jurisdiction. For human beings in this but not every respect take the place of God.

5. Does the way of virtue fall under command of the law?[42]

I answer that commands of the law have the power to compel compliance. Therefore, what the law compels falls directly under command of the law. But that for which legal punishment is inflicted falls strictly under command of the law. Therefore, the law compels compliance by fear of punishment. And the divine law and human law are differently disposed in regard to ordering punishment. For legal punishment is inflicted for things regarding which lawmakers have the power to judge, since law punishes by passing sentence. Human beings, who lay down human laws, have the power to judge only regarding external acts, but only God, who lays down the divine law, has the power to judge regarding interior movements of the will.

The way of virtue consists of three things, the first of which is whether one acts knowingly. Both the divine law and human law judge this, since one does accidentally what one does unknowingly. And so both the divine law and human law deem deeds worthy of punishment or pardon depending on a person's knowledge or ignorance.

The second consideration is whether one acts willingly, that is, by choice and by choosing to do something for its own sake. And we thereby signify two interior movements, namely, willing and intending. Only the divine law, not human law, judges these two movements. For human law does not punish one who wants to kill and does not, but the divine law does.

---

[42]ST I–II, Q. 100, A. 9.

The third consideration is whether one has the power to act firmly and consistently and does so. Such firmness, properly speaking, belongs to habits, namely, that one act by reason of ingrained habit. In this respect, the way of virtue does not fall under command of the law, whether the divine law or human law. For example, neither human beings nor God punish as transgressors of the law those who give requisite honor to their parents but do not have the habit of filial piety.

6. Does the way of charity fall under command of the divine law?[43]

I answer that we can consider acts of charity in one way as such, and they in this respect fall under commands of the law that lay down specific commands (e.g., *Thou shalt love the Lord thy God*, and *Thou shalt love thy neighbor*). It is possible to observe these precepts concerning acts of charity, since human beings can dispose themselves to possess charity and can exercise charity when they have possessed it.

We can consider acts of charity in a second way insofar as they are the way of acts of other virtues, that is, as acts of other virtues are ordered to charity. For the intended end is a formal modality of acts ordered to the end. In this respect, the way of charity does not fall under command of the law. For example, the commandment *Honor thy father* only commands that one honor one's father, not that one honor one's father out of charity. And so those who honor their fathers, although they do not possess charity, do not become transgressors of the precept to honor one's father, although they are transgressors of the precept regarding acts of charity. And they deserve punishment for the latter transgression.

Precepts of the Old Law Regarding Rulers

Thomas claims that the regime established by Moses to govern the Israelites was (and presumably remains) the best regime. It was best because it took and mixed the best features of monarchy, aristocracy, and democracy. Moses and his successors, the Judges, ruled as monarchs because of their virtue. Seventy-two elders assisted in governing because of their virtue. (The principal virtue in both cases is political wisdom, the special kind of practical wisdom involved in governance.) And Thomas claims that all citizens should participate in the best regime. Popular participation was desirable because it helped to legitimate the regime, thereby insuring domestic peace and broad support for the regime. But

[43]ST I–II, Q. 100, A. 10.

contrary to contemporary democratic standards, the people participated only in the choice of rulers, and the business of government was the sole responsibility of Moses and the elders.

1. Did the Old Law ordain fitting precepts regarding rulers?[44]

I answer that we should note two things regarding the right institution of rulers in any political community or people. First, we should note that all citizens should participate in the regime, since this maintains civic peace, and since all citizens love and protect such an institution. Second, we should note about types of regimes that the chief forms are kingdoms, in which one person rules by reason of the person's virtue, and aristocracy (i.e., government by the best), in which a few persons rule by reason of their virtue. And so the best institution of rulers belongs to a city or kingdom in which one person is chosen by reason of his virtue to rule over all, and other persons govern under him by reason of their virtue. And yet such a regime belongs to all citizens, both because its rulers are chosen from its citizens, and because all citizens choose its rulers. This is the best constitution, a happy mixture of kingdom, since one person rules, and aristocracy, since many govern by reason of their virtue, and democracy (i.e., government by the people), since rulers can be chosen from the people, and since the choice of rulers belongs to the people.

And the divine law established such a regime. For Moses and his successors governed the people, individually ruling over all, as it were, and this regime is a form of kingdom. And seventy-two elders were chosen by reason of their virtue, and this was aristocratic. And the regime was democratic in that the rulers were chosen from all the people, and in that the people chose the rulers. And so the best institution of rulers was the one that the Old Law established.

---

[44]ST I–II, Q. 105, A. 1.

Glossary

Accident: *an attribute that inheres in another and cannot subsist in itself.* What subsists in itself and does not inhere in another is a substance. John, for example, is a substance, while his height is an accident; his height does not exist apart from him. *See* Actuality, Property, Substance.

Action: *activity*. There are two basic kinds of action. Immanent action, the activity of living things, perfects the being that acts. Plants have the immanent activities of nutrition, growth, and reproduction. Animals have, in addition, the immanent activities of sense perception and sense appetites. Human beings have, in addition, the immanent activities of intellection and willing. God alone has perfectly immanent activity, that is, activity without any accompanying transitive effect. Transitive activity produces an effect in something other than the active cause. In other words, transitive action is efficient causality. *See* Cause.

Actuality: *the perfection of a being*. Existing is the primary actuality of every being. A specific (substantial) form actualizes finite beings and distinguishes one kind of being from another. Particular (accidental) characteristics further actualize finite beings. Joan, for example, is perfected and actualized by her act of existing, her human form, and her particular attributes (her knowledge, her virtue, her physical attributes). *See* Accident, Form, Matter, Potentiality, Substance.

Appetite: *the desire or striving of finite beings to actualize potentialities*. Nonliving material beings have natural appetites. Plants have, in addition, the vegetative appetites of nutrition, growth, and reproduction. Animals have, in addition, sense appetites (concupiscible, irascible). Human beings have, in addition, an intellectual or rational appetite, the will. *See* Concupiscible, Irascible, Will.

Cause: *something that contributes to the being or coming-to-be of something else*. The term refers primarily to an efficient cause, that is, a cause that by its activity produces an effect. For example, a builder and those who work under the builder are efficient causes of the house they are building. A final cause is the end for the sake of which an efficient cause acts. For example, a builder builds a house to provide a dwelling suitable for human habitation (objective purpose) and to make money if the house is to be sold (subjective purpose). An exemplary cause is the idea or model of a desired effect in the mind of an intellectual efficient cause that preconceives the effect. For example, a builder conceives the form of the house the builder intends to build. Efficient, final, and exemplary causes are extrinsic to the effects they produce. In addition, form, which makes an effect to be what it is, and matter, which receives the form, are correlative intrinsic causes. For example, houses are composed of bricks and mortar (the matter), which are given a structure or shape (the form). *See* End, Form, Intention, Matter.

Charity: *the supernatural virtue whereby one is characteristically disposed to love God above all things, and all other things for his sake. See* Virtue.

Coming to Be, Passing Away: *the process of substantial change.* In substantial change, matter (prime) gains a form (substantial), and so a new material substance comes to be. The same matter also loses a substantial form, and so the previous material substance ceases to exist. *See* Form, Matter.

Concupiscence: *the inclination of human beings' sense appetites toward actions contrary to the order of reason, with the inclination not completely subject to reason.* Concupiscence is not to be identified with the concupiscible appetites as such. *See* Concupiscible, Will.

Concupiscible: *a sense appetite for something pleasant.* Love and hate, desire and aversion, joy and sorrow are movements of concupiscible appetites. *See* Appetite, Irascible.

Conscience: *the dictate of reason that one should or should not do something. See* Synderesis.

Efficient Cause: *See* Cause.

Emotions: *movements of sense appetites.* Emotions may be ordinate (in accord with right reason) or inordinate (contrary to right reason). Emotions involve either desire for the pleasant or repugnance regarding difficult things. *See* Concupiscible, Irascible, Moral Virtues.

End: *the object for the sake of which something acts.* The end may be intrinsic or extrinsic. The end is intrinsic if it is built into the nature of an active thing. The end is extrinsic if it is the conscious object of a rational being's action. *See* Cause.

Essence: *that which makes things what they substantially are.* For example, the human essence makes human beings be what they are as substances, namely, rational animals. When the essence of a being is considered as the ultimate source of the being's activities and development, it is called the being's nature. For example, human nature is the ultimate source of specifically human activities (activities of reason and activities according to reason). *See* Form, Property, Substance.

Exemplary Cause: *See* Cause.

Final Cause: *See* Cause.

Form: *what makes things be the kind of thing they are or to possess additional characteristics*. For example, the human form makes human beings human, and other forms make them so tall and so heavy. *See* Accident, Essence, Matter, Substance.

Formal Cause: *See* Cause.

Genus: *See* Species.

Habit: *the characteristic disposition or inclination to be or to act in a certain way*. Habits belong chiefly to the soul, that is, to the intellect and the will. They may be innate or acquired, natural or supernatural, good or bad. For example, the habit of logical argumentation belongs to the intellect; the habit of justice belongs to the will; the habits of the first principles of theoretical and practical reason are innate; the habit of cleanliness is acquired; the habit of courage is natural; the habit of faith is supernatural; the habit of generosity is good; the habit of stinginess is bad. Habits belong secondarily to the body, as the latter is disposed or made apt to be readily at the service of the soul's activity. *See* Virtue.

Happiness: *the perfect or complete attainment of the good or end that nature constitutes human beings to desire and strive for*. As such, happiness is an objective state of perfection and not a subjective state of euphoria, although possession of the ultimate objective perfection of human beings will entail joy and satisfaction. For Aristotle, human beings become happy, that is, reach a state of perfection, when they engage in activities of reason and live in accord with right reason. For Thomas Aquinas, human beings can only become completely happy when they behold God as he is in himself, although activities of reason and activities in accord with right reason in this life will bring human beings to a state of incomplete and imperfect happiness. Aquinas typically uses different words to denote this-world and next-world happiness: *felicitas* to denote this-world happiness, and *beatitudo* to denote next-world happiness.

Ideas (Divine): *the forms or natures of actual or possible creatures in God's mind*. Because God knows himself as imitable, he knows the forms or natures of every being that he creates or could create. These ideas are identical with God's knowing himself, and God's knowing is in turn identical with his substance.

Intellect: *the human faculty of understanding, judging, and reasoning*. Thomas Aquinas, following Aristotle, holds that there is an active power of the intellect that moves the passive or potential power of the intellect to understand the essence of material things, form judgments, and reason deductively. *See* Reason.

Intellectual Virtues: *virtues consisting of the right characteristic disposition of the intellect toward truth.* Theoretical intellectual virtues concern understanding first principles, scientific knowledge, and theoretical wisdom. Practical intellectual virtues concern practical wisdom and skills. *See* Practical Wisdom (Prudence), Principle, Science (Aristotelian), Skills, Theoretical Wisdom.

Intention: *striving for things.* Human beings, in their specifically human acts, strive for things as their reason understands the things to be good. Irrational animals strive for things as their senses perceive the things to be good. Other material things strive for things as their natures determine them to act. *See* Appetite, Cause, End.

Irascible: *a sense appetite for a useful object that can be attained only with difficulty.* The object does not seem pleasant and can be obtained only by overcoming opposition. Hope and despair, fear and anger are movements of irascible appetites. *See* Appetite, Concupiscible.

Justice: *the moral virtue consisting of the right characteristic disposition of the will to render to others what is due them.* This is the special virtue of justice, and there are two particular kinds. One kind, commutative justice, concerns the duties of individuals and groups to other individuals and groups. The other kind, distributive justice, concerns the duties of the community to insure that individuals and groups receive a share of the community's good proportional to the individuals' and groups' contributions to the community. But justice in general is moral virtue in general, insofar as all moral virtues can be directed to the common good. Thomas Aquinas calls such justice legal justice. *See* Moral Virtues, Virtue.

Law: *an order of reason, for the common good, by one with authority, and promulgated.* For Thomas Aquinas, the archetypal law is God's plan for the universe and everything he creates. Aquinas calls this plan the eternal law. Human beings, as rational creatures, can understand God's plan for them and judge what behavior it requires of them, and they in this way participate in the eternal law. Aquinas calls this participation in the eternal law the natural law. And human beings need to establish laws for their communities. These human laws either adopt conclusions from the general precepts of the natural law (e.g., do not commit murder) or further specify the precepts (e.g., drive on the right side of the road). Aquinas calls those human laws that are proximate conclusions from the general precepts of the natural law the common law of peoples (*jus gentium*), and those human laws that are more remote conclusions from, or further specifications of, the general precepts civil laws.

Material Cause: *See* Cause.

Matter: *the stuff or subject matter out of which things are constituted. See* Cause, Form.

Moral Virtues: *virtues consisting of the right characteristic disposition of the will toward requisite ends (e.g., just, courageous, moderate deeds).* Reason directs moral virtues, theoretical reason by understanding their ends, and practical wisdom by choosing means to those ends. Moral virtues concern the mean between too much and too little. One moral virtue, justice, concerns external things. Other moral virtues concern control of emotions. *See* Emotions, Justice, Practical Wisdom (Prudence).

Motion: *movement.* Motion literally and primarily refers to locomotion, that is, change of position. But the term can refer more broadly to any change or transition from one state or condition to another. According to Aquinas, it is a self-evident first principle of understanding that whatever undergoes motion does so as a result of causal action by something else.

Nature: *See* Essence.

Passing Away: *See* Coming to Be.

Political Community: *the organized community wherein and whereby human beings are fully able to achieve their proper excellence or well-being.* Like Aristotle, Thomas Aquinas holds that human beings are by their nature social and political animals. Human beings need to associate with one another for self-defense and economic development, but they also and especially need to associate with one another for their full intellectual and moral development. Only an organized community of a certain size can be self-sufficient to achieve these goals. Political community thus differs from the state, which is the supreme agency responsible for organizing the community, and from government, which is the machinery and personnel of the state. Unlike Aristotle, however, Aquinas envisioned a supernatural end for human beings beyond their temporal well-being, and by reason of that supernatural end, the membership of Christians in another, divinely established community, the church. The relation between the natural and supernatural ends of human beings, and the relation between the two communities promoting these ends, were an important concern of Aquinas. *See* Polity.

Polity: *the regime or constitution that gives a political community its distinctive form.* For Thomas Aquinas, polity also has the meaning of a particular regime or constitution that mixes or combines elements of monarchic rule (rule by one person), aristocratic rule (rule by the few best persons), and democratic rule (rule by the multitude). Such a regime includes only limited popular participation. *See* Political Community.

Potentiality: *the capacity to be or to become something.* The potentiality of a being limits its actuality; frogs, for example, can swim, but they cannot fly. Finite beings can change accidentally; John, for example, can go bald. Finite material things can also change from one substance into another; grass, for example, when consumed by a cow, becomes part of the cow. Potentiality in the active sense is the same as power. *See* Accident, Actuality, Matter, Power.

Power: *the active capacity to perform a certain kind of activity.* For example, the intellect and the will are powers of human beings.

Practical Wisdom (Prudence): *the intellectual virtue consisting of the right characteristic disposition to reason about what human beings should or should not do.* Practical wisdom concerns human action and so differs from theoretical wisdom, which concerns the ultimates causes of things irrespective of related human action. Theoretical wisdom understands the ends of moral virtues, and practical wisdom chooses the means to achieve those ends. As the most important natural virtue connected with human action, practical wisdom is sometimes considered as if it were one of the moral virtues. *See* Habit, Moral Virtues, Theoretical Wisdom, Virtue.

Principle: *the universal major premise of an argument.* Principles presupposing no principle, or at least no principle other than the principle of contradiction, are called first principles. There are theoretical first principles (e.g., everything coming to be has a cause) and practical first principles (e.g., do good, avoid evil, live sociably with others).

Property: *a quality or characteristic that necessarily belongs to something but is neither part of the thing's essence nor part of the thing's definition.* For example, the ability of human beings to use speech to convey ideas is a characteristic proper to them but not part of their essence or definition (rational animal).

Reason: *(1) the process of drawing conclusions from principles; (2) the power to draw conclusions from principles; and (3) the power of the intellect in general.* Thomas Aquinas frequently uses the word in the third sense. *See* Intellect.

Science (Aristotelian): *knowledge about things through knowledge of their causes.* Science studies the efficient, final, material, and formal causes of things. Physical, psychological, and social sciences study the secondary causes of material and human things, and philosophy (metaphysics) studies the first causes of being as such. For Aristotle, philosophy is the highest science. For Thomas Aquinas, theology, the study of God in the light of Christian revelation, is the highest science. *See* Cause, Intellect, Intellectual Virtues, Theoretical Wisdom.

Senses: *faculties of perception through bodily organs.* The external senses (sight, hearing, smell, taste, touch) have proper objects, that is, objects that each sense alone perceives, and common objects, that is, objects related to quantity that more than one sense can perceive. The internal senses (the common or unifying sense, imagination, memory, and the cogitative sense) derive from data provided by the external senses.

Skills: *practical intellectual virtues that consist of right reasoning about how to make things. See* Intellectual Virtues.

Soul: *the substantial form of a living material thing.* The soul is the ultimate intrinsic source whereby living material things differ from nonliving material things. There are three kinds of souls: the vegetative soul capable of nutrition, growth, and reproduction; the sensory soul capable of sense perception; the rational soul capable of intellection. According to Aristotle and Thomas Aquinas, the only soul in human beings is the rational soul, which also has the powers of the vegetative and sensory souls. The rational soul is intrinsically independent of matter for its existence and activity. *See* Form, Substance.

Species: *the substantial identity of material things insofar as that identity is common to many things.* The species concept (e.g., human being) is composed of a genus concept (e.g., animal), which indicates the essence of particular material things in an incompletely determined way, and a specific difference (e.g., rational), which distinguishes different kinds of things of the same genus. The species concept, or definition, thus expresses the whole substance or essence of a particular kind of material thing.

Specific Difference: *See* Species.

Subject (1): *that in which something else inheres.* In the strict sense, subjects are the substances underlying accidental characteristics. For example, human beings are the subjects of their powers and acts. In a broader sense, powers can be considered the subjects of the powers' acts. For example, the intellect is the subject of intellectual acts.

Subject (2): *a human being bound to obey another human being*. For example, British citizens are British subjects, that is, bound to obey British authorities.

Substance: *what exists in itself and not in another*. Finite individual substances "stand under" (Latin: *substare*) accidents and persist through accidental changes. Human beings, for example, are composed of substance (the body-soul composite) and accidents (size, shape, color, etc.) *See* Accident, Property, Subject (1).

Synderesis: *habitual understanding of the first principles governing human action*. This is an innate disposition. Human beings are disposed by their rational nature to recognize that they should seek the good proper to their human nature and should avoid things contrary to it. The human good includes preserving one's life in reasonable ways, mating and educating offspring in reasonable ways, and living cooperatively with others in an organized community. *See* Habit, Virtue.

Theoretical Wisdom: *the intellectual virtue consisting of the right characteristic disposition to reason about the ultimate causes of things*. *See* Intellectual Virtues, Practical Wisdom (Prudence), Virtue.

Virtue: *human excellence*. Virtue is a perduring quality and so a characteristic disposition. Thomas Aquinas distinguishes three kinds of virtue: intellectual, moral, and theological. Intellectual virtues have intellectual activities as their object. Concerning theoretical truth, intellectual virtues comprise understanding first principles, scientific knowledge, and theoretical wisdom. Concerning practical truth, intellectual virtues comprise practical wisdom and skills. Moral virtues consist of characteristic readiness to act in practical matters as practical wisdom dictates. Practical wisdom and moral virtues may be acquired or infused. There are three infused theological virtues: faith, hope, and charity. *See* Charity, Habit, Intellectual Virtues, Moral Virtues, Practical Wisdom (Prudence), Principle, Science (Aristotelian), Theoretical Wisdom.

Will: *the human intellectual (rational) appetite; the intellectual faculty of desire*. The will necessarily desires the ultimate human perfection, happiness, but freely desires particular goods, since the latter are only partially good.

Wisdom: *See* Practical Wisdom (Prudence), Theoretical Wisdom.

Select Bibliography

Complete Translations of the Summa Theologica

Summa Theologiae. Translated, with Latin text, introductions, notes, appendices, and glossaries, by the English Dominican Fathers. 60 vols. New York: McGraw-Hill, 1964–1966.

The Summa Theologica of St. Thomas Aquinas. Translated by the English Dominican Fathers. 3 vols. New York: Benziger, 1947–1948; reprint ed., Allen, TX: Christian Classics, 1981.

Partial Translations of the Summa Theologica

God and Creation. Translated, with introduction, by William P. Baumgarth and Richard J. Regan. Scranton, PA: University of Scranton Press, 1994.

The Human Constitution. Translated, with introduction, by Richard J. Regan. Scranton, PA: University of Scranton Press, 1997.

Law, Morality, and Politics, 2nd edition. Translated, with introduction, by Richard J. Regan. Edited by William P. Baumgarth and Richard J. Regan. Indianapolis: Hackett Publishing Company, 2002.

Summa Theologiae: A Concise Translation. Translated and edited by Timothy McDermott. Westminster, MD: Christian Classics, 1989.

Treatise on Law. Translated, with introduction, by Richard J. Regan. Indianapolis: Hackett Publishing Company, 2000.

Virtue: Way to Happiness. Translated, with introduction, by Richard J. Regan. Scranton, PA: University of Scranton Press, 1999.

Life and Works of Thomas Aquinas

Torrell, Jean-Pierre. *St. Thomas Aquinas.* Vol. 1: *The Person and His Work.* Translated by Robert Royal. Washington, DC: The Catholic University of America Press, 1996.

Tugwell, Simon. "Introduction to St. Thomas," in *Albert and Thomas: Selected Writings*, pp. 201–351. Edited by Simon Tugwell. New York: Paulist Press, 1988.

General Commentaries

Aertsen, Jan. *Nature and Creation: Thomas Aquinas' Way of Thought.* Leiden: Brill, 1988.

Clarke, W. Norris. *The One and the Many: A Contemporary Thomistic Metaphysics.* Notre Dame: University of Notre Dame Press, 2001.

Davies, Brian. *The Thought of Thomas Aquinas*. Oxford: Oxford University Press, 1992.

———. *Aquinas*. London: Continuum, 2002.

Elders, Leo J. *The Philosophical Theology of St. Thomas Aquinas*. Leiden: Brill, 1990.

Gilson, Etienne. *The Christian Philosophy of St. Thomas Aquinas*. New York: Random House, 1956.

Kretzmann, Norman, and Eleanore Stump. *The Cambridge Companion to Aquinas.* Cambridge: Cambridge University Press, 1993.

McInerny, Ralph. *A First Glance at St. Thomas Aquinas: A Handbook for Peeping Thomists.* Notre Dame: University of Notre Dame Press, 1990.

Pieper, Joseph. *Guide to Thomas Aquinas*. Translated by Richard and Clara Winston. New York: Pantheon, 1962.

Stump, Eleanore. *Aquinas*. London: Routledge, 2003.

Thomas Aquinas: Contemporary Philosophical Perspectives. Edited by Brian Davies. Oxford: Oxford University Press, 2002.

Wippel, John F. *The Metaphysical Thought of Thomas Aquinas*. Washington, DC: The Catholic University of America Press, 2000.

God and Creation

Clarke, W. Norris. *The Philosophical Approach to God*. Winston-Salem, NC: Wake Forest University Philosophy Dept., 1979.

Dewan, Lawrence. "The Number and Order of St. Thomas's Five Ways," *Downside Review* 92 (1974):1–18.

McCabe, Herbert. *God Still Matters*. Edited, with introduction, by Brian Davies. London: Continuum, 2002.

Schmitz, Kenneth L. *The Gift: Creation*. Milwaukee: Marquette University Press, 1982.

Sillem, Edward. *Ways of Thinking about God*. New York: Sheed and Ward, 1961.

The Human Constitution

Adler, Mortimer. *Intellect: Mind over Matter*. New York: Collier-Macmillan, 1990.

Clarke, W. Norris. *Person and Being*. Milwaukee: Marquette University Press, 1993.

Donceel, Joseph F. *Philosophical Psychology*, 2nd edition. New York: Sheed and Ward, 1961.

Klubertanz, George P. *The Philosophy of Human Nature.* New York: Appleton-Century-Crofts, 1953.

Pegis, Anton C. *At the Origins of the Thomistic Notion of Man*. New York: Macmillan, 1963.

Ethics in General

Aquinas, Thomas. *Commentary on the Ethics.* Translated by Charles I. Litzenger. Chicago: Regnery, 1963.

Donagan, Alan. *Human Ends and Human Action: An Exploration in St. Thomas's Treatment.* Milwaukee: Marquette University Press, 1985.

———. *Choice: The Essential Element in Human Action.* New York: Routledge, 1987.

Elders, Leon J., and K. Hedwig, eds. *The Ethics of St. Thomas Aquinas.* Studi tomistici 25. Vatican City: Libreria Editrice Vaticana, 1984.

———. *Lex et Libertas: Freedom and Law According to St. Thomas Aquinas.* Studi tomistici 30. Vatican City: Libreria Editrice Vaticana, 1987.

Finnis, John M. *Aquinas: Moral, Political, and Legal Theory.* Oxford: Oxford University Press, 1999.

Flannery, Kevin L. *Acts amid Precepts.* Washington, DC: The Catholic University of America Press, 2001.

Lonergan, Bernard. "The Natural Desire to See God," in *Collection,* 2nd edition, pp. 81–91. Edited by Frederick E. Crowe and Robert M. Doran. Toronto: University of Toronto Press, 1988.

Mullady, Brian T. *The Meaning of the Term* Moral *in St. Thomas Aquinas.* Studi tomistici 27. Vatican City: Libreria Editrice Vaticana, 1986.

Powell, Ralph. *Freely Chosen Reality.* Washington, DC: University Press of America, 1983.

Sokolowski, Robert. *Moral Action: A Phenomenological Study.* Bloomington: Indiana University Press, 1985.

Virtue

Geach, Peter. *The Virtues.* Cambridge: Cambridge University Press, 1977.

Hibbs, Thomas. *Virtue's Splendor: Wisdom, Prudence, and the Human Good.* New York: Fordham University Press, 2001.

Hursthouse, Rosalind. *On Virtue Ethics.* Oxford: Oxford University Press, 1999.

Pieper, Joseph. *The Four Cardinal Virtues: Prudence, Fortitude, Justice, and Temperance.* New York: Harcourt, Bruce, and World, 1965.

Porter, Jean. *The Recovery of Virtue: The Relevance of Aquinas for Christian Ethics.* Louisville, KY: John Knox Press, 1990.

Westberg, Daniel. *Right Practical Reason: Aristotle, Action, and Prudence in Aquinas.* Oxford: Oxford University Press, 1994.

Natural Law and Political Philosophy

Armstrong, Ross A. *Primary and Secondary Precepts in Thomistic Natural Law Teaching.* The Hague: Nijhoff, 1966.

Finnis, John M. *Aquinas: Moral, Political, and Legal Theory.* New York: Oxford University Press, 1999.

Fortin, Ernest L. "St. Thomas Aquinas," in *History of Political Philosophy*, 2nd edition, pp. 223–50. Edited by Leo Strauss and Joseph Cropsey. Chicago: University of Chicago Press, 1981.

Kaczor, Christopher. *Proportionalism and the Natural Law Tradition.* Washington, DC: The Catholic University of America Press, 2002.

Lee, Patrick. "Permanence of the Ten Commandments: St. Thomas and His Modern Commentators," *Theological Studies* 42 (1981):422–43.

Regan, Richard J. "The Human Person and Organized Society: Aquinas," in *Moral Dimensions of Politics*, pp. 37–46. New York: Oxford University Press, 1986.

Reilly, James P. *St. Thomas on Law*. Etienne Gilson Series 12. Toronto: Pontifical Institute of Medieval Studies, 1990.

Rhonheimer, Martin. *Natural Law and Practical Reason: A Thomist View of Moral Autonomy*. Translated by Gerald Malsbary. New York: Fordham University Press, 1999.

Simon, Yves. *The Tradition of Natural Law: A Philosopher's Reflections.* New York: Fordham University Press, 1965.

Recent Bibliography

Davies, Brian. Bibliography in *Aquinas,* pp. xiv–xxii. London: Continuum, 2002.

Ingardia, Richard. *Thomas Aquinas: International Bibliography, 1977–1990.* Bowling Green, OH: Philosophical Documentation Center, Bowling Green State University, 1993.

Index